Dream States

Dream States

A Lurking Nightmare for World Order

BENJAMIN J. COHEN

OXFORD
UNIVERSITY PRESS

Oxford University Press is a department of the University of Oxford.
It furthers the University's objective of excellence in research, scholarship,
and education by publishing worldwide. Oxford is a registered trade mark of
Oxford University Press in the UK and in certain other countries.

Published in the United States of America by Oxford University Press
198 Madison Avenue, New York, NY 10016, United States of America.

© Oxford University Press 2025

All rights reserved. No part of this publication may be reproduced, stored in a retrieval system, transmitted, used for text and data mining, or used for training artificial intelligence, in any form or by any means, without the prior permission in writing of Oxford University Press, or as expressly permitted by law, by license or under terms agreed with the appropriate reprographics rights organization. Inquiries concerning reproduction outside the scope of the above should be sent to the Rights Department, Oxford University Press, at the address above.

You must not circulate this work in any other form
and you must impose this same condition on any acquirer

CIP data is on file at the Library of Congress

ISBN 9780197811641
ISBN 9780197811634 (hbk.)
DOI: 10.1093/9780197811672.001.0001

Paperback printed by Integrated Books International, United States of America

Hardback printed by Bridgeport National Bindery, Inc., United States of America

The manufacturer's authorized representative in the EU for product safety is
Oxford University Press España S.A., Parque Empresarial San Fernando de Henares,
Avenida de Castilla, 2 – 28830 Madrid (www.oup.es/en).

The manufacturer's authorised representative in the EU for product safety is Oxford University Press España S.A. of El Parque Empresarial San Fernando de Henares, Avenida de Castilla, 2 – 28830 Madrid (www.oup.es/en or product.safety@oup.com). OUP España S.A. also acts as importer into Spain of products made by the manufacturer.

Sometimes, the only realists are the dreamers.

– Paul Wellstone

Reality is wrong. Dreams are for real.

– Tupac Shakur

Contents

Abbreviations and Acronyms	ix
Prologue	x

PART. I SETTING THE STAGE

1. Pretenders to Sovereignty	3
2. Supply and Demand	17

PART. II A SEPARATIST'S GUIDE

3. The Disunited States of America	29
4. Fantasies	44
5. Daydreams	54
6. Drexits	67
7. Rebels with a Cause	78
8. Clients	95

PART. III FUTURE HOT SPOTS

9. Familiar Faces	107
10. Special Cases	121
11. Fragile Federations	132
12. Russia	140
13. India	154

viii CONTENTS

PART. IV SOLUTIONS?

14. The Challenge		173
15. A Modest Proposal		181
Notes		194
References		199
Index		208

Abbreviations and Acronyms

BCE	Before the Common Era
BJP	Bharatiya Janata Party
CE	Common Era
COW	Correlates of War
ETA	Basque Homeland and Liberty
EU	European Union
Fretilin	Revolutionary Front for an Independent East Timor
IRA	Irish Republican Army variations: Provisional IRA, Real IRA, New IRA
ISIS	Islamic State
NATO	North Atlantic Treaty Organization
NMLA	National Movement for the Liberation of Azawad
NGO	Non-governmental organization
PKK	Kurdistan Workers' Party
PLO	Palestine Liberation Organization
RSS	Rashtriya Swayamsevak Sangh
SNP	Scottish National Party
UAE	United Arab Emirates
UK	United Kingdom
UN	United Nations
UNADS	United Nations Agency for Dream States
UNPO	Unrepresented Nations and Peoples Organization
US	United States

Prologue

A fable for the future

Dateline: September 9, 2035

CALIFORNIA SECEDES, OTHERS MAY FOLLOW

After years of festering discontent with the direction of politics in Washington, California today formally declared its independence as a sovereign nation. California's secession comes exactly 185 years to the day since the Golden State was admitted to the Union on September 9, 1850. Henceforth, the date is to be known as California Independence Day.

The secession comes as no surprise. Ever since the re-election of Donald Trump back in 2024 despite several indictments for criminal and civil offenses, the gap between "blue" California and the increasingly "red" Federal government has grown ever wider. Differences now seem irreconcilable. Liberal Californians no longer feel much in common with the deeply conservative states of America's south and mid-section.

The turning point came when the Republican-dominated Congress voted to repeal the Twenty-second Amendment, allowing Mr. Trump to gain a third term in 2028. His successor, Vice President JD Vance, took office in 2030 following Mr. Trump's fatal heart attack during a private dinner with his old acquaintance Stormy Daniels. By this time public opinion in California was moving swiftly toward overwhelming support for separation. Last year's Calexit referendum approving secession won with a majority in excess of 80 percent.

The breakup with Washington fulfills the dream of long-active secession movements in California such as Yes California. Separatists argue that with the fifth largest economy in the world, dominating global production of everything from lettuce to moon landers, and a population in excess of 40 million, California is well placed to go its own way.

PROLOGUE   xi

California's dramatic decision is expected to breathe new life into other secession movements elsewhere in the increasingly fragmented US federation—now far more disunited than united. Oregon and Washington State have already petitioned to join California in a new Union of Pacific States. Alaska's long-dormant independence party has sprung back to life, as have secession movements elsewhere, most notably in Hawaii, New England, and Texas. Separatist dreams at the state level are becoming an ever more scary nightmare for Washington.

The question on everyone's mind is: Can violence be avoided? President Vance has threatened a military takeover of the state government in Sacramento, backed by National Guard troops from nearby red states. In turn, California's governor LeBron James has mobilized the California National Guard to defend its hold on key state offices and infrastructure. James came to power four years ago in the same manner as Arnold Schwarzenegger as a result of a recall election. Armed conflict looks increasingly possible. America may be facing its second civil war in less than two centuries.

******

Could this alarming scenario come to pass? Our dispatch from the future, with its prospect of an independent California, might seem unrealistic, even ludicrous. But, then again, maybe not. When the United Nations (UN) was born at the end of World War II, its founding membership included just fifty-one sovereign nations. Today, that number is 193—nearly a fourfold increase. Many of the scores of countries that have joined the UN since 1945 began with a dream of secession. They were "dream states." So why not California?

In fact, escapist dream states are found just about everywhere—not only in California and not only in the United States (US). In dozens of countries around the globe, on every continent and in every ocean, separatists actively pursue the dream of secession: a nation of their own, with their own frontiers, institutions, anthem, and flag—even their own postage stamps. The aim of secessionists is to redraw established borders, laying claim to a coveted homeland. Their cause is self-determination: to live free as a recognized sovereign state. They want their own place under the sun.

xii PROLOGUE

Should we care? The answer is: Absolutely! By definition, secession movements are troublemakers. Trouble *must* be made if secessionists are to realize their aspirations. They are, in short, *disruptive*. Their aim is to challenge the existing world order, by force if necessary. And more often than not, they are likely to be met with stiff resistance. The threat of deadly strife, therefore, is ever present—like it or not.

That is not a judgment on the *merit* of any particular secessionist movement, of course. A people's separatist hopes may be quite reasonable. Indeed, it is difficult not to feel sympathy for anyone's desire to break loose from the dominion of others. But we cannot deny objective reality. Whatever you think of a secession movement's claims for validation, secessions are inherently destabilizing, a form of rebellion. For untold millions of people, therefore, dream states are a lurking nightmare, and that is as true for the United States as it is for other nations.

Indeed, the nightmare is especially scary for the United States, since America is such a big and diverse country with so many far-flung global engagements and responsibilities. Separatist struggles could originate in our own domestic political divisions, which in the era of Donald Trump are growing deeper and more intense with every passing year. Or they could originate abroad in areas of particular importance to America for economic or security reasons. For most nations, secession is a *domestic* threat. For Americans, the challenge of dream states is twofold: not just *internal*, as it is for most other countries, but *external* as well. It is no exaggeration to say that both types of challenges are serious.

First is the specter of secession *at home*. From the very beginning, America's remarkable diversity has invited dreams of separation in many of our states and regions. A century and a half ago, a bloody civil war was fought over the South's wish to secede from the Union. Today, independence movements are rife all across America, from New England and the Old South to California, Alaska, and Hawaii. In an era of widening differences between "red" Republicans and "blue" Democrats, the idea of secession in the United States is attracting more attention than ever. The risk of violent conflict within or between America's fifty states becomes more urgent year by year. It is tempting to dismiss domestic separatist campaigns as implausible, little more than the vanity projects of a few headline-seeking malcontents. But isn't that precisely the sort of thing that was also said of the thirteen original colonies before 1776? Dream states are a chimera—until they're not.

Second is the specter of secession *abroad*, which could draw the United States into conflicts far from our own shores whether we like it or not. Separatist uprisings in distant lands may seem to be none of our business. Why care about a simmering dispute in some "far away country, between people of whom we know nothing" (to mimic the memorable words of British prime minister Neville Chamberlain back in 1938, when he confidently promised "peace in our time" less than a year before the outbreak of World War II)? The US public may feel that it has little at stake in a tribal insurgency in rural Myanmar or an obscure territorial dispute in the Caucasus region. Indeed, few Americans may even know where to look for Myanmar or the Caucasus on a world map. Isolationism has its appeal.

In practice, however, we may have no choice. America is a global power with vital interests and commitments virtually everywhere. In a globalized world that looks to Washington for some measure of leadership, isolation just may not be possible. In the face of threats to global order, indifference is rarely the best option. How can we ignore secession movements in countries like the Congo or Indonesia, with their rich mineral resources? Can we afford to turn our backs on the risk of Yugoslavian-style disintegration in fragile multiethnic federations like Nigeria, Pakistan, or—most important of all—Russia? What about present-day independence campaigns in Catalonia or Scotland, which threaten to distract key European allies? Or what about the sovereignty aspirations of Canada's francophone province of Quebec, which is just a stone's throw away across our northern border? In many cases, the United States simply cannot avoid involvement, even at the risk of becoming mired in armed combat.

******

The book is divided into four parts. Chapters 1 and 2 set the stage. Chapter 1 explains the importance of dream states as a wide-ranging threat to the global order and outlines the principal dangers they pose for the United States and others. Chapter 2, in turn, briefly explores both the potential barriers to secession and the motivations that drive separatists. These two chapters together establish that the lurking nightmare is real and may indeed be serious. In essence, the contemporary system of sovereign states is like a private club. Secession is all about gaining admission to an exclusive fraternity. Entry is difficult but by no means impossible. These chapters explain why.

xiv PROLOGUE

Part II (Chapters 3 –8) offers a concise guide to the vast galaxy of separatist movements to be found scattered around the globe, many of which might pose a serious challenge to the United States. Chapter 3 considers America's internal challenge: the specter of secession at home. Americans like to think of our nation as "exceptional." Nothing could render us asunder. We are one nation, indivisible. In reality, though, our federation is no more immune to disintegration than most other countries. Increasingly, in domestic political discourse, we hear talk of widening social and political divisions—giant chasms opening up between conservatives and progressives; between the coasts and the interior; between "red" states and "blue" states. That is the language of separatism. More and more Americans are beginning to dream of going their own way. A Disunited States of America, at war with itself, is not beyond the realm of possibility.

Chapters 4 –8 then take up America's external challenges: the multiple specters of secession abroad that could, in one way or another, entangle the United States. To aid in assessing risks, five types of dream state are distinguished, in ascending order of the dangers that they might pose. Many separatist movements are harmless fantasies or little more than daydreams. But many others are much more serious, prepared to go to war if necessary or even call in help from influential allies. Before the Arab Spring, who would have expected America to intervene in a separatist struggle in far-off Syria on behalf of beleaguered Kurds? Before the breakup of Yugoslavia, who would have expected the US air force to start dropping bombs on the city of Belgrade on behalf of a secessionist Kosovo? The possibilities for conflict are virtually endless.

The five chapters in Part III (Chapters 9 –13) peer into the cloudy future to consider where in the world the greatest risks are likely to emerge in the years to come. Where are the most incendiary hot spots, and where among them could the flames of secession begin to singe the United States? A few dangerous brush fires can be found in Europe and the Western Hemisphere. But the most serious threats are located in places like Africa, the Middle East, the Caucasus region, and Asia where political borders carelessly sketched out back in the heyday of European imperialism have left a broad residue of dissatisfaction among countless minorities today. Dangerous separatist challenges in these areas abound, from Morocco in western Africa to the Philippines in East Asia. At risk are countries of every size, from tiny statelets like the Solomon Islands to large and fragile multiethnic federations like

Russia and India. If not managed effectively, any one of these hot spots could fatally embroil the United States.

Finally, Part IV (Chapters 14 –15) takes up the difficult question of solutions. What, if anything, can be done about the lurking nightmare of dream states? Is there any chance that we can reduce the danger of separatist hostilities in years to come? The most workable approach, I contend, would begin by abandoning the traditional dichotomous conceptualization of statehood typical of most discussions of secession. Standard practice insists on a strict binary choice: communities are either fully sovereign or else completely subordinate. In fact, options are more elastic than that, since sovereignty can in practice be disaggregated, allowing for various hybrid forms of political authority. Powers can be redistributed between different levels of government; territorial authority can also be shared in some form of joint governance. The risk of separatist violence might be reduced significantly if more possibilities can be contemplated between the extremes of either disruptive secession or quiet assimilation. My "modest proposal" may not be ideal. Indeed, it may be more hopeful than political circumstances generally warrant. But surely it is worth a try. The world has enough troubles as it is. It would be comforting to think that here, at least, there might be some way to thwart the prospect of ever-more destructive eruptions.

Overall, my position is aptly captured by an old joke about the difference between an optimist and a pessimist. An optimist is someone like Dr. Pangloss in Voltaire's epic satire *Candide*—an eternally happy individual who repeatedly insists that this is the best of all possible worlds. A pessimist is someone who wearily replies, "Yes, I'm afraid that I agree with you."

PART I
SETTING THE STAGE

1

Pretenders to Sovereignty

Creatures of the passions

Have you been to Abkhazia lately? Puntland? Sahrawi? Or perhaps the Conch Republic? If you've never heard of any of these places, it's no surprise. Don't feel embarrassed. Even expert cartographers would be hard-pressed to find them all. They rarely appear on world maps. Most people wouldn't even know where to look. These are "dream states."[1]

Like most nocturnal reveries, dream states have only a tenuous relationship with reality. They would like you to believe that they really do exist—or, at a minimum, *should* exist. Their aim is *secession*: to redraw established borders, laying claim to a separate territory of their own. Their cause is *self-determination*: to live free as a distinct sovereign state. They want their own place under the sun.

Many dream states have some form of government, a flag, and at times even their own sports teams. But that does not make them sovereign nations as the term is commonly understood. Most lack legal recognition. They are not members of the United Nations (UN). Indeed, they are largely excluded from the prevailing international system. Though their cause may hold merit, their grasp on reality is more aspirational than substantial—more an assertion of ambition than a description of fact. They are akin to the fleeting mental images that swim through our minds as we sleep. Their existence is a matter of faith in a collective sense of identity.

Fundamentally, dream states are creatures of the passions. Like the progeny of defunct royal dynasties who advertise themselves as the "pretender" to such and such a crown, dream states are driven ultimately by an exercise of will. Their goal is validation as sovereign states. They seek recognition as members in good standing in the community of nations. They are *pretenders to sovereignty.*

Dream States. Benjamin J. Cohen, Oxford University Press. © Oxford University Press (2025).
DOI: 10.1093/9780197811672.003.0001

4   DREAM STATES

Secession

The core issue addressed in this book is the highly contentious challenge of *secession*. By definition, pretenders to sovereignty are secessionists. The word secession has its roots in the Latin words *se,* meaning "apart," and *cedere,* meaning "to go." Hence, secession is associated with leaving or withdrawing from some place. Secessionists seek to separate from an already existing sovereign state. Popular synonyms for secessionism are self-determination or separatism.

Technically, secession has been defined as "the formal withdrawal from an established, internationally recognized state by a constituent unit to create a new sovereign state. Secession movements are groups of people within a state that actively seek to break away from the larger country and obtain independence."[2] That is a good starting point. The devil, however, is in the details, as we shall see. Key questions remain to be addressed.[3] Is separation partial or complete? Is the divorce consensual or contested? Is withdrawal achieved peaceably or by force? Is the former sovereign state (the "incumbent" or "host" state) to be erased from the world map or will it continue to exist in diminished form? Such details matter.

In practical terms, dream states emerge for all kinds of reasons. Abkhazia was an autonomous region of the Republic of Georgia, one of the fifteen successor states of the former Soviet Union, until military intervention by Russia in 2008. With backing from Moscow, Abkhazia then declared itself a sovereign nation. Puntland, by contrast, took shape as a byproduct of the disintegration of the "failed state" of Somalia in the Horn of Africa. Puntland's aim was primarily to defend its people against the anarchy that erupted elsewhere in Somalia some decades after independence in 1960. And Sahrawi, also known as Western Sahara, was a colonial dependency of Spain until the territory was handed over to neighboring Morocco and Mauritania in 1975 against the wishes of the local populace. (Four years later, Mauritania relinquished any claim to the area.) An on-and-off war of resistance has been fought against Morocco ever since in the name of the notional Sahrawi Arab Democratic Republic. The Conch Republic, meanwhile, is a tiny pretender declared in 1982 as a tongue-in-cheek secession of the city of Key West, Florida. The make-believe country has since expanded to encompass all of the Florida Keys (jokingly described as the Conch Republic's "Northern Territories").

The origin stories of dream states vary enormously. What they share in common is a shadowy existence at the fringes of the global community.

Importance

Shadowy, however, does not mean trivial. On the contrary, dream states actually play an outsized role in world politics that we can ignore only at our peril. Their salience is grievously underappreciated. In practical terms, they are important for three reasons.

First, there are an awful lot of them, with millions of people. They even have their own support group, the Unrepresented Nations and Peoples Organization, based in the Netherlands, to plead their case before the world community. We may not pay dream states much attention; indeed, we may be oblivious to their existence. But once we start looking for them, each one seeking to carve out a territory of its own, we find them just about anywhere. They are active on every continent and in every ocean. We live in an "age of secession," declares one expert,[4] who calculates that there have been, on average, some fifty-two separatist movements actively pursuing their cause in any single year since 1945.[5] By one count, there were as many as seventy active secession campaigns to be found around the world in 2008;[6] by another estimate a decade later, there were at least sixty.[7] Plainly, pretenders to sovereignty are not limited just to obscure corners of the globe in Africa or the volatile Caucasus region. Just ask the Scots or Catalans in Europe, the Palestinians or Kurds in the Middle East, or the Moros or Karen people in Asia. Millions around the world are firm in their allegiance to a dream state of their own.

Second, there is a sizable potential for many more dream states. Experts agree that secession movements emerge for any number of proximate reasons, both domestic and international.[8] At issue, in practical terms, is usually some sense of deprivation, discrimination, or injustice. Sovereignty may be sought to resist political oppression, overcome economic disadvantage, or preserve threatened religious or cultural traditions. Or it may be simply a matter of emotional resentment and distrust of rival communities. Stripped to their essence, however, most secession movements have a common root. At their core, they are first and foremost an expression of *identity politics*, driven by a sense of communal distinctiveness. Some would call it tribalism.

6 DREAM STATES

It would be a mistake to underestimate the intensity of feeling underlying secession movements. As one source puts it, "loyalty to state and homeland appears to be an extremely strong motivator."[9] Indeed, psychologists argue that identity-driven tribalism is a fundamental element of human nature—the product of eons of evolution. In the words of another authoritative source:

> Selective pressures have sculpted human minds to be *tribal,* and group loyalty and concomitant cognitive biases likely exist in all groups .... The human mind was forged by the crucible of coalitional conflict. For many thousands of years, human tribes have competed against each other. Coalitions that were more cooperative and cohesive not only survived but also appropriated land and resources from other coalitions and therefore reproduced more prolifically, thus passing their genes (and their loyalty traits) to later generations .... Tribalism, therefore, is natural.[10]

Secession movements, in short, are tribal separatists operating under the banner of self-determination. Their driving force is loyalty to the group. Their goal is to live apart—to formalize their group's unique and legitimate place in the community of nations. If we live in an "age of secession," it is because more and more groups are demanding to be validated as distinct sovereign states, splitting off from older, already established national units. Like single-cell amoebae, they seek to subdivide. The notion of self-determination has an enormously powerful appeal.

Indeed, everywhere we look, conceptions of national identity today seem driven to fragment into smaller and smaller entities. A prime illustration is provided by the defunct federation of Yugoslavia ("Land of the South Slavs"), which first came into existence in southeastern Europe after World War I. In the 1990s after the end of the Cold War, Yugoslavia suddenly disintegrated, first into its six constituent "republics" (Bosnia, Croatia, Macedonia, Montenegro, Serbia, and Slovenia) and then, a few years later, even further with the secession of Kosovo from Serbian jurisdiction. From one state emerged seven, and the jury is still out on Bosnia, where the hostile Serbian population seems still determined to consolidate its own Republika Srpska. Similar centrifugal forces are also to be found in many other countries elsewhere—perhaps, if our dispatch from the future is to be believed, even in the United States (US). Subdivision is in the air. William Shakespeare wrote of the "stuff as dreams are made on." For many people around the world, dream states are the stuff that local politics are made of.

Third, most importantly, dream states have become a dominant source of friction on the global stage—"downright dangerous," in the blunt phrasing of one informed observer.[11] More and more armed conflicts in the world today can be traced to the aspirations of pretenders to sovereignty.

Traditional interstate disputes over territory have, of course, by no means disappeared. Just think of the continuing antagonisms between unhappy neighbors like India and Pakistan or Armenia and Azerbaijan. But for the most part, territorial ambitions have become less expansive than they once were.[12] Indeed, with relatively rare exceptions—such as Saddam Hussein's failed grab for Kuwait in 1990 or Vladimir Putin's "special military operation" in Ukraine in 2022—outright territorial wars have become quite rare. These days, few governments aspire to gobble up other states. Instead, we generally see widespread respect for the borders between sovereign states—a proscription that has come to be known as the "territorial integrity norm."[13] Existing international borders are treated almost as if they were sacrosanct; and even on the relatively rare occasions when lines between sovereign states are redrawn, they tend to follow previous administrative frontiers.[14] I will have more to say about the territorial integrity norm in Chapter 14.

Today, armed combat around the world tends to occur much more often *within* national borders rather than *across* them. Well over half of all conflicts in recent years have been separatist wars of secession triggered by the aspirations of dream states—a striking development.[15] Indeed, the proliferation of secessionist conflicts is of historical proportions. As one respected expert puts it, separatism has become the "chief source of violence in the world today."[16] Another scholar contends that we live not in an "age of secession" but in an "age of *wars* of secession."[17] Consider these words of a middle-aged German journalist published on Christmas Day 2022:

> To my generation war was a distant and gloomy impossibility, something that happened elsewhere, if at all. We thought that "never again," the country's postwar slogan, designed to expunge war from the national psyche, accurately described the world. We thought we grew up in peace. In truth, the '90s and 2000s saw a lot of violence in Europe. The brutal Balkan wars started in 1991, the conflict over Transnistria's secession from Moldova in 1992. Mr. Putin's war in Chechnya … lasted a decade. In 1998, war broke out in Kosovo; ten years later, Russia attacked Georgia. The war in Ukraine, of course, started in 2014 when Mr. Putin annexed Crimea and fomented separatist conflict in the Donbas region.[18]

8 DREAM STATES

All these were wars of secession. Nor, during this time, was separatist violence limited only to Europe. In fact, wars of secession have become remarkably common in much of the world. They may even be considered endemic. Over the decades since World War II, there has been an average of fifteen secessionist conflicts boiling along in any given year.[19] The Balkan wars of the former Yugoslavia were only one example. Many similar conflicts have flared up elsewhere as well, in all sorts of far-flung places. Just since the start of the twenty-first century, murderous hot spots have erupted in Ethiopia, Iraq, Libya, Myanmar, Palestine, the Philippines, Somalia, Sri Lanka, Sudan, Syria, and Yemen, to name just a few.

As dream states proliferate, each one seeking its own place in the sun, so too does the risk of deadly strife. Worse, while wars of secession may be easy to start, once ignited they turn out to be remarkably difficult to extinguish. Many persist for years, even decades, adding more and more to the number of separatist struggles raging at any given moment. The average conflict in the mid-1980s had been going on for about thirteen years; by 2021, the average was up to nearly twenty years.[20] Though not all wars of secession can be expected ultimately to succeed, most are apt to become increasingly costly over time in terms of both blood and treasure.

In short, dream states can become a nightmare.

Types

Not all dream states are equally disruptive, of course. Distinctions must be made between different kinds of dream states and the threats that each type might pose. Some pretenders to sovereignty are more likely to provoke conflict than do others. No one fears that Canada's *Québécois* are about to launch an armed rebellion, however much francophone Canadians may yearn for a *Québec libre*. On the other hand, few observers doubt that the aspirations of the Palestinians can at any time explode into bloody violence (and often do). Dream states are by no means all alike.

The need to differentiate among different types of dream states is routinely emphasized by academic specialists. Consensus on a standardized taxonomy, however, is lacking. Perhaps the most refined effort has come from Ryan Griffiths, a leader in the field of secession studies, who distinguishes among six identifiable types of secession movements—what he calls democratized, indigenous legal, weak combative, strong combative, decolonial, and de facto.[21] Regrettably, however, his taxonomy is not very useful for our purposes, since each of his categories is merely, as he puts it, a pragmatic "cluster of characteristics." The categories are not directly comparable among themselves on a common scale.

For our purposes, the common scale of most interest is the risk of violence, with particular emphasis on any dangers involved for the United States. In the chapters that follow, therefore, I will rely on a system of classification that focuses directly on the *degree of conflict risk* posed by individual dream states. Five separate categories of secession movements can be distinguished, moving in sequence from the least disruptive to the most destabilizing. Many dream states, we shall see, are wholly benign, a threat to no one, or at worst a petty nuisance, while others are contentious but unlikely to resort to military force. Only a minority of separatist movements pose a real danger of armed combat that could involve the United States— but that minority is more than enough to threaten peace in many parts of the world.

With my tongue firmly in cheek, I offer the following labels for my quintet of categories:

(1) *Fantasies.* These are dream states that no one is expected to take very seriously. They are included here mainly for a sense of completeness and perhaps a little comic relief. Most fantasy dream states are little more than jokes. Some may be promoted for the purpose of evading government regulations. A few may be a scam of some sort.

(2) *Daydreams.* These dream states are a bit more serious than fantasies but have only limited ambition. They are mainly an expression of a cherished desire: a sentimental yearning for acknowledgment of an authentic ethnic, racial, or linguistic identity. Their goal is more social than political. They build no organized secession movement of significance, and the United States is not likely to become directly involved.

(3) *Drexits.* These are dream states that do more than just dream. They are more ambitious, more daring, than daydreams. Ultimately, their goal is to formally exit an older state (hence, "drexit")—in other words, to secede. But they are not inclined to go beyond peaceable means in pursuit of their goal. There may be an organized separatist movement of significance, but its preferred means are political

10   DREAM STATES

rather than militarized. Here too, US involvement is most likely to be limited.

(4) *Rebels with a cause.* These are dream states that, as compared with daydreams or drexits, are even more radical in their ambition. In pursuit of recognition, they are prepared to go beyond strictly peaceable means, up to and including fully armed rebellion. They too want to exit an older state, but in contrast to daydreams or drexits, they are willing to fight for their cause. In these cases, the United States could well become involved, indirectly if not directly.

(5) *Clients.* These dream states are essentially a cover for the concealed ambition of an outside patron. The previous categories could all be considered endogenous, an expression of local preference. Clients, by contrast, are largely exogenous in nature, more an extension of the geopolitical aspirations of a powerful sponsor that is pledged to defend and promote the dream state's interests, by force if necessary. Some kind of US involvement is much more likely.

Westphalia

Hypocrisy, it is said, is the homage that vice pays to virtue. In a similar vein, dream states may be said to be the homage that non-states pay to states— or, to be more precise, the homage that non-states pay to the state system that defines world politics in the modern era. With few exceptions, school children are taught a global map that is colorfully divided into fixed and mutually exclusive entities that we call states (or countries or nations). Jurisdiction is said to be territorially based. In principle, each state is assumed to be sovereign within its own inviolable frontiers.

It hasn't always been that way. Indeed, for most of human history, political geography was far more complex. There were as yet no fixed or exclusive sovereignties. It was taken for granted that governing authority was diffuse, often shifting, and certainly more permeable. Think of the conclusion of Shakespeare's historical drama *Henry V*, when the Duke of Burgundy mediates a peace agreement between the King of England and the King of France. Though nominally autonomous, the Duke was considered a vassal of both monarchies. Legally, he owed fealty to each of them.

The nation-state system that we take for granted today only emerged in the centuries following the Peace of Westphalia of 1648, which ended the Thirty Years War in Europe. Westphalia is generally recognized as a watershed in world politics—the first treaty to carefully codify basic elements of international law. A lengthy and complicated document, it contained provisions to address a variety of contentious issues, including diverse dynastic claims, divisions of territory, religious practices, and the constitution of the Holy Roman Empire. But today, the Peace is most remembered for its assertion of the principle of sovereign equality among states: absolute rule for each state within its own physical borders. In effect, the treaty formally established territoriality as the sole legitimate basis for the distribution of authority across the map. The spread of Westphalian norms took time. But by the twentieth century, their triumph was complete. The territorial state has come to be accepted as the world's basic unit of governance. Global politics is conceived in terms of the familiar state system—the so-called Westphalian model of political geography.

The limitations of Westphalia's territorial imagery, however, are clear—or should be. The idea that world politics can be understood simply in terms of "neatly divided spatial packages," as one scholar has put it,[22] is deceptively innocent, even naive. Critical to the Westphalian model is an assumption that states are, in some sense, "natural," each gathering together a distinct community under the banner of national identity. Each is implicitly thought to share a common culture of some sort, including such features as language, customs, and religious beliefs. In reality, however, the notion of the homogeneous territorial state is sadly misleading—a distortion at best, a caricature at worst. In the words of one recent commentary: "Humans don't group into tidy and geographically distinguishable communities. Rather, we all bear multiple identities."[23]

As a practical matter, it is impossible to think of a single country that does not have minority populations of some kind, each with its own distinctive identity and culture. Americans are taught the slogan *e pluribus unum*—"out of many, one"—but how many of us actually believe it? How many Muslims in India or Tamils in Sri Lanka count themselves as full citizens of the country in which they happen to reside? How many Amharas in the heartland of Ethiopia feel a true societal kinship with rival ethnic groups like the Oromo or Tigrayans?

The famed cultural anthropologist Benedict Anderson said it best when he described states as "imagined communities"—not natural units but, rather, entities that have been deliberately *created*, usually through some

12 DREAM STATES

combination of force and loyalty.[24] States, he pointed out, do not emerge spontaneously. Rather, they must be cultivated, as much in the mind as in geography. A nation, someone once quipped, is "a people with a common confusion as to their origins and a common antipathy to their neighbors."[25] National identity rests on a critical distinction between Us and Them. The difference must be inculcated and may be heightened by all manner of tangible symbols such as flags, anthems, public architecture, and even national sports teams. States are imagined, Anderson argues, "because the members of even the smallest nation will never know most of their fellow-members, meet them, or even hear of them, yet in the minds of each lives the image of their communion."[26] The Westphalian model of a concert of "natural" states was plainly a product of a particular time and place. It can lay no claim to general truth or eternal validity. As one observer aptly summarizes:

> A little comparative history goes a long way. It shows us that the sovereign state is not naturally occurring. In fact, by comparison with other forms of rule and ways of organizing space, it is historically exceptional ... a distinctively modern way of conceiving and organizing space ... No other civilization either imagined or organized the known world in this way.[27]

Today, nearly four centuries after Westphalia, absolute state sovereignty still prevails as a judicial norm, a core constitutive rule firmly enshrined in the canons of international law. The presumed authority of governments over a defined geographic space remains, in principle, inviolate. But in terms of actual practice, the concept has always been a convenient fiction—in the words of a noted political geographer, a "territorial trap"[28] for the unwary. To some degree, practical sovereignty has always been more contingent than categorical: contested rather than conceded, pliant rather than immutable, diffuse rather than indivisible. De facto, states are perpetually engaged in negotiating or renegotiating elements of their nominal national authority. Sovereignty, in the blunt phrase of Stephen Krasner, a leading scholar of international relations, has always been "up for grabs."[29]

That is where dream states come in. If sovereignty is indeed up for grabs, what is to discourage sub-groups of all kinds from aspiring to their own statehood? A community that is a minority within existing borders might well feel that it has every right to become a majority within revised frontiers. We should not be surprised, therefore, that there are so many dream states around the globe. As Anderson noted, "many 'old nations,' once thought fully consolidated, find themselves challenged by 'sub'-nationalisms within their borders—nationalisms which, naturally, dream of shedding this sub-ness one happy day."[30] In that sense, sub-nationalisms may claim as much legitimacy as any older incumbent nationalism. What could be more "natural?"

Sovereignty

The challenge, of course, is obvious. Who belongs? The Westphalian state system is like a private club. Entrance is not automatic. You have to be admitted. Sub-nationalisms may dream of shedding their "sub-ness," but there is no guarantee that any of them will succeed in gaining entry. Remember, they are *pretenders*—claimants. As candidates, they must *qualify*. They must be *accepted*. Meeting the necessary qualifications for membership is by no means easy.

The key qualification is *sovereignty*. Indeed, the club is often referred to as the "sovereignty club."[31] But what do we mean by sovereignty? At its core, the Westphalian model equates sovereignty with a meaningful degree of control over a defined parcel of land. Statehood is both "empirical" and "juridical."[32] In the famous words of the German sociologist Max Weber, states may be defined as political communities that "[successfully] claim a monopoly on the legitimate use of physical force within a given territory."[33] At first glance, that would seem to make matters easy: a simple binary choice. A candidate state either exercises territorial control or it does not. We might expect that admission to the club would be conceded to the former but not to the latter.

In practice, however, outcomes are rarely so straightforward. Historically, territorial control alone has proved neither necessary nor sufficient to gain entrance. Exceptions abound. Just a few years ago, the notorious Islamic State (known as ISIS) gained command over a wide swath of land in the remote border regions of Syria and Iraq, yet was never considered a legitimate member of the international state system. Territorial control was not enough to realize its ambitions. By contrast, Palestine has been formally recognized by a sizable number of governments as an independent state despite its lack of undisputed domain over either the West Bank or Gaza. For the Palestinians, territorial control has not been needed to get a foot in the sovereignty club's door.

14　DREAM STATES

Why are there exceptions like these? The answer lies in the meaning of sovereignty, which in reality encompasses much more than just territorial control. Krasner, for instance, identifies at least four core dimensions of national sovereignty,[34] which are defined as follows:

(1) *Domestic sovereignty*, referring to the organization of public authority within a candidate state and to the level of effective control exercised by those holding authority.
(2) *Interdependence sovereignty*, referring to the ability of public authorities to control transborder movements of goods, services, money, and people.
(3) *International legal sovereignty*, referring to the mutual recognition of states or other entities.
(4) *Westphalian sovereignty*, referring to the exclusion of external actors from domestic authority configurations (in other words, the core idea of territorial control).

With so many dimensions in play, it is evident that matters are by no means as simple as they might seem at first glance. As Krasner emphasizes, none of the four dimensions are logically linked, nor do they necessarily covary in practice. Hence, candidates may score high on some dimensions but lower on others, complicating the simple binary choice.

At the extremes, of course, there is little doubt. If a candidate appears to satisfy all four dimensions, the dream state almost certainly will become a reality sooner or later. An apt example is Timor-Leste, a small island nation located at the eastern end of the Indonesian archipelago just north of Australia. A former Portuguese colony that passed to the control of Indonesia in 1976, Timor-Leste struggled for years to qualify for membership in the community of nations. Ample resources were invested in building its domestic and Westphalian sovereignty and lobbying vigorously for formal recognition. The goal of independence was finally achieved in 2002. Conversely, if none of the four dimensions are fully attained, a candidate most likely will remain a dream state indefinitely. Abkhazia, Puntland, and Sahrawi all fit unhappily into that category. Until now, despite years of effort, they have yet to be admitted to the club. The fate of outliers is relatively easy to predict.

The problem is that in the real world, most cases tend to fall between the extremes—strong in some dimensions of sovereignty, weaker in others. That means that most cases are apt to be rather more controversial than outliers like Timor-Leste on the one hand or Abkhazia, Puntland, and Sahrawi on the other. Where one or more of Krasner's four dimensions are lacking, the door to full club membership will not be shoved open without effort. To succeed, therefore, any bid for acceptance by newer nationalisms may have to be vigorously pressed, which in turn can be expected to turn up the heat in relations with older established governments. The harder candidates push for admission, the more likely it is that they will be met with some degree of resistance and may even be contested militarily. Incumbent governments will be particularly loath to make concessions if they are at risk of additional separatist challenges in the future.[35] Is it any wonder, then, that there are so many wars of secession around the globe?

Dangers

My aim in this book is to highlight just how disruptive dream states can be. Two questions define my agenda. First, how serious is the threat of separatist conflict? And second, what can be done about it? My answers are not necessarily reassuring.

As we shall see, there truly are a lot of dream states—an astonishing number, in fact. Some, such as the Conch Republic, are not to be taken seriously. Many are mere jokes or publicity stunts; others, nothing more than clever gambits to escape taxes or regulations. Few of these more fanciful constructs pose any real danger. They are essentially harmless. But even if they are all excluded, the number of more serious dream states remains impressively large.

Worse, as noted, there is a potential for a lot more dream states in the years to come. Centrifugal forces in the modern state system clearly dominate centripetal pressures. Since World War II, there have been only four mergers of sovereign states attempted anywhere on the globe: Egypt and Syria (1958); Tanganyika and Zanzibar (1964); South Yemen and North Yemen (1990); and East Germany and West Germany (1990).[36] Moreover, of these four, only two survive. One is Tanzania, where the tiny island of Zanzibar was effectively swallowed up by its much larger neighbor Tanganyika. The other is the special case of Germany, where two halves of a once-single nation were reunified at the end of the Cold War. Yet during the same period, we have seen the disintegration of two larger political unions, Yugoslavia and the Soviet Union, as well as the emergence of other new states like Timor-Leste

16   DREAM STATES

or South Sudan as a result of successful wars of secession. The membership of the sovereignty club keeps growing. Who is to say that pressures for further fragmentation might not intensify in the future? The possibilities are virtually endless.

And that means that the possibilities for armed conflict are virtually endless as well. When it comes to international relations, most of us tend to focus on the risk of conflict between the great powers or struggles with rogue states like Iran or North Korea. That is all quite understandable, of course, particularly if nuclear weapons might come to be involved. Less attention, meanwhile, is paid to the multitude of brush fires that smolder around the world, driven by the separatist aspirations of dream states. That is a mistake. As any resident of California (where I happen to live) knows, it doesn't take much for a small local wildfire to suddenly swell into an all-consuming inferno. Dream states may seem innocuous, not much of a menace for those of us who are not directly involved. In fact, they are a grave danger to all of us if the flames are allowed to spread, leaving death and destruction in their wake. The threat should not be underestimated. Dream states are indeed a lurking nightmare.

2

Supply and Demand

Paramount considerations

How bad is the nightmare? Are there really many brush fires out there that could swell into an inferno? Or can I be accused of exaggeration?

It's not easy to say. Two considerations are paramount. First is the matter of credentials. How hard might it be to gain admission into the sovereignty club? The easier it is to qualify for membership, the greater will be the number of dream states that might be tempted to give it a try, even at the risk of sparking armed combat. And second is the question of motivation. How strong is a "sub-nationalism's" urge to sharpen the distinction between itself and older incumbent nationalisms? The more "natural" an imagined community might seem to its proponents, the more determined it will be to pry the door open and force its way in. Resorting to the arcane language of economics, the first of these considerations may be said to highlight the *supply* side of the issue, while the second defines the *demand* side. Both sides matter, and both point to the same conclusion. It is no exaggeration to say that the lurking nightmare is indeed serious.

The supply side

On the supply side, the question is one of accessibility: How much room is there in today's state system for new members? The number of eager dream states will very much depend on the degree of difficulty in gaining admission. The stricter the barriers to entry, the shorter will be the queue of potential applicants.

At first glance, constraints on supply would seem to dominate. As indicated in the previous chapter, the key qualification for club membership is sovereignty. But fully meeting all four of Stephen Krasner's core dimensions of sovereignty is clearly a tall order, not easily achieved in practice. Getting a foot in the club's door would appear to be quite a challenge.

Dream States. Benjamin J. Cohen, Oxford University Press. © Oxford University Press (2025).
DOI: 10.1093/9780197811672.003.0002

18   DREAM STATES

Yet history suggests otherwise. Over the years—particularly since 1945—the number of sovereign states around the globe has increased dramatically. Club members have multiplied like rabbits, from no more than a few dozen nations a century ago to nearly 200 today. Expansion like that implies that while the qualifications for admission may be arduous, they are by no means insurmountable. At the same time, the average size of recognized states has noticeably shrunk, implying some relaxation of standards for smaller candidates in particular. Overall, it seems evident that resistance to new members, even the tiniest, is far from prohibitive.

Defining statehood

Multiple attempts have been made over the years to give empirical precision to the notion of a global sovereignty club. Academic experts have competed to produce what amounts to a census of the Westphalian world.

The first step is to define "statehood." What may be considered a state? Without a proper understanding of the meaning of statehood, obviously, it would be difficult to come up with an accurate count of the club's membership roster. The earliest formal estimate was compiled more than half a century ago[1] and has since been maintained and periodically updated by a well-known research initiative known as the Correlates of War project.[2] More recently, rival counts have been proposed by a variety of researchers in the United States (US) and elsewhere,[3] each producing a standardized list of entities that could be reckoned as fully independent states.

Though empirical efforts differ on many details, they all agree that the expansion in the number of club members since 1945 has been phenomenal. Indicative is membership in the United Nations (UN), which has risen exponentially since the organization's birth at the end of World War II. The UN itself does not recognize countries; the organization's General Assembly simply votes on whether a new nation will be allowed to join the club. But absent any other qualifying procedure, election to UN membership may be seen as the closest equivalent we have to a formal admissions process. From fifty-one founding members in 1945, the number of full UN member states has swollen to a total of 193 today—nearly a fourfold increase in less than eight decades. Can such a rate of growth be regarded as anything short of astonishing? As one scholar wryly observes, if the rate of state birth were to continue at the same pace, there would be 260 countries in the world by 2050 and 354 by the end of the century.[4]

In good part, of course, the striking expansion of the UN roster may be said to be a reflection of two one-time special events. One was the massive wave of decolonizations that swept across the globe in the first decades after World War II. Out of the fading colonial empires of Europe came dozens of new states in the Global South, all eager for recognition of their political sovereignty. The other special event was the breakup of Yugoslavia and the Soviet Union, which between them added yet another score of new members. Bewildered school children had to learn a whole bunch of new country names. But these events were hardly the whole story. Also important were a number of prolonged but ultimately successful secession struggles that produced additional new members like South Sudan and Timor-Leste.

The standards used for election to UN membership rely broadly on customary international law going back to the Montevideo Convention of 1933 (formally, the Montevideo Convention on the Rights and Duties of States). The Convention was signed by some nineteen Western Hemisphere countries, including the United States. It set out four criteria for statehood: (1) a defined territory; (2) a permanent population; (3) a government; and (4) a capacity to enter into relations with other states. In updated form, any or all of the same four criteria are typically stressed in rival estimates of who rightfully belongs to the sovereignty club and who doesn't.

(1) *Territorial control.* The importance of territorial control, stressed by Max Weber's famous aphorism,[5] is universally assumed to be a minimum qualification for admission. This is what Krasner calls Westphalian sovereignty. Others refer to it as "empirical statehood."[6] Estimates of club membership generally exclude pretenders that are subject to formal rule from outside their frontiers. Candidates must have a meaningful degree of authority over some exclusive fraction of the earth's surface.

(2) *Population.* A permanent population, however minuscule, is also considered an essential criterion for statehood. Effectively, there may be no lower limit to the size of a state's population. Very small states are generally referred to as "microstates" (not to be confused with "micronations," which is the term typically assigned to very small dream states).

20 DREAM STATES

(3) *Effective control.* Also considered essential is a reasonable degree of command over political and economic activities both within and across the entity's frontiers—a combination of what Krasner calls domestic sovereignty and interdependence sovereignty.

(4) *Diplomatic recognition.* A final requirement is widespread formal recognition by other states, through either direct accreditation of diplomatic missions or membership of the United Nations. This is what Krasner calls international legal sovereignty. Others refer to it as "juridical statehood."[7]

Taken together, these four criteria add up to a formidable set of requirements. Gaining standing in the global club does indeed appear to be a challenge.

Exceptions

Exceptions, however, are common. In practice, some entities come to be accepted as states despite their failure to meet one or more of the four criteria, while others that might seem qualified are nonetheless left sitting out in the cold. Almost every standardized list includes decisions that are essentially ad hoc and might be questioned.

To illustrate, consider again the matter of UN membership. On the one hand, there have been (and still are) some questionable inclusions in the UN's roster. Perhaps the most egregious came up at the time of the organization's birth when Soviet leader Joseph Stalin insisted on full membership for two of his domestic "republics," Belarus and Ukraine. (Reportedly, when challenged on this demand by President Franklin Roosevelt, Stalin offered in exchange to accept UN membership for two US states, such as New York and Texas.) In more recent times, membership has been preserved for badly fractured or failed states, where the writ of the recognized government may not extend any further than the gates of the presidential palace. Prime examples today include Libya, Somalia, Myanmar, and Yemen.

On the other hand, there have also been some glaring omissions. Most prominent these days are a lonesome foursome—Kosovo, Taiwan, Palestine, and Western Sahara—all well-known but highly controversial would-be candidates for club membership. Each has been effectively blackballed by an influential neighbor with competing territorial claims: Serbia in the case of Kosovo, Israel in the case of Palestine, Morocco in the case of Western Sahara, and China vis-à-vis Taiwan. The closest any of these four candidates has come to entry is the putative state of Palestine, which has long been granted status at the UN as a "permanent non-member state observer" despite its lack of control over any piece of land to call its own. Although the Palestinians have received formal diplomatic recognition from more than 140 countries, full UN membership has been repeatedly vetoed by the United States, Israel's close ally—most recently in May 2024. (The only other entity with permanent non-member observer status at the UN is Vatican City, also known as the Holy See.) In all four instances, the problem, plainly, is politics. Decisions on membership at the UN, whether to admit or to reject, are inevitably politicized, tainted by local or global rivalries.

Exceptions like the lonesome foursome suggest that the dichotomous conceptualization of statehood typical of most empirical studies may be too rigid.[8] Standard practice insists on a strict binary choice: Entities either are full-fledged states or they have no international standing at all. In reality, the dichotomous approach is crude and makes no allowance for various hybrid forms of political power that might be considered possible. Cases can be found where governments find a way to accommodate demands by diverse sub-nationalisms for greater autonomy while at the same time keeping the incumbent state intact as a political unit. One familiar example is Puerto Rico, whose "commonwealth" relationship with the United States acknowledges the island's subordinate legal status even while allowing residents to exercise some independence as an autonomous political entity. (Of particular symbolic importance to Puerto Rico's is its right to participate in the Olympics or other international sporting events under its own flag.) Another example is Canada's francophone province of Quebec, which enjoys a high degree of home rule within the broader Canadian federation. Quebec is even permitted to operate its own Ministry of International Relations with some thirty-three offices in eighteen foreign countries.

In practice, therefore, there really is room for elasticity in the interpretation of entry standards, particularly if we conceptualize statehood as a continuous attribute—more sovereign or less sovereign—rather than either/or. (I will have more to say about this matter in my concluding chapters.) Elasticity can cut both ways, of course, both in favor of candidates that might not be adequately qualified as well as against fully qualified candidates who

22 DREAM STATES

happen to have powerful enemies. But for ambitious dream states, the implication is clear. The qualifications for admission are not strictly prohibitive. Validation as club members in good standing is not impossible.

Size

Elasticity in the interpretation of statehood is particularly evident when it comes to the matter of size. Whether measured by population or area, an entity's size—however small—has never been an absolutely prohibitive barrier to entry. The UN's rules, for instance, have allowed admission of microstates with some really tiny populations. Many number well under 100,000. One familiar example is San Marino, often held to be the world's oldest continuously existing republic. Entirely surrounded by Italy, San Marino was admitted to the UN in 1992 with a population of less than 40,000. Other microstates include Andorra and Liechtenstein in Europe, Dominica and St. Kitts in the Caribbean, and Nauru and Palau in the Pacific. UN rules also permit entry for many territories that are little more than specks on the map—tiny places like the city-state of Singapore or scattered island-nations in the Caribbean, Indian Ocean, or Pacific. The size criterion included in most empirical studies—as measured by either population or territory—does not appear to have much influence on definitions of statehood in practice.

Quite the contrary, in fact. In practice, it appears that resistance to membership on the grounds of size alone is not at all a problem. The evidence from history is clear. Over time, average state size has contracted sharply and for the most part continuously—a process that has been going on for over a hundred years, since before World War I. Today, average state size is less than half of what it was a century ago.[9] Scholars speak of "the incredible shrinking state."[10]

Obviously, shrinkage does not mean that existing states are actually getting smaller. Rather it simply reflects the fact that, more often than not, new states tend to be smaller than older states, thus lowering the average. That can easily be seen in the two developments that have accounted for so much of the growth of the club since 1945: the massive waves of decolonization and the disintegration of the Soviet Union and Yugoslavia. Most newly emancipated colonies were considerably smaller than their former metropolitan powers; of course, the individual successor states of Yugoslavia and the Soviet Union were, by definition, more diminutive than the broader federations from which they sprang.

All in all, therefore, the conclusion is clear. On the supply side of the issue, the door to the club is not tightly locked. As tough as it may seem to gain admission, inclusion is by no means impossible—not even for midget microstates. A temptation to make a serious bid for membership, therefore, is not at all unreasonable, no matter how hopeless the cause may seem to others. You don't have to be crazy to be a pretender to sovereignty.

The demand side

But there is also the matter of motivation—the demand side of the issue. How strong is the urge to secede? Are there really many communities out there just aching to join the club? Or is the dream of sovereignty, in many cases, little more than a whim?

In the absence of comprehensive opinion polls, it is of course impossible to give a direct answer. More indirectly, however, a strong clue is offered by a body of political economy theory, now some two decades old, that aimed to specify in material terms the optimal size of nations.[11] The basic approach of most such models was to make the size of nations a function of decisions about the provision of goods and services to constituents. A critical trade-off was posited. On the one side were the benefits of economic integration, in the form of lower transaction costs within a single market. Economists label this economies of scale. On the other side were the costs of political integration, in the form of policies that might be less reflective of divergent social preferences and identities. When barriers to international trade are high, the benefits of economic integration at the domestic level can be assumed to be substantial, owing to economies of scale. That suggests that as far as state size is concerned, bigger is better. But where populations are more heterogeneous, increasing the risk of identity-driven disputes over policy choices, the costs of political integration will also be large, suggesting contrarily that the optimal size of nations might be smaller, not larger. Breaking big states into smaller units, either voluntarily or via secession, would allow individual sub-national groups to congregate more with their own kind.

In short, according to this body of theory, the optimal size of nations is hostage to two contrasting variables: the level of trade barriers and the degree of domestic heterogeneity. A cursory glance through recent history

24 DREAM STATES

would suggest that in the contemporary era, at least one of these variables—domestic heterogeneity—is moving unmistakably in a direction that favors ever smaller state size.

That may not be the case with the trade-barrier variable. For decades, the trend of the world economy was all in the direction of greater and greater openness, meaning that even very small states could share in the benefits of economic integration without sacrificing their political independence. We called it globalization. More recently, however, many governments seem more inclined to reverse—or, at least, to moderate—the degree of their international commercial exposure. The global financial crisis of 2008, the Great Recession that followed, the Covid-19 pandemic that started in 2020, the Russian invasion of Ukraine in 2022, and Israel's war with Hamas and other Iranian proxies that began in 2023—all have persuaded many policy makers that economic openness could turn out to be too much of a good thing. More and more, governments are turning to tariffs, subsidies, and other protectionist measures to reduce the risks of foreign exposure. Observers increasingly talk of "slowbalization," "deglobalization," or "homeland economics," which suggests that on strictly economic grounds, bigger states might now be more favored in order to preserve the benefits of economic integration. We still don't know how strong this trend may be or whether it will persist.

However, as far as the heterogeneity variable is concerned, the trend is unmistakable. Across the globe, allegiances to diverse sub-nationalisms seem to be taking increasing hold. Some, like the Catalans in Spain or the Scots in Britain, are contained largely within the borders of a single older nation. Others, like the Kurds in the Middle East or the Berbers in northern Africa, occupy a stretch of land spread across two or more established states. Each one of these minority groups imagines itself to be as "natural" a community as any other. For most of them, existing frontiers or administrative divisions are just lines drawn on a map. Reality exists in the minds and hearts of communities. Again, we call it identity politics.

The trend can gain momentum over time as separatist movements come closer to realizing their distinctive preferences. The process can also become recursive, as ostensibly homogeneous groups within a more heterogeneous society themselves splinter into yet thinner and thinner shards. In academic circles, this is known as the "minorities-within-minorities" issue.[12] An apt example is provided by Lithuania, once a tiny minority within the nine million square miles of the Soviet Union. Today, Lithuania is an independent state that finds itself dealing with its own homegrown minority, the Karaims. These are descendants of immigrants from Crimea who were invited centuries ago by the Grand Duke of Lithuania to serve as bodyguards and traders. Today the Karaims in Lithuania—though numbering no more than a few hundred—campaign actively on behalf of their own singular ethnicity. The irony is not lost on the Lithuanian majority.

Potentially, the recursive "minorities-within-minorities" process is endless. As Boutros Boutros-Ghali, a former secretary-general of the United Nations, once remarked, "If every ethnic, religious or linguistic group claimed statehood, there would be no limit to fragmentation."[13] Reputable scholars have suggested there might be as many as 3,000–5,000 ethnic groups that could offer a plausible claim to self-determination.[14] Many stress language as a basic determinant of identity. The United Nations recognizes some 6,700 spoken languages and dialects worldwide. Ernst Gellner, a pioneering student of nationalism back in the 1980s, went even further. On the basis of linguistic diversity, Gellner suggested that in the final analysis, there may be as many as 8,000 potential nations in the world.[15] As one expert concludes, identity "is ultimately a fluid category .... In the end, the closest thing to a fundamental (or atomic) unit ... is the individual."[16]

On balance, therefore, we should not be surprised to find strong motivations to secede in many different places around the globe. Dreams of sovereignty are not a mere whim.

The challenge

Hence the challenge of secession is difficult to deny. There are indeed potentially disruptive nightmares lurking out there. On the supply side, it is evident that the door to club membership can be pushed open. Serious pretenders to sovereignty have no reason to eschew all hope of validation. Conversely, on the demand side, there would seem to be plenty of drive on the part of diverse communities to get through the door to full recognition. A priori, it hardly seems unreasonable for any group to fight for its own distinctive identity. Supply and demand considerations both point in the same direction—toward more and more dream states and, most likely, more and more conflict.

PART II
A SEPARATIST'S GUIDE

3

The Disunited States of America

America's internal challenge

We can begin with the United States (US), an "imagined community" if there ever was one. Ranking third among all countries in population and fourth in land mass, America can hardly claim to be a homogeneous nation. Few cultural traits are shared universally across the country's vast expanse beyond a nominal allegiance to a Constitution drafted by a bunch of bewigged gentlemen more than two centuries ago. Otherwise, Americans differ widely in almost every possible way—social customs, religious practices, political beliefs, and even modes of daily speech. I am old enough to recall when Jimmy Carter of Georgia was elected president in 1976 and southerners celebrated that, finally, we had a chief executive who could speak without an accent. No one could accuse the United States of being a "natural" entity. From the start, a sense of national identity has had to be cultivated and regularly refreshed in the face of all sorts of fissiparous forces. So far, the Union has held together. The question, looking forward, is: Can it remain together? Can America surmount its *internal* challenges?

Constitutional order

The constitutional order of the United States is more complex than most Americans realize. On the rare occasion when we may reflect on the structure of the US system, we naturally think of the fifty states that are represented by the fifty stars on the national flag, known to every schoolchild as the Star Spangled Banner or Old Glory. Originally, there were just thirteen stars on Old Glory, representing the original baker's dozen of colonies along the Atlantic coast that joined together to declare their independence from the British crown. The most recent additions to the flag's stars were for Alaska and Hawaii, which were admitted to the Union in 1959. The span of

Dream States. Benjamin J. Cohen, Oxford University Press. © Oxford University Press (2025).
DOI: 10.1093/9780197811672.003.0003

30 DREAM STATES

time since their admission is the longest period in US history without the addition of another new state.

The fifty states are the core constituents of the US federation. Votes in the House of Representatives, the lower chamber of the Congress, are allocated in proportion to each state's population. In the Senate, the upper chamber, each state has two votes. And every four years, the president is elected by an electoral college comprising representatives from all fifty states, each state by tradition voting as a unit. But that is just the top tier of America's union. Below the top tier, there is a second tier comprising a complex constellation of some fifteen dependencies of varying size and diverse links to the federal government in Washington. In this second tier, four groups may be distinguished.

First is the District of Columbia—effectively a unique group of one— where the federal government is seated. From the beginning, the Founding Fathers felt that the government's home should be as politically neutral as possible. Hence, the District of Columbia was constituted as a federal district, not part of any state and under the exclusive jurisdiction of the Congress. Over time, however, as the District's population has grown, the arrangement has come to seem increasingly anomalous. The District of Columbia today has almost three-quarters of a million residents—more than Vermont or Wyoming—with no voting rights in the Congress.

Second are two dependencies that are formally designated as commonwealths: Puerto Rico and the Northern Mariana Islands. Each is for most purposes self-governing, and both are authorized to send a non-voting representative, known as a delegate or resident commissioner, to the House of Representatives. Delegates may participate in debates and serve on Congressional committees, but may not cast votes on the House floor. The District of Columbia also sends a non-voting delegate to the Congress.

Third is a trio of dependencies with more limited autonomy that also enjoy the privilege of sending a non-voting delegate to the Congress. These are American Samoa, Guam, and the US Virgin Islands. All three are formally designated as overseas territories of the United States.

Finally, there are some nine more obscure dependencies that are governed directly from Washington. All but one are located in the Pacific Ocean. (The one exception is Navassa Island, in the Caribbean near Haiti.) Formally designated as US Minor Outlying Islands, these include Baker Island, Howland Island, Jarvis Island, Johnston Atoll, Kingman Reef, Midway Islands, Navassa Island, Palmyra Atoll, and Wake Island. All are considered too small to exercise any meaningful degree of self-government. These too are designated as US overseas territories.

Secession

How does secession fit into this constitutional structure? For most Americans, the answer is simple: It doesn't. From 1861 to 1865, a bloody civil war was fought over the Southern Confederacy's attempt to secede from the Union. The struggle was nasty and cost more than 750,000 lives on the two sides—more fatalities than suffered by Americans in the two world wars, Korea, and Vietnam combined. But with the South's decisive defeat, the matter was seemingly settled and then formally codified in 1869 by the Supreme Court in a historic case known as *Texas v. White*. By a vote of 5–3, the Court established what came to be called the principle of perpetuity—the view that the Union, once launched, could never be dissolved by the states. Secession was ruled out under any circumstance. In the words of the chief justice at the time, Salmon P. Chase, writing for the majority:

> When Texas entered the Union, she entered into an indissoluble relation. All the obligations of perpetual union, and all the guaranties of republican government in the Union, attached at once to the State. The act which consummated her admission into the Union was something more than a compact; it was the incorporation of a new member into the political body. And it was final. The union between Texas and the other States was as complete, as perpetual, and as indissoluble as the union between the original States. There was no place for reconsideration, or revocation, except through revolution, or through consent of the States.

We are reminded of an image popularized half a century ago by the Eagles, a once popular rock band. The Union might be said to resemble the mythical Hotel California. You can check in, but you can never leave.

Or can you? Despite *Texas v. White*, the legitimacy of secession continues to be debated. Many interested parties keep looking for a key that might conceivably unlock the Hotel California's exits. The constitution itself was silent on the matter, which from the start seemed to leave the question moot. Throughout the antebellum era, prior to the Civil War, defenders of the right of secession—mostly from below the Mason–Dixon line—energetically

32 DREAM STATES

sought a loophole of some kind. Technically, they conceded, secession by a sub-national unit could, in principle, be regarded as illegal—a violation of the Westphalian model of political geography, which prizes the absolute primacy of sovereignty at the top national level. But they also noted that sovereignty in practice is often treated as an "extralegal" matter that can be resolved, ultimately, only by political or military means. For them, the Union was more like a "compact" that legitimized secession as one possible option. The compact theory of the Union became the classic viewpoint of the southern slave states.[1] Maybe there could be exits from the Hotel California after all.

By contrast, opponents of secession disagreed, appealing to what appeared to be prior commitments in the Constitution as well as in the Articles of Confederation that preceded it. The Articles of Confederation explicitly stated that the Union, limited as it was, was "perpetual." The constitution, in turn, then went on to declare that its purpose was to build on the Articles of Confederation to form a "more perfect union." The system, therefore, could be considered to be like a contract without an escape clause. The Hotel California had no exits. The compact theory was firmly rejected by Chief Justice Chase in the *Texas v. White* opinion. "The ordinance of secession," he wrote, "adopted by the convention and ratified by a majority of the citizens of Texas, and all the acts of her legislature intended to give effect to that ordinance, were absolutely null. They were utterly without operation in law."

In practical terms, of course, secession's opponents prevailed, first on the battlefield and then at the Supreme Court. Yet even so, not everyone was convinced. The search for loopholes has persisted to the present day, with notable contributions over the years from some of the nation's leading constitutional scholars.[2] Collectively, at least seven potentially justifiable reasons for secession have been identified and highlighted by legal experts. These are:

(1) *Political morality.* Are civil liberties persistently oppressed? An identifiable sub-national community—a religious, ethnic, or linguistic minority—may come to believe that its political rights are being systematically sacrificed on behalf of the priorities of more favored social groups. Some would call that the "tyranny of the majority." Secession may be thought to be the only way to escape adverse discrimination.

THE DISUNITED STATES OF AMERICA   33

(2) *Economic self-interest.* Is a sub-national community economically exploited? Parallel to the political morality argument, this justification refers to the possibility of adverse discrimination in the economic realm—another form of tyranny by the majority. A sub-national minority may feel itself to be systematically deprived of access to material resources by way of taxes, regulations, or outright prohibitions.

(3) *Cultural integrity.* Is a sub-national community's social heritage threatened? The community may feel that its cultural traditions are at risk—a third form of tyranny by the majority. Its history may be ignored or distorted in school curriculums; use of its language may be banned or discouraged; or its holy days and festivals may be effectively repressed. Secession may come to seem the only way to preserve the group's sense of collective identity.

(4) *Origins.* Was the original act of unification voluntary? In many cases, union was imposed on a sub-national community, often by military conquest at some moment in the more or less remote past. Secession is justified as a means to correct what may be regarded as an historical wrong.

(5) *Centrifugal forces.* Have the nation's diverse sub-national communities lost any sense of common purpose? Successful unions are held together by strong centripetal forces, whether material or psychological. In some cases, however, political or social ties may fray over time, weakening resistance to the centrifugal forces of diverse sub-nationalisms. The more any sense of common destiny decays, the greater will be the attraction of secession.

(6) *Mutual suspicion.* Has there been an irreparable loss of civic trust? As any good divorce lawyer will tell you, a marriage cannot endure if the partners lose confidence in one another. Good will is essential. When mutual trust is lost, secession (divorce by another name) may be the only solution.

(7) *Dysfunction.* Has the central government lost its ability to exercise effective control, either domestically (what Krasner had in mind when he spoke of domestic sovereignty and Westphalian sovereignty) or in the management of transborder exchanges (Krasner's interdependence sovereignty)? The more any of these dimensions of sovereignty are weakened, the greater will be the temptation for sub-national communities to seek to go their own way.

34 DREAM STATES

As a matter of legal principle, all seven of these putative reasons for secession are logically sound. Any of them, on its own or in combination, could provide a lawful justification for secession. It is obvious, of course, that to some extent, each of the arguments is, in practical terms, subjective, calling for a necessarily qualitative judgment. How serious is perceived political, economic, or cultural discrimination? How deep was opposition to the original act of unification? How strong is the erosion of common purpose or the growth of mutual suspicion? Can nothing be done to reverse dysfunction at the center? Clearly, secession cannot be justified casually. The legitimacy of every claim has to be examined closely on a case-by-case basis.

The essential point, however, is that separatists are not without plausible legal arguments. There might yet be a key to the Hotel California's exits. Secession remains a possible option, even if only as a long shot. The issue is empirical. It all depends on how strong a case can be made for separation, given the facts.

Secession movements

Long shot or no, a good number of Americans have been willing to try. Secession movements in the United States are anything but scarce. Relatively few citizens, until now, have seemed eager to mount an armed rebellion on the model of the Old Confederacy. But most are clearly determined to make their presence felt by more peaceable means such as petitions, plebiscites, or local polls. Their aim, first and foremost, is to keep their dream alive. If many separatists remain unfamiliar to the general public, it is not for lack of effort.

Who are these separatists? Essentially, activism comes in two flavors— mild and bold. Mild separatists have only limited ambitions. Their aim is not to leave the Union but merely to redraw its internal lines in one way or another. The ultimate authority of the federal government in Washington is not disputed. But within the Union, it is hoped, a new dream state (or two or three) might be carved out of the existing fifty-state configuration. A precedent from earlier American history is Kentucky, which was part of Virginia until it was admitted as a separate state on its own in 1792. Another was Maine, which separated from Massachusetts in 1820. And a third was West Virginia, which split from Virginia at the outset of the Civil War and was admitted to the Union in 1863. There is nothing in the Constitution to prevent consideration of yet more adjustments like these in years to come.

Today, mild-type separatists seem to be most active in America's West and Northwest. Perhaps best known is a long-running campaign for approval of a new state of *Jefferson*, which would combine portions of northern California and southern Oregon.[3] Secessionists recently took over the board of supervisors of Shasta County, at the northern tip of California's Central Valley, promoting what one commentary labels their "utopian dream" of "a rural idyll of a state more to their liking."[4] Other similar campaigns include the *Liberty Star* movement, which aims to create a fifty-first state in the Pacific Northwest to be called Liberty,[5] and the *Greater Idaho* movement, which would transfer the predominantly rural counties of Eastern Oregon into the state of Idaho.[6] Any one of these initiatives, if enacted, would undoubtedly be disruptive. But the Union itself would survive. Mild separatists are not a threat to US sovereignty as such.

Bold separatists, by contrast, *would* be a threat—a radical one, at that. Their challenge is self-consciously existential. Bold separatists seek not only to reconsider existing lines within the Union. They aim to challenge the borders of the Union itself in order to make room for a new independent state of their own. They *do* dispute the authority of the national government, and they are found in almost every corner of the country and its diverse dependencies.

Not surprisingly, some of the most active of these bolder separatists are rooted in the Deep South—essentially, the same eleven states that fought a losing battle against the Union a century and a half ago. The Old Confederacy's secession may have been successfully suppressed. But for many in the region, the dream lives on. Many southerners truly believe that, one fine day, "the South will rise again." The dream is kept alive by a constellation of militant organizations with names like Dixie Republic, Identity Dixie, and League of the South. All are part of what the Southern Poverty Law Center calls the *Neo-Confederate Movement*, stingingly described as a "reactionary, revisionist branch of American white nationalism typified by its predilection for symbols of the Confederate States of America, typically paired with a strong belief in the validity of the failed doctrines of nullification and secession—in the specific context of the antebellum South—that rose to prominence in the late 20th and early 21st centuries."[7] The Neo-Confederate Movement includes some of the most radical secessionist groups in the country.

36   DREAM STATES

In the South, we also find the *Texas Nationalist Movement*, which advocates a revival of the independent Lone Star State that existed for a decade before Texas joined the Union in 1845. Texans call it "Texit." In the Northeast, activists promote independence for a putative *Second Vermont Republic*.[8] (A first Vermont Republic, which had been part of New York State in colonial times, existed briefly on its own before being admitted to the Union in 1791.) In the Upper Midwest, the Lakota people of Nebraska and the Dakotas seek recognition of a sovereign *Republic of Lakota*. Likewise, in Oklahoma, the *Cherokee Nation* of Oklahoma lays claim to fourteen counties in the state's northeastern corner. In Alaska, the *Alaska Independence Party* plays a prominent role in state politics. In Hawaii, a *Hawaiian Sovereignty Movement* calls for the restoration of the monarchy that ruled the territory prior to its takeover by the United States in the 1890s. And of course there is California, which has a number of active secessionist movements, including most notably *Yes California*.

Finally, among America's dependencies, there is the well-known case of *Puerto Rico*, where the goal of separation has long been nurtured by several local political parties, including the Puerto Rican Independence Party and the Puerto Rican Nationalist Party. Dissatisfaction with the island's commonwealth status is certainly present, though when given the opportunity to express their preference in non-binding referendums in 1993, 2020, and 2024, voters rejected independence as an alternative to the status quo.

In short, one thing that America does not lack is dream states. Separatists of both flavors roam the country from "sea to shining sea."[9]

Public opinion

How seriously should we take initiatives like these? Many observers would argue: not much at all. Secession movements may not be scarce, but the number of people directly involved in any of them tends to be rather limited. Activists are thin on the ground. Hence, it is tempting to dismiss separatist dreams as futile, little more than the fanciful ravings of a few crazies at the fringes of society. Tempting—but almost certainly a mistake. In reality, opinion polls find that Americans today are surprisingly receptive to the idea of secession in one form or another. They may not agree on who should secede or in what combinations. But they no longer seem quite so committed as once thought to the sanctity of the Union as such. Some would argue that separatism is a hidden thread that runs through all of American history.[10]

Representative was a 2010 poll by the esteemed Pew Research Center, which asked respondents if they would favor allowing an American state to secede if a majority of people from that state wanted to become independent. Overall, some 25 percent said "Yes"—one American in four.[11] A 2013 poll by CBS News asking the same question found 30 percent in favor.[12] Among the CBS poll's youngest respondents (aged eighteen to twenty-nine), those in agreement actually topped 40 percent. In 2017, a Zogby International poll found that as many as 69 percent of Americans were open to the idea of secession in some form.[13] In 2020, a Hofstra University poll found that nearly 40 percent of likely voters would support state secession if their presidential candidate were to lose.[14] And in 2021, substantial support was found in a poll by Bright Line Watch, a research group made up primarily of academics.[15] Respondents were asked "Would you support or oppose [your state] seceding from the United States to join a new union with [list of states in a new union]?" In every region, at least 30 percent of respondents—roughly one American in three—endorsed the idea of secession in some form. In the South, as many as two-thirds of Republicans supported secession into a southern union. On the Pacific coast, nearly half of Democrats supported secession into a Pacific union.

Interest in secession is particularly strong in big, potentially self-sustaining states like Texas and California. In Texas, the state's Republicans famously voted in 2022 to add a secession referendum to their party's platform. The Lone Star State, they said, "should reassert its status as an independent nation."[16] No action, however, has yet been taken by the state legislature. In a similar vein in California, the idea of secession received a significant boost in a 2017 poll for a state ballot initiative proposed by the *Yes California* movement. Some 32 percent of respondents expressed approval of separation.[17]

Results like these suggest that it would indeed be a mistake to underestimate the seriousness of America's many secession movements. As children in elementary school, we all learned to recite the Pledge of Allegiance, with its ideal of "one nation, indivisible." Today, however, it would appear that America is no longer necessarily one nation, and quite possibly no longer indivisible.

38 DREAM STATES

Dissolution?

What, then, does the future portend? Is the Union heading for a breakup? Or will the center hold? The odds in favor of dissolution remain long—but it's a good bet that they are getting shorter.

Naturally, there are many Americans who dismiss the idea of dissolution as nothing more than fantasy. The Hotel California's exits, they contend, were firmly locked shut by the Civil War and *Texas v. White*. Diehards continue to cling stubbornly to the principle of perpetuity. For them, there simply can be no legitimate basis for something like the Texas Republican Party's proposed referendum. In the words of one influential commentary, "Texas can't legally secede from the U.S., despite popular myth: The theme of independence has recurred throughout the history of Texas ... But the Civil War established that a state cannot secede."[18] Absolutist declarations like this are unyielding and ignore or deny all the possible justifications for secession identified by subsequent decades of legal scholarship.

Increasingly, however, sentiment appears to be shifting under the pressure of events. It is no secret that American society has grown increasingly fragmented in recent years, especially after Donald Trump arrived on the national scene. Ours, laments one veteran observer, has become "a season of coming apart ... a period of dissolution."[19] Indeed, apart from the antebellum era, when the nation was torn by the issue of slavery, America has never seemed so deeply divided over basic social values. We appear to be in the midst of a "slow civil war."[20] In principle, it ought to be possible to avert outright conflict through legislative or judicial processes or, more deliberately, through constitutional amendment. As Jill Lepore, a prominent commentator, writes, "Amendment is a constitutional mechanism necessary to avoid insurrection."[21] In practice, however, the Constitution's elaborate provisions for amendment have become an immovable barrier to change. Laments Erwin Chemerinsky, one of the country's leading constitutional scholars, "Amending the Constitution, let alone replacing it entirely, appears to have little chance of happening right now."[22] In Lepore's words, our founding document has become "frozen in time."[23] The Constitution has not been meaningfully amended in over fifty years.

More and more, therefore, partisanship is driving Americans into two seemingly irreconcilable tribes—"red" Republicans versus "blue" Democrats. Republicans like to think of themselves as "conservative," though in the eyes of Democrats they are actually unredeemably "radical" and perhaps authoritarian. Democrats, conversely, take pride in the label "progressive," though for Republicans that word is little more than camouflage for "socialism" or "communism." In states where they are in control, Republicans push for new curbs on abortion, sweeping new restrictions on gender transitions for youths, and laws limiting discussion about sexuality in school classrooms. In states where Democrats dominate, legislatures pass new gun control measures, set limits on carbon emissions, and enact bills legalizing recreational marijuana. In the century and a half since the Civil War, partisan animosity has never been higher. As journalist Kevin Baker summarizes, "The common ground is gone."[24]

Illustrative is the state of Oregon. Historically, a tradition of bipartisan cooperation, known as the "Oregon Way," had long prevailed in the state. More recent years, however, have seen a steady rise of partisan strife. In several eastern counties, conservatives have campaigned successfully for ballot measures calling for secession from Oregon in favor of joining Greater Idaho. And in the state senate, in 2023, minority Republican members boycotted sessions for weeks in order to stall Democratic legislative initiatives. Said one local academic, "The 'Oregon Way' has really almost vanished from the scene .... The current situation is just poisonous."[25]

Violence is in the air. For many informed observers, the mob occupation of the US Capitol on January 6, 2021 was just the beginning.[26] Particularly since Donald Trump's indictment under the Espionage Act in June 2023, militant calls to action have been on the rise, making the idea of organized insurrection more and more acceptable. During the presidential campaign in 2024, rumor had it that Trump, if elected, might create a private "red-state army" comprising National Guard troops from sympathetic Republican-controlled states. Ostensibly, the purpose would have been to wage a massive deportation program against undocumented immigrants. In practice, however, armed resistance could not have been ruled out. The possibility of conflict could then have been used as a justification for deploying federal forces into Democratic jurisdictions. The last barrier to civil strife would have fallen. A commercial film offering a vivid portrayal of what might come next, entitled simply "Civil War," was released in the spring of 2024, drawing sizable audiences. "Civil War" envisioned fragmentation of the Union into at least four successor entities.

Surprising numbers of Americans believed that Donald Trump, for all his flagrant misbehavior, was anointed by God himself to lead the nation to salvation. That conviction remains pervasive even after the election of

November 2024. In the vanguard of Trump supporters are many of America's white evangelicals, for whom partisan animosity is nothing less than a contest between the forces of good and evil. Democrats are not just "woke." They are demonic disciples of Satan. As one Iowa pastor put it: "This is more than a fight between left and right, Democrats and Republicans .... This is good and evil. Biblically."[27] In late 2023, a video began circulating on right-wing social media entitled, simply, "God Made Trump."

In such a heated atmosphere, it would not be difficult to make a persuasive case for separation in one part of the country or another. As the director of governance studies at the venerable Brookings Institution puts it, secession "is the logical culmination of political polarization. There's just been a dramatic increase in our internal divisions .... Secession is basically polarization on steroids."[28] Many perceptive observers fear that the risk of some form of secession will steadily increase. Others, going even further, suggest that we are already in a slow, low-intensity civil conflict.[29] Formally, the nation remains the *United* States of America. But in reality, seemingly, we are becoming more and more the *Disunited* States of America.

In fact, at least three of the seven possible arguments for secession highlighted by legal scholars would now seem, manifestly, to apply. One is the centrifugal forces argument: the evident weakening of political and social ties across the more than 3.7 million square miles of US territory. America's sense of common destiny has dramatically eroded. As F.H. Buckley, an ardent fan of secession, contends, "we've sacrificed ... the fellow feeling that a common national identity used to provide .... If we split apart, we'd be more likely to find ourselves living with people ... with whom we share bonds of solidarity."[30] Separation, he continues, would be "a cure for our social ills."[31]

A second is the mutual suspicion argument: the equally obvious loss of civic trust, which has drained any residue of good will between different segments of society. The red and blue tribes increasingly regard each other as untrustworthy, if not downright demonic. It used to be said that in Washington, politicians would fight by day and then sit down for a cocktail together in the evening. Today, those halcyon times seem gone forever. Where once there might have been a degree of tolerance, even respect, we now see mutual loathing and more and more outlandish conspiracy theories—bitter accusations of "deep state" manipulation, Satan worship, pedophilia, or worse. In marriage disputes, when it becomes clear that a couple has reached the point of "irreconcilable differences," divorce may appear to be the least unattractive option. So might secession.

THE DISUNITED STATES OF AMERICA 41

And a third is the dysfunction argument: the breakdown of effective governance at the center. In the words of one recent manifesto: "The United States has become too big .... We have created an unworkable meganation which defies central management and control."[32] Or as another pro-secessionist puts it: "Our government appears to be irrevocably broken, and we are running out of time."[33] With every passing year, it seems, gridlock in Washington grows worse. Legislative initiatives by one chamber of the Congress are ignored by the other or vetoed by the President. Policy initiatives by the Executive branch are nullified by the Congress or by increasingly partisan courts. And lobbyists of all stripes have long since become expert at profitably gaming the system. On a growing list of critical issues, from immigration and guns to social welfare and climate control, government seems increasingly impotent, unable to meet even the most basic demands of sovereignty. More and more, the nation seems adrift.

For some, the loss of common ground can mean only one thing: a second civil war. A brief survey of "smart national security thinkers" in 2017 produced a consensus estimate of a 35 percent chance of civil war in the next ten to fifteen years.[34] Another expert source put the risk even higher, at 60 percent.[35] Given this level of gloom, the idea of secession seems almost benign. Who wouldn't prefer a calm parting of the ways over a bloody—and possibly interminable—armed conflict? The point was well made by John Quincy Adams in a memorable speech in 1839 marking the fiftieth anniversary of George Washington's inauguration:

> If the day should ever come, (may Heaven avert it,) when the affections of the people of these states shall be alienated from each other; when the fraternal spirit shall give way to cold indifference, or collisions of interest shall fester into hatred ... far better will it be for the people of the disunited states, to part in friendship from each other, than to be held together by constraint.

Complications

But is a calm parting of the ways even feasible? Even if all sides agree in principle—and the raw emotions of divorce can be overcome—a peaceful breakup of the Union might not be easy to achieve in practice. Complications abound.

42 DREAM STATES

First is the question: Who would secede from whom? Most analyses assume that states would be the key actors, pushing for secession either singly or in regional groupings. But what states? What regions? Would Vermont seek a second Republic on its own or instead join together with neighboring states in New England or the Mid-Atlantic region? Would California go it alone or seek a wider union with other western states? Would southern states seek to revive the Old Confederacy, in whole or in part? Reshuffling the deck of cards would not be easy.

A second question is: Who should go first? Democrats and Republicans disagree. On the blue-state side, left-leaning progressives like Kevin Baker think it ought to be the blue states that break away from what he sees as a Union increasingly structured to disadvantage Democrats. He calls it "Bluexit." By seizing the initiative, blue states would be able to choose their own friends, leaving the rest on their own.[36] The opposite viewpoint is illustrated by hard-right conservatives like Georgia's Marjorie Taylor Greene, who contends that red states should act first in a "national divorce" in order to liberate themselves from the rest of the country. Says Greene: "We are absolutely disgusted and fed up with the left."[37] Both sides take for granted that actions will be unilateral. Neither side appears to anticipate a peaceful negotiated settlement.

A third question is: Might state lines be redrawn? Once a process of dissolution begins, there is no reason to assume that the map would continue to juggle the same fifty "neatly divided spatial packages." The approach is traditional but reckons without the preferences of secessionists who are more interested in new configurations like the states of Jefferson, Liberty, or Greater Idaho. Or what about the Cherokee Nation of Oklahoma or the Lakota people, who aspire to independent states of their own? Existing state lines are by no means inviolate.

Finally, if indeed state lines can be redrawn, what should they look like? By convention, we tend to speak of states that are either red or blue (or some shade of purple), but that is obviously misleading. The approach reckons without the presence of political heterogeneity within existing states. Even in as deep a red state as Alabama or Wyoming, blue urban pockets are to be found; conversely, even in deep blue states like Massachusetts or Oregon, we find red enclaves in many rural locations. What would prevent the emergence of smaller-scale secession movements within individual states—a blue Houston seeking to separate from a Republican-dominated Texas or a red Upper Peninsula trying to escape a Democrat-dominated Michigan? A map drawn to more accurately represent the distribution of political preferences could end up looking like a Jackson Pollock action painting—something like a disorderly collection of messy archipelagos.

Worse, recall the "minorities-within-minorities" issue: the recursive process described in the previous chapter where ostensibly homogeneous groups within a more heterogeneous community may splinter into yet thinner and thinner shards. Once the sanctity of state lines is breached, where do you stop? Here too the closest thing to a fundamental unit could be the individual. Indeed, for libertarians, the defense of personal rights provides the most convincing rationale for secession.[38] But few people (other than, perhaps, identical twins) are absolutely the same in terms of ideas or preferences. Hence, redrawing the map on the basis of anything other than the individual would necessarily be unrepresentative to a degree and therefore a source of potential disagreement. That way lies anarchy, where the likelihood of armed violence is high.

A house divided

The challenge to the United States is real. Despite the Union's victory in the Civil War and the subsequent Supreme Court ruling in *Texas v. White*, the possibility of secession remains very much alive. Legal scholarship identifies at least seven plausible justifications for secession, depending on circumstances; America does not lack for determined separatist organizations prepared to act on those justifications; and public opinion appears increasingly receptive to the whole idea. Hence, the odds in favor of dissolution are getting shorter with every passing year.

In the face of this challenge, can the Union hold together? *Should* it be held together? On the one hand, the many complications of secession, which are serious, could act as a deterrent to separatists. But on the other hand, there is the discontent that motivates secessionist sentiment, which is most likely to keep growing the longer it remains unsatisfied. "A house divided against itself cannot stand," Abraham Lincoln declared in 1858, two years before the start of the Civil War. His cautionary words ring as true today as they did then.

4

Fantasies

Mostly Benign

The threat of secession at home is not the only challenge that America faces these days. There is also the *external* challenge—the menace of secessions abroad that could draw in the United States (US) in one way or another. America is not the only house that seems divided against itself. As I have emphasized, dream states are found almost everywhere, and many put vital US interests seriously at risk, directly or indirectly. Involvement in many separatist struggles, at high cost in terms of blood and treasure, could turn out to be unavoidable. All types of secession movements are possible.

We begin with *fantasies*, the most benign of all secession types. Fantasy dream states are mostly harmless, though they may turn out to be a bit of a bother for some. Ostensibly, they are about an assertion of sovereign rights. In reality, the idea of secession is for most of them simply a handy device intended to achieve some entirely unrelated goal. They present no real threat to existing states—no nightmare to keep Americans or others up at night.

Fantasy dream states come in three main varieties. Many are frivolous or eccentric—mere jokes that are more attention-seeking than anything else. Most are good for little more than a hearty laugh. Others, a bit more serious, take their aim at public policies of one kind or another. Some seek to provide a loophole for the evasion of government regulation, while others are intended to encourage supervisory initiatives that might be thought to be in the public interest. And then, on occasion, there is a downright fraud aiming to hoodwink incautious citizens via one criminal activity or another. Fantasy dream states are so numerous that small libraries of books have been written about them, often quite amusing.[1] There are even comic "how-to" books instructing readers on how to create a microstate of their own.[2] But ubiquitous though they may be, fantasy dream states pose little risk of violent conflict.

Dream States. Benjamin J. Cohen, Oxford University Press. © Oxford University Press (2025).
DOI: 10.1093/9780197811672.003.0004

Jokes

Joke fantasies are dream states with a sense of humor. In one way or another, they have fun at the expense of more sober governments. They play on the conventions of statehood for purposes of satire or to draw attention to themselves or to some cause. Typically, they are minuscule and involve only a few individuals.

Examples

The number of joke fantasies is remarkably large. Examples abound and can be found in virtually every corner of the globe. In the United States, we have, among many others, the Conch Republic, which I have already mentioned. Founded in 1982 by the then-mayor of Key West, the Conch Republic was born as part of a protest against a checkpoint established by the US Border Patrol that inconvenienced residents and tourists. Initially encompassing just Key West alone, the venture was later expanded northward to include all of the Florida Keys (the Republic's "Northern Territories"). Today, it serves mainly as a tourism booster for the area. Its lack of any more serious intent is demonstrated by its motto: "The Mitigation of World Tension Through the Exercise of Humor."

Comparably, in Canada, we have the Aerican Empire, founded in 1987, an eccentric jest asserting sovereignty over various terrestrial and interplanetary territories. In Britain, we have the Grand Duchy of the Lagoan Isles, three tiny islands in a pond near the city of Portsmouth claimed by a self-styled Grand Duke Louis, who declared the islands independent in 2005. In France, we have Le Saugeais, a make-believe mini-republic nestled up against the Swiss border. Le Saugeais first made an appearance under the protection of a neighboring duke as long ago as 1150. Its modern manifestation can be traced back to a jocular query posed to a visiting state official by a local hotel owner: "Do you have a permit allowing you to enter the Republic of Saugeais?" In New Zealand, we have Whangamōmona, a tongue-in-cheek micronation created in 1989 as a tourism booster. Past elected presidents of the republic have included a goat and a poodle. The list of joke fantasies goes on and on.

46 DREAM STATES

Kingdom of Lovely

One of the most elaborate of all joke fantasies was a faux-documentary comedy series aired on British television in the summer of 2005 and later released on DVD.[3] The show, entitled "How to Start Your Own Country," was presented by a comedian named Danny Wallace and followed his quixotic quest to start his own state in his apartment in London. The sovereign micronation he created was eventually dubbed the Kingdom of Lovely. The king, of course, was Wallace himself.

The series proceeded in six episodes. In the first episode, "Birth of a Nation," Wallace investigated territory for his new state. After a variety of madcap encounters—including a meeting with a man who claimed to own the moon—he eventually settled upon the area of his apartment and issued a formal declaration of independence. In subsequent episodes, he chose a design for the flag of his country, recorded a national anthem, and visited several other joke micronations. When having trouble paying his electricity bill, he designed his own currency and applied for international aid (which was refused). He even traveled to New York to apply for UN membership (which was also refused). At the conclusion of the series, he addressed a gathering of would-be citizens in a London square and pronounced that the country was henceforth to be called "Lovely." Its motto would be "Have a Lovely day."

At its peak, nearly 60,000 "citizens" were registered on the micronation's website. Today, the site is no longer active and the kingdom is considered defunct.

Regulatory fantasies

Almost as numerous as joke fantasies are regulatory fantasies—dream states that are motivated by dissatisfaction with allegedly onerous public policies. Though regulatory fantasies typically are a bit more serious than joke fantasies, humor can be involved here as well. Their aim is to use a declaration of independence to draw attention to a cause.

Frequently, the cause is broadly libertarian: a desire to live free, shedding all the shackles of noxious governmental authority. A prime historical example is Seborga, a tiny Italian village thought to be the oldest micronation in existence. Its roots go back more than a thousand years, to the time of the Holy Roman Empire, and to this day it continues to name its own ruler and to issue its own currency. A more modern counterpart is Liberland (officially the Free Republic of Liberland), a micronation claiming an uninhabited parcel of disputed land on the bank of the Danube River between Croatia and Serbia. Roughly the same size as Gibraltar, Liberland was proclaimed an independent state in 2015 by a right-wing Czech politician and activist named Vít Jedlička, who claimed to gain his inspiration from other European ministates like Monaco and Liechtenstein. His goal, he says, is to create "a society where righteous people can prosper with minimal state regulations." More pithily, an Argentine disciple of his declares that the goal is "to kick Keynesians and collectivists in the ass."[4]

Nor are these all. Many similar projects can be found elsewhere, each promoting its own idiosyncratic brand of libertarianism. In Denmark, we have Freetown Christiania, also known simply as Christiania, a self-proclaimed sovereign neighborhood of the capital city of Copenhagen. Most of the Christiania community, dating back to 1971, occupies the site of an old army barracks and is home to almost 1,000 residents. Likewise, in Lithuania's capital city of Vilnius, we have the Republic of Užupis, also a self-proclaimed sovereign neighborhood, which declared itself an independent republic in 1997. And for a time in the United States, we had the Principality of Freedonia, which was started as a "hypothetical project" by a group of teenagers in 1992 and formalized as a new country in 1997, only to fade away in subsequent years. The name Freedonia was inspired by the mythical micronation featured in the classic 1933 Marx Brothers film *Duck Soup*.

In other cases, a venture's cause may be much narrower—indeed, at times, bordering on the trivial. In Austria, for instance, we have Kugelmugel, an orange ball-shaped house in Vienna that proclaimed its independence in 1984 after a dispute with city authorities over building permits. Likewise, in the United States, we had North Dumpling, an island in Long Island Sound that declared itself independent in 1986 after its wealthy owner was denied permission to build a wind turbine. In Israel, there was the micronation of Akhzivland, founded in 1971 as a protest against the Israeli government's demolition of an illegally inhabited house. And in Australia the sovereign state of Wy was established in the city of Sydney during a dispute over the construction of a driveway.

Only occasionally are sovereignty projects ignited in order to encourage, rather than discourage, some form of government action. Perhaps the most notable recent example is the Glacier Republic, which was founded in

48 DREAM STATES

southern Chile in 2014 by Greenpeace activists for the sole purpose of drawing attention to the Chilean government's lack of environmental protection for glaciers. Chile contains 82 percent of South America's glaciers but had no laws in place to safeguard them. Greenpeace admitted that the real purpose of the republic was to induce the Chilean government to protect its glaciers, not to create a long-lasting sovereign state.

Rose Island

One of my favorites among the world's many regulatory fantasies is (or, more properly, was) the Republic of Rose Island, a dream state built upon an artificial platform in international waters off the eastern coast of Italy, opposite the province of Rimini.[5] The project's aim was to escape what its inventor considered the corrupt and oppressive rule of the government in Rome—in brief, to create a home for free men and women. Construction was completed in May 1968. Months later, the platform was temporarily occupied by Italian police forces, subjected to a naval blockade, and eventually demolished in February 1969. Rose Island has gone down in history as the only nation ever to have been directly attacked by the post–World War II Italian Republic.

The story, as might be expected, is operatic. It began in 1967 when an inventive Italian engineer named Giorgio Rosa persuaded a friend to join him in building an artificial island in the Adriatic Sea. The platform, which measured no more than some 400 square meters, was carefully placed to be just outside Italy's sovereign territorial waters. With money that Rosa's friend reportedly stole from his own father and with innovative building techniques cleverly developed by Rosa himself, construction proceeded speedily. On May 1, 1968, independence was declared, with Rosa, not surprisingly, designated as the newborn republic's first president. The island quickly established its own government, currency, and post office. It even adopted an official language, which curiously enough was chosen to be Esperanto.

Rose Island soon became popular as a tourist destination and in short order was furnished with a variety of commercial amenities, including a restaurant, bar, nightclub, and souvenir shop. All that, in turn, aroused the ire of the Italian government, which feared that the venture might become an illicit channel for tax evasion. Technically, since the island was in international waters, it was beyond Rome's direct legal jurisdiction. Rosa pleaded the case for his republic before the Council of Europe, which agreed to look into the matter (the diplomatic equivalent of kicking the can down the road). But the Italian authorities moved anyway, flouting international law, and ultimately decided to do away with the nuisance by blowing it up. The challenge to Italy's sovereignty was resolved, though not without some cost to the country's reputation.

In the years since, the memory of Rose Island has served as an inspiration for similar efforts elsewhere to set up self-governing hamlets in international waters—what their libertarian sponsors call "seasteading" (a seaborne version of homesteading). In 2019, for instance, an American-Thai couple spent time living in a small cabin floating in international waters some 12 miles off the coast of Thailand until the Thai government decided to tow their "seastead" ashore. Here too, the fear was that the venture would become a vehicle for tax evasion.[6] For years, the idea of floating cities, free of regulation, has been loudly promoted by the Seasteading Institute, a research organization backed initially by Peter Thiel, co-founder of PayPal.

The whole farcical tale of Rose Island was subsequently celebrated in a feature-length film, "The Incredible Story of Rose Island," released by Netflix in December 2020.[7] Reviews were generally favorable. Typical was one critic who wrote that the film's creators "successfully mix whimsy and pathos to give us something truly inspiring."[8] Rose Island may have been sent to the bottom of the Adriatic Sea, but it lives on in celluloid.

The mouse that roared

Another of my favorites is a fantasy dream state that was never anything but fictional. That was the Duchy of Grand Fenwick, said to be located somewhere in the Alps between France and Switzerland. No one in the real world actually tried to create a micronation called Grand Fenwick. But back about six decades ago, the imaginary Duchy gained a considerable degree of notoriety as "the mouse that roared," first in a satirical novel by British author Leonard Wibberley published in 1955,[9] and then in a memorably comic 1959 film starring Peter Sellers (in three separate roles).[10] The aim of both the novel and the film was to bring a critical eye to the nuclear arms race that at the time, in the midst of the Cold War, seemed to threaten the end of all human civilization. The story was a favorite of picketers carrying signs demanding that governments "Ban the Bomb."

50 DREAM STATES

In both the novel and the film, the story starts when the Duchy finds itself facing bankruptcy. An American company has come up with a less expensive imitation of Fenwick's sole export, its fabled Pinot Grand Fenwick wine. In response, the prime minister devises a seemingly foolproof plan. The Duchy will declare war on the United States and then surrender, taking advantage of America's well-known largesse toward its defeated enemies to rebuild Fenwick's economy. If the Americans could be so generous toward post–World War II Germany and Japan, why not Fenwick? But through a comedy of errors, the Duchy unexpectedly finds itself in sole possession of a prototype doomsday device that could destroy the entire planet if triggered. The mouse, now in a position to roar, then forces all the nuclear powers to accept strict controls over their weapons programs, and the tale concludes happily. The world is rescued by one of its tiniest states.

Frauds

As compared with jokes and regulatory fantasies, fraud dream states are—happily!—relatively rare. Like jokes and regulatory fantasies, they aim to play cleverly on the conventions of statehood. But unlike the other two types, which are comparatively good natured, frauds are nefarious in purpose and aim to separate some class of victims from their fortunes. The goal is to profit at the expense of the gullible.

In the modern era, the best known example of a fraud dream state was the Dominion of Melchizedek, a micronation known largely for facilitating large-scale banking scams in several parts of the world.[11] Melchizedek, which borrowed its name from a biblical Israelite king, was unilaterally declared by a US citizen, Mark Pedley, in 1990. At various times, it laid claim to a diverse range of territories, including a small Colombian island, a French-owned islet off the coast of Nicaragua, a handful of shoals and atolls in the South Pacific, and even an unclaimed portion of Antarctica known as Marie Byrd Land. Only one established state ever offered formal diplomatic recognition to the Dominion. That was in 1993. The obliging country was the Central African Republic, which has never been known for its scrupulous standards regarding the concept of international legal sovereignty. Commented the Washington Post, "you get the feeling that the Central African Republic would recognize the State of Denial if it had a letterhead."[12]

FANTASIES 51

Almost from its start, Melchizedek was involved in one fraudulent activity after another. The Dominion began by selling documents purporting to charter or license companies to do business in the fake country. These charters and licenses were then, in turn, used as collateral to secure loans or to open bank accounts. Other criminal activities included insurance fraud schemes, passport sales, and a crooked investment program—effectively, a Ponzi scheme—that convinced at least 1,400 people to invest a total of over $4 million. One of the Dominion's most notorious victims was the brother of a one-time president of Portugal, who was conned out of some $35,000 supposedly meant to guarantee a loan to build a hotel. Eventually, most of those associated with Melchizedek's diverse schemes were apprehended, convicted, and sentenced to years in jail.

Poyais

Blatant as it was, however, Melchizedek could not compare with the grand-daddy of all fraud dream states—Poyais, a totally fictitious kingdom alleged to exist two centuries ago somewhere on the Mosquito Coast of Central America near the border between Honduras and Nicaragua. Poyais was the invention of Sir Gregor MacGregor, a British war hero and popular man about town in early nineteenth-century London. The name Poyais derived from the purported territory's local population, the Paya or Poyer people (today called the Pech). After years of successful service with the British army, rising eventually to the rank of General, MacGregor appeared in London in 1821 calling himself "Cazique" (or Prince) of Poyais, using a Spanish-American word for a native chief. In the next two years, Mac-Gregor was able to carry out one of the most brazen confidence tricks in history.[13]

London in the early 1820s, following the end of the Napoleonic Wars, was ripe fruit for the picking. British interest rates were generally low, encouraging the wealthy classes seeking higher returns for their savings to take a plunge on more risky foreign debt. At the same time, a wave of revolutions in the Western Hemisphere sparked the creation of a score of penurious new states in desperate need of funds. That brought a flood of seemingly lucrative investment opportunities to the historic City of London, by then home to the world's largest bond market. A boom ensued. Amid the crowd of new Latin American borrowers, not many plungers paused to inquire if a place

52 DREAM STATES

like Poyais really even existed. MacGregor was ideally positioned, therefore, to exploit the public's gullibility.

To convince the unwary, MacGregor put his imagination to work, devising convoluted constitutional arrangements, along with commercial and banking mechanisms, for the non-existent nation. He designed distinctive uniforms for the Poyaisian Army, a system of grand honors, landed titles, and a national flag. He even composed popular ballads to help advertise his dream state. Remarkably, the ruse worked. As one historian puts it, the Cazique soon became "a great adornment for the dinner tables and ballrooms of sophisticated London."[14] Investors snapped up Poyaisian land certificates at two shillings and three pence per acre, roughly equivalent to a working man's daily wage at the time (later raised, owing to excited demand, to as much as four shillings an acre). By 1823, as many as 500 eager speculators had bought Poyaisian land, some investing their lifesavings. In 1822, MacGregor also organized a Poyaisian government loan on the London Stock Exchange that attracted a great deal of interest. The bond issue was for some 200,000 pounds sterling, a massive sum at the time, and was to be underwritten by one of the City of London's most reputable banks. MacGregor stood to amass a fortune.

But at that point, the bubble burst, as defaults suddenly spread through the former Spanish and Portuguese colonies. The markets crashed, turning investor sentiment firmly against Latin American loans of any kind. Starting in late 1822, frantic buying of debt issues was replaced by panicked selling, and the Cazique's cash flow was all but wiped out. A year later, Poyais bonds were trading for less than 10 percent of their face value. Soon the fiction of Poyais was revealed, and MacGregor was forced to go into hiding in the French countryside for a time before returning to Britain in 1826. By then, however, his reputation—along with that of his fictional creation—was in tatters. An attempt to market another Poyaisian loan in 1827 failed, and ultimately he emigrated to Venezuela, where he died in 1845.

Largely harmless

Melchizedek and Poyais were the exceptions. Over the years, many fantasy dream states have popped up in one place or another. But few, apart from the occasional scam, have caused much pain for anyone. Most are little more than publicity stunts meant to gain attention for a cause or perhaps to do no more than boost the ego of their creators. Only rarely, as in the case of Rose Island, has any government felt the need to take forceful action in opposition. In most instances, the attitude has been largely forbearing: simply live and let live.

If all dream states were of this type, clearly, there would be few lurking nightmares to worry about. But, of course, there are other types that are indeed much more threatening, as we shall now see.

5

Daydreams

Sentimental attachments

Next on our list are *daydreams*—dream states that embody a sentimental attachment to a unique ethnic, racial, or linguistic identity, more often than not linked to a particular territory on cultural or historical grounds. People daydream about a dream state.

Daydreams may be considered an intermediate category in my taxonomy. On the one hand, they are quite a bit more serious than fantasy dream states. They are about much more than mere fun or fraud. They are about *identity*, which is by definition a weighty matter. They are about group pride and are typically anchored in what a community considers its traditional "homeland." They are anything but trivial. They are, in fact, the key to understanding what motivates a community to become a pretender to sovereignty in the first place.

But on the other hand, daydreams as such are also less threatening than the formal secession movements that we will encounter in subsequent chapters. Typically, they are less self-consciously organized for direct political action. Their emphasis is more on cultural heritage than public policy. The degree of conflict risk, therefore, is limited, though not negligible. There is little risk of an armed struggle that could draw in outsiders like the United States (US). On my scale, daydreams fall between fantasies on the one hand and more organized separatist campaigns on the other—neither blithely comedic nor dangerously combative. Mainly, they are about celebrating a community's allegiance to its sense of self.

Daydreams are "crowd sourced," arising spontaneously from the collective emotions of a specific population. But that does not mean that they are the product of free choice. In practice, an emotional tie to a common history or homeland can be a powerful driver, not at all easy to erase or override. It may not even rise to the level of consciousness. The eminent African-American author James Baldwin puts the point well in his seminal novel *Giovanni's Room*, when the narrator spots a sailor in crisp whites striding

Dream States. Benjamin J. Cohen, Oxford University Press. © Oxford University Press (2025).
DOI: 10.1093/9780197811672.003.0005

across a boulevard in Paris. He looks at the sailor with a longing he doesn't quite understand. The sailor reminds him of home, he ultimately realizes, before concluding: "Perhaps home is not a place but simply an irrevocable condition."[1]

Fragility

It is the rare sovereign state that does not have minority populations of some kind, complete with their own distinctive identities—their own ethnicity, language, or religion. Many of these minorities tend to be located in what they consider to be their native habitat, their *homeland*, where the group's ancestors may have originated or lived for centuries. Homelands are set amid bigger and more established nationalities. Their populations are among the many "sub-nationalisms" that Benedict Anderson talked about, yearning to shed their "sub-ness." They want to see their distinctive identity validated. In that respect, daydreams are no different from most other secession movements.

What distinguishes daydreams is their limited ambition. Many secession movements, I have warned, may be quite combative. They may even be prepared to go to war to achieve their goals. But not daydreams, whose aims are more modest. Daydreams are rooted in the subconscious rather than the frontal cortex. They are reflexive, not cerebral. It is not necessarily their intention to seek formal secession, nor in most instances do they seek to wholly supplant one national identity with another. Rather, their part in an older national state remains more or less unquestioned so long as their unique contribution to a complex society is respected. Their goal is largely to *supplement* an older incumbent nationalism with an additional layer of identity, thus expanding the overall meaning of statehood. The idea can be summarized concisely: "I am a part of the nation. I am also a member of a minority. My identity includes both."

Based as they are in emotions, daydreams operate most crucially at the level of symbols. Identity is projected through popular culture and every known means of social communication—including even posters, tee shirts, and bumper stickers. Success is gauged by standard measures of diversity and inclusion. My own personal history provides testimony. When my father arrived in the United States a century ago, a penniless immigrant fleeing pogroms in his native Belarus, his dream was to live openly in the Land of the Free as a member of the Jewish community. Not unreasonably, he wanted both identities, American and Jewish, for himself and for his family. His dream was achieved by his firstborn son, who had the good fortune to study at one Ivy League university and to launch a modestly successful academic career at another, all the while identifying as a Jew. Lucky, Jerry lived the dream.[2]

But not all daydreams are equally blessed. In many instances, sub-national identities are effectively cursed, discouraged, or even actively suppressed in favor of a broader concept of nationalism. Narrow devotion to an ancient homeland is discouraged; assimilation is encouraged. You are not "real" members of the national community, minorities may be told, if you do not seek to blend in: speak the same language, practice the same religion, observe the same customs. The result often is frustration and anger, which in turn can lead to increased militancy or perhaps even violent conflict— the nightmare lurking behind the scenes today. The alternatives, blessing or curse, are inherent in the nature of an intermediate category. Outcomes could go either way.

In practice, therefore, daydreams are fragile things and may turn out to be little more than a transition—a bridge to some other more definitive attitude. They are like what economists with their specialized jargon would label an "unstable equilibrium": a constellation of mutually interrelated variables, exquisitely balanced, that could explode apart at any moment. More colorfully, daydreams may be likened to a delicate soap bubble. At any moment, they might pop.

Four R's

The questions are obvious. *Will* the bubble pop? And if it does, what happens *next*? What is the most likely "other" attitude? Will the daydream fade into obscurity, carried away in the breeze? Or will it intensify, turning political or possibly even become nightmarishly violent? Some scholars would have us believe that daydreams are deterministic, leading us through several distinct stages of a more or less standardized life cycle.[3] In practice, however, outcomes are far less predictable. Any of four broad possibilities may emerge. I call them the four R's: reconciliation, repression, reform, and rebellion.

First is reconciliation. That is the possibility that the sub-nationalism's daydream will gradually yield to the superior attraction of the more encompassing nationalism in which it finds itself embedded. The minority community need not give up all claim to a distinctive identity. Its customs and homeland may still be quietly revered. But its "sub-ness" within the broader nation will no longer be contested. Rather the community will become *reconciled* to its politically subordinate status. History is replete with outcomes like that. Think of France, which is far from the homogeneous nation that naive tourists might take it to be. In fact, it is largely a collection of regions that have gradually coalesced over the course of centuries to emerge today as one avowedly *French* state. The regions of France today generally accept the overriding authority of the central government in Paris. But from Alsace or Brittany in the north to Occitania or Corsica in the south, many of them still strive as well to preserve elements of their own original culture—for instance, in the food they eat or the flags they fly. But few dream any longer of a sovereign state to call their own.

Second is repression. At the first signs of separatist sentiment, the incumbent national government may take action to keep minority groups in line. The aim, in the lingo of old Hollywood westerns, would be to "cut them off at the pass": to *repress* emergent daydreams before they can coalesce into an organized secession movement. The use of distinctive "sub-national" symbols may be discouraged, while efforts to encourage assimilation are redoubled. Repression has always been a favorite tactic of authoritarian governments, which naturally feel more comfortable relying on sticks rather than carrots. The approach remains common in many states today. Think of the Uyghurs in China or the Rohingya people in Myanmar. Hundreds of thousands of Uyghurs—possibly more than a million—were herded into internment camps in recent years and subjected to arduous re-education programs. Many of Myanmar's Rohingyas have been driven from their ancestral homes into exile in neighboring Bangladesh.

Third is reform. That is the obverse of repression: the use of carrots rather than sticks. The idea is that the discontent of minority communities can in effect be "bought off" by concessions and compromises of various kinds— *reforms* meant, we might say, to stabilize the unstable equilibrium. The idea is not to suppress identity-driven daydreams but rather to accommodate them without at the same time promoting formal secession. Expressions of distinctive sub-national cultures might actually be encouraged. For instance, instruction in historical languages might be allowed in school curricula or the practice of ancient faiths might be given formal protections. Alternatively, elements of political autonomy might be introduced to give a sense of practical reality to traditional homelands, up to and including the option

58   DREAM STATES

of full internal self-rule. With luck, measures like these might be enough to keep the bubble from popping—at least for a time.

Finally, there is the possibility of rebellion. That is what happens when the bubble does in fact pop. The minority *rebels*. An organized secession movement takes shape, demanding independence. The minority becomes a genuine (and disruptive) pretender to sovereignty. Concessions and compromises, up to full autonomy, will no longer be enough to satisfy the dissatisfied. Now the goal is maximal: recognition as a full member in good standing of the global sovereignty club. And if that goal cannot be attained by peaceful means—via, say, referendum or negotiation—resort to force may be felt necessary. A war of secession could follow, one more addition to the long list of separatist hot spots around the world.

A few examples from the northwestern corner of Europe will suffice to illustrate the four R's in practice.

Celtic Fringe

Northwestern Europe is home to what is often referred to as the *Celtic Fringe*—a roughly crescent-shaped area stretching from Scotland in the north to the French region of Brittany further south. In addition to Scotland and Brittany, the six so-called Celtic nations include Cornwall, Ireland, the Isle of Man, and Wales. Scotland occupies the northern half of the island formally known as Great Britain (with England in the southern half), Cornwall is located in the southwestern corner of Great Britain, Wales is on Great Britain's western coast, and the Isle of Man is found in the middle of the Irish Sea between Great Britain and Ireland. Brittany, just across the English Channel, sits on a peninsula at the northwestern tip of France. The term nation is used in a traditional sense to mean people who share a common culture and are identified with a traditional territory.

Technically, five of the Celtic nations today are what Anderson called sub-nationalisms. Only the Republic of Ireland, occupying the bulk of the "Emerald Isle," exists on its own as an independent state. Brittany is an administrative region of France, while the others—including the six counties of Northern Ireland—all fall, in one way or another, under the jurisdiction of the central government in London. Sovereignty resides in what is officially known as the United Kingdom—UK, for short. Differences among the Celtic nations are by no means insignificant, whether we are speaking of language, religion, or other cultural traditions. But they all share in common one key element: their Celtic identity. Each of them firmly considers itself to be a distinct Celtic nation.

History

The Celts long played a prominent role in European history. For millennia, a significant part of the European continent was dominated by Celtic-speaking tribes. During the European Iron Age, dating back some 2,500–3,500 years, the ancient Celts extended their territory to most of western and central Europe. But with the imperial expansion of Ancient Rome and then the invasion of Germanic and Slavic-speaking populations, most Celts were gradually forced to retreat westward toward the fringe that they occupy today. The Celtic Fringe is also sometimes known as the "Celt Belt" or the "Celtic Crescent."

Furthest north in the Celtic Fringe was a mixture of ethnic groups and monarchies that over time melded into a single Scottish sense of nationhood. Though the name Scots was borrowed from the Irish, by the late Middle Ages the label came to be used for subjects of the Scottish king. To a large extent, Scottish identity was forged in opposition to attempts by England, their mortal enemy, to annex the kingdom. Of particular importance was the Declaration of Arbroath (1320), which asserted the ancient distinctiveness of the Kingdom of Scotland. Written by some fifty-one Scottish magnates and nobles in the form of a letter to the Pope in Rome, the document highlighted the kingdom's antiquity and denounced English attempts to subjugate it. The letter has been described as the first "nationalist theory of sovereignty."[4] Three centuries later, however, after the death of Elizabeth I, the Scots voluntarily agreed to the unification of the Scottish and English crowns under James VI King of Scots, who would subsequently reign in London as James I. Scotland has since existed as an integral part of the United Kingdom.

By contrast, Cornwall, Wales, and the Isle of Man were all incorporated into the Kingdom of England more by overt force. After a series of defeats by superior armies from Wessex and other neighboring English monarchies, Cornwall lost its independence as early as 875 when the last recorded Cornish king died. It has since survived as a county of England. Wales held onto its independence longer but finally succumbed in the sixteenth century during the reign of Henry VIII, when the Westminster Parliament passed the

60   DREAM STATES

Law in Wales Act, also referred to as the "Acts of Union." The Acts gave Wales, like Scotland, full political representation in London. The Isle of Man passed back and forth between the kings of Scotland and England for centuries until coming under the feudal lordship of the English Crown in 1399. It exists today as a self-governing British Crown Dependency and is best known to outsiders as a tax haven and offshore banking destination.

Ireland, after centuries of resistance to English occupation, formally joined the UK in 1801 under the Acts of Union, creating a new political entity called the United Kingdom of Great Britain and Ireland. But sporadic rebellions persisted, especially after the notorious Irish famine of the 1840s, culminating in the so-called Easter Rising of 1916. Several years of guerrilla war led ultimately to the creation in 1921 of an Irish Free State, intended to be a self-governing Dominion of the British Commonwealth in the manner of Canada and Australia. The Free State later declared itself a republic in 1949. The Irish Republic incorporated all of the Emerald Isle apart from the six predominantly Protestant counties of Northern Ireland, which elected to remain part of what now became known as the United Kingdom of Great Britain and Northern Ireland. Nearly a century later, the political fate of Northern Ireland, centered on the industrial city of Belfast, remains a matter of hot dispute.

And then there is Brittany, the only Celtic nation of substantial size remaining on the European continent. Traces of Celtic culture can be found in scattered locations elsewhere in Europe, particularly on the Iberian Peninsula, but are too faint to rouse a spirit of ethnic nationalism. On the continent, Brittany alone continues to celebrate its Celtic identity. The name of Brittany derives from the Britonnes tribes in Roman Britain who migrated across the English Channel after the fall of the Roman Empire and subsequently blended with the local population to form the later Bretons. The region was unified as a duchy (dukedom) in the ninth century and then in the sixteenth century was taken over by the King of France, who converted the duchy into a French province. To this day, Brittany remains an integral part of the French state even though many of its people retain their sense of identity as a Celtic nation.

Promoting identity

The daydream of Celtic nationalism is expressed in a variety of ways by the six nations (seven if you count Northern Ireland as a separate entity). Formal cooperation is encouraged by two long-standing bodies: the Celtic

Congress, founded in 1917, and its more recent cousin the Celtic League, dating from 1961. The Celtic Congress bills itself as a non-political charitable organization whose goals, in its own words, are to "perpetuate the culture, ideals, and languages of the Celtic peoples and to maintain an intellectual contact and close cooperation between the respective Celtic communities." An International Celtic Congress is convened each year in one of the Celtic nations. The Celtic League, by contrast, is a bit more political and campaigns actively for the linguistic and cultural rights of the Celtic nations. Additionally, albeit in a minor key, it also advocates for more self-governance in the Celtic nations and ultimately for each nation to become an independent state in its own right. The Celtic League is an accredited non-governmental organization with roster consultative status at the United Nations Economic and Social Council.

Celtic identity is also promoted by popular festivals showcasing the living culture of the Celtic nations, including inter-Celtic music festivals like Celtic Connections (Glasgow) and the Hebridean Celtic Festival, also known as HebCelt (Isle of Lewis). Sports also contribute in the form of competitions between the Celtic nations. Prominent examples include rugby (Pro14, formerly known as the Celtic League), athletics (Celtic Cup), and soccer (Nations Cup). Heavy coverage of all these activities in the local news media cannot help but heighten awareness of the Celtic Fringe's common roots.

Of importance as well are the many symbols of Celtic identity that can be seen everywhere in the six nations. One cultural icon common to all is the triangular-framed Celtic harp, known to many outsiders as the Irish harp but is in fact traditional to all the Celtic nations. Separately, Scotland can boast of its kilts and tartans; Wales has venerated the leek, a pungent member of the onion family, since before Shakespeare wrote of it in *Henry V*; and Brittany has its *crêpes*. Even the Isle of Man has a well-known icon that it can call its own—the Manx cat, a unique breed of felines with short or no tails.

Finally there are the flags, which are displayed as often as possible. Scots proudly fly the blue-and-white Cross of St. Andrew, which was adopted as a national symbol centuries ago. Cornwallers and Bretons each have their own black-and-white design. Ireland, of course, has its familiar tricolor of green, white, and orange. Wales has a fierce-looking dragon posed dramatically on a green and white field, while the Isle of Man has its enigmatic "three legs of Man," a design of three armor-covered legs conjoined at the hip on a field of bright red. Icons like these, which cultivate allegiance to the nation, are precisely what Benedict Anderson had in mind when he wrote about "imagined communities."

62 DREAM STATES

Not surprisingly, the cumulative impact of all these cultural influences is substantial. If public opinion polls are to be believed, commitments to some form of Celtic identity are remarkably strong across much of the region, even if they vary somewhat in intensity. In Scotland, for example, fully three-fifths of Scottish residents polled in 2014 and 2015 responded "Scottish" when asked whether they would describe themselves as either British or Scottish.[5] By contrast, in Wales in 2016, only about one-quarter of respondents said "Yes" when asked if Wales should be an independent country—though by removing non-committed voters, the share of those polled who would vote for independence rose above 35 percent.[6] In Cornwall, surveys have suggested that as many as 44 percent identify as Cornish rather than British or English,[7] while in Brittany some 37 percent of residents polled in 2013 said they would describe themselves as Breton first.[8] Overall, it is clear that for many in the area, their respective communities may be "imagined," but they are by no means imaginary. For these people, the Celtic daydream is real.

Outcomes

Outcomes, however, differ considerably. At one extreme is the Isle of Man, which continues quietly to go about its business as an offshore financial center. Its choice has long been reconciliation. The island's population, some 85,000 in all, may think of itself as Celtic, but few Manx seem to harbor any ambitions for genuine political independence. They know that any serious effort to live alone as a sovereign microstate would be costly. They already enjoy full domestic self-rule. Moreover, oversight from London, which is responsible only for foreign affairs and security, is benign. So, as the saying goes, if it ain't broke, don't fix it. There seems little risk that, in this case, the bubble might pop.

At the other extreme is Ireland, where repression ruled for centuries until the bubble finally popped a century ago with the Easter Rising, leading to the formal partition of the Emerald Isle. In Northern Ireland, which remained part of the UK, violent rebellion has persisted on and off ever since. Worst was the thirty-year struggle known as the Troubles that began in the late 1960s and was not brought to an end until the so-called Good Friday Agreement in 1998. At the heart of the violence was the Provisional Irish Republican Army (Provisional IRA), which saw itself as the legitimate successor to the original Irish Republican Army that had achieved independence for the Irish Free State back in 1921. The Troubles claimed over 3,500 lives and injured as many as 50,000 others. To this day, tensions simmer between mostly Catholic secessionists, seeking merger with the Irish Republic, and mostly Protestant unionists, loyal to the British crown. Northern Ireland is a classic avatar of the nightmare that lurks in so many parts of the world today.

Between the extremes, in the other Celtic nations, we find reform—a variety of political adaptations intended to stabilize the unstable equilibrium. For Brittany, this has meant preservation of the area's status as an autonomous administrative region within France, on a par with other historical provinces such as Normandy, Burgundy, Aquitaine, and Corsica. For Scotland and Wales, the key move came in the late 1990s in the form of *devolution*, a strategy of administrative decentralization. Two new legislative bodies were established—a Scottish Parliament and a Welsh Assembly—each with authority to act in areas of policy not expressly "reserved" for the UK government in London. The reforms were prompted by a growing intensity of nationalist feeling in both regions. Electoral support for leading separatist parties—the Scottish National Party, first created in 1934, and Plaid Cymru in Wales—was reaching unprecedented heights. In all three of these Celtic nations, the hope was that the statutory delegation of powers might succeed in blunting calls for referendums on political independence. In Brittany, the reform tactic seems to have been successful, at least for now. In Scotland and Wales, the jury is still out.

Ubiquity

The Celtic Fringe is illustrative, but it is by no means alone. In fact, there is not much that is truly unique in the devotion of the Celtic nations to their identity and their respective homelands. Similar examples can be readily found elsewhere, near and far. Scholars like Ernst Gellner may have exaggerated a bit in their estimates of the number of potential nations in the world (cited back in Chapter 2), but they are not wrong. Potentially secessionist daydreams are ubiquitous.

Across Europe, for instance, it is difficult to travel more than a few kilometers without stumbling into some restless minority's homeland, from

Catalonia and the Basque Country on the Iberian Peninsula to the Caucasian countries of Armenia, Azerbaijan, and Georgia. In the far north, we find Sápmi, the ancestral territory of the indigenous Sámi people scattered across Scandinavia and Russia's Kola Peninsula. And in the Balkans we have the fragmented and persistently feuding South Slavs, remnants of the old Yugoslavia.

Many of Europe's historical communities, like the cantons of Switzerland or the *Länder* of Germany, appear quite content with their status as sub-nationalisms within an established national state. Others, however, never seem to quit in their struggle for validation. A prime example can be found in the Baltic region where the trio of Estonia, Latvia, and Lithuania, once administrative divisions of the Russian Czarist Empire, gained recognition as sovereign states after World War I, only to lose their independence once again when they were absorbed into the Soviet Union at the end of World War II. Governments-in-exile never ceased fighting to keep alive the dream of national renewal of their homelands. I recall seeing pro-Baltic demonstrations at the United Nations many years ago and wondering how these people could continue to pursue such a futile cause. But they turned out to be right. Persistence paid off. In 1991, at the end of the Cold War when the Soviet Union disintegrated, their tenacity was finally rewarded. The Baltic trio are now all members in good standing in the global sovereignty club.

In areas of the world that were once known as the "regions of recent settlement," early indigenous populations have become increasingly vocal in defense of their identity and traditional homelands. In the United States, where they used to be called Indians (or, more pejoratively, Redskins), it is now considered politically correct to use terms like Native Americans or Indigenous People. Elsewhere they are variously dubbed the First Nations in Canada, First Peoples in Australia, or the Maori in New Zealand. Many long to return to the lands of their ancestors from which they were driven generations ago. Their daydream was well captured in fictional form in a 2018 Canadian film, "Falls Around Her," about the frustrations of a First Nation in northern Ontario that is denied access to its historical territory. Laments one lead character, sarcastically: "Everyone loves Indians—they just don't want us to have a home."[9]

At times, efforts to improve the status of native populations reach the highest levels of government. Particularly noteworthy was the decision of US president Joe Biden in 2023 to throw his support publicly behind the efforts of an indigenous lacrosse team to be allowed to compete in the 2028

Olympics under its own flag.[10] The team represents six tribes of indigenous people in the United States and Canada known as the Haudenosaunee Confederacy (earlier, the Iroquois Confederacy). Considered to be among the best players in the world, the Haudenosaunee have competed internationally since 1990, though never yet in the Olympics. Ancestors of the Haudenosaunee are credited with inventing lacrosse—or at least a game that closely resembles modern lacrosse.

Efforts like these are not always successful. In Australia in late 2023, the country's First People lost a campaign for the creation of a national advisory body to be called a "Voice to Parliament." Intended to give the indigenous population a greater say over laws and policies that directly concern them, the Voice was soundly defeated in a referendum. Opponents argued that the plan would simply codify racial divides in Australia. Over 60 percent voted "No." Likewise in New Zealand, also in late 2023, a new conservative government was elected pledging to scrap policies that had been introduced by the previous incumbents to boost Maori influence in the country's politics. Voters decisively rejected the idea of some form of "co-governance" with indigenous tribes.

And of course there are even more tribal or religious minorities to be found in developing nations across the vast territories of Africa and Asia. In many cases, where political frontiers date back to colonial days, cultural communities find their homelands divided between two or more contemporary states. Perhaps the most striking example today highlights the dilemma of the Kurds in the Middle East, who have been described as the largest minority in the world without a jurisdiction to call their own. In all, the Kurdish population numbers somewhere in the range of 30–45 million. Following the collapse of the Ottoman Empire at the end of World War I, when lines on the region's maps were hastily redrawn, the Kurds found themselves scattered across parts of no fewer than four sovereign states: Iran, Iraq, Syria, and Turkey. To varying degrees in all four places, the Kurds continue to dream of validation of their ancient—and badly fractured—homeland.

Lessons

What, then, do we learn from all these examples? Three lessons stand out. First, it is evident that daydreams are *commonplace*. They can be found virtually anywhere. Boutros Boutros-Ghali was right. Potentially, there is no

66 DREAM STATES

limit to fragmentation.[11] The recipe is the simplest possible: Find a minority, stir in some cultural heritage and an attachment to a historical homeland, and voilà! You have a people dreaming of validation. You have possible pretenders to sovereignty.

Second, it is also evident that daydreams are best thought of as *transitional*—a necessary first step toward a more definitive expression of identity. An organized secession movement does not appear suddenly out of nowhere, like Athena from the forehead of Zeus. It begins with the celebration of cultural or historical identity, which acts as a fundamental motivator: the dream state's driving force. Without a sense of its own uniqueness, a "sub-national" community is unlikely to go to the trouble of seeking formal validation of what it regards as its special character. A daydream is a necessary condition for every pretender to sovereignty, an essential starting point.

Finally, it is evident that some daydreams can become truly *disruptive*. The four R's tell us that four alternative outcomes are possible. While many minorities may well in time come to be content with their "sub-ness," reconciled to their submergence in an older and broader incumbent state, others may well be stifled by repression or perhaps bought off with reforms of various kinds, up to and including the possibility of full home rule. At any given time, however, there will be a handful of minorities for whom rebellion seems to be the only viable option. For them, the formula could turn out like a few of the experiments I tried with my childhood chemistry set. They might just explode.

6

Drexits

Mild-mannered separatists

Secessionist explosions are by no means rare. Dangerous hot spots are found all over the globe. Most of them, we can be sure, were sparked by a captivating daydream before erupting into a secessionist inferno.

However, the leap from daydream to conflagration—from sentimental yearning to active rebellion—is not inevitable. In between, there remains the possibility that policy differences might be resolved peaceably, by way of negotiation and compromise. That is the goal of *drexits*—dream states that are more ambitious than daydreams but not inherently violent. With drexits, the degree of conflict risk is significant yet contained. Embedded in older national states, drexits dream of exiting their "sub-ness" (hence the mix of dream and exit) and are ready to organize a secession movement for direct political action. But their preference is to attain their goals, if possible, by non-violent means, not to the point of provoking armed combat. They are mild-mannered separatists: disrupters who would prefer to gain validation by way of reform rather than rebellion. If outsiders like the United States come to be drawn in, it is most likely to be as informal advisors or mediators.

Around the world

Like fantasy dream states and daydreams, drexits are remarkably commonplace. Recall the estimate of some fifty-two secession movements, on average, in action in any given year since World War II (Chapter 1). Drexits, too, can be found seemingly everywhere. Indeed, if the familiar Westphalian model of political geography were to be redrawn to highlight all the secession movements that are politically active today, the globe would end up looking like a giant jigsaw puzzle, with scores of small, oddly shaped pieces scattered across the map.

Dream States. Benjamin J. Cohen, Oxford University Press. © Oxford University Press (2025).
DOI: 10.1093/9780197811672.003.0006

68 DREAM STATES

In 1872, the French author Jules Verne published his justifiably famous adventure novel, *Around the World in Eighty Days.* An alien visiting from another planet might need even more than eighty days to make sense of the dream-state puzzle. A representative sample of examples circumnavigating the globe will demonstrate the point. Our friendly alien would certainly be impressed by the number and variety of drexits in virtually every region.

Canada

In Canada, next door to the United States, we find one of the best-known drexits in the world today: the storied province of Quebec. With origins going back to the first French settlers in the New World, in the sixteenth and seventeenth centuries, Quebec became the jewel in the crown of France's North American empire—then known simply as New France—until it was lost to the British during the French and Indian Wars of 1754–1763. For the next two centuries, Quebec chafed under the rule of Canada's Anglophone majority. The *Québécois* particularly resented their inferior economic status as compared with Ontario, Canada's richest province next door, and other areas further west. As a popular expression had it: "In Canada, money speaks English."

Starting in the 1960s, however, a so-called Quiet Revolution ushered in a period of rapid modernization, which did much to restore Quebec's pride in its own identity and homeland. Soon separatist sentiment began to capture the public's imagination, encapsulated in the slogan *"Vive le Québec libre"* ("Long live free Quebec"). By the time Charles de Gaulle, president of France at the time, loudly shouted the phrase before a huge crowd of *Québécois* at the Montreal World's Fair in 1967, the die was cast. A new separatist movement was born, led by the pro-independence Parti Québécois, which first came to power in 1976. Enthusiasm for secession waned, however, after two lost referenda on exit in 1980 and 1995 (the latter failing by less than one percentage point).

In more recent years, attention has shifted to a model known as "sovereignty association"—a less ambitious hybrid form of separatism. Quebec's national identity would be reaffirmed, but the province would nonetheless retain its place in a broad economic partnership with the rest of Canada. In effect, the *Québécois* would settle for the option of reconciliation. In 2003, the provincial government voted unanimously "that the people of Quebec form a nation," and three years later, Ottawa responded with a symbolic resolution declaring "that this House recognizes that the *Québécois* form a nation within a united Canada." The model, clearly, is the United Kingdom (UK), where Scotland and Wales have long been formally acknowledged as nations within a larger sovereign state. The shift of sentiment was confirmed most recently in 2022, when a provincial election was decisively won by the ruling *Coalition Avenir Québec* (Coalition for Quebec's Future), which first came to power in the province in 2018. The Coalition ran on an agenda emphasizing identity-based nationalism within the Canadian state. The old Parti Québécois, by contrast, was virtually wiped out, managing to gain no more than three seats in Quebec's National Assembly. Lamented a disappointed Parti Québécois strategist, the election said, "You don't have to love Canada, but you don't have to leave it either."[1]

Latin America

Though not as well known as Quebec, a number of drexits can also be found scattered around Latin America. In Argentina, there are two secession movements of note. One is located in the country's affluent wine country, the Mendoza district, where there is much talk of self-rule or even secession. Activists call it "Mendoexit." The purported goal is a sovereign Republic of Mendoza. The other is in Patagonia, Argentina's remote southern region, where the Movimiento Independentista Patagónico campaigns for independence. In Bolivia, Nación Camba promotes the idea of secession for the southeastern department of Santa Cruz, the state's wealthiest area. The mainly European-descended "lowlanders" of Santa Cruz, perched at the edge of the Amazon basin, resent being asked to share more of Bolivia's natural-resource wealth with the country's indigenous "highlanders" living mostly far up in the Andes. In Brazil, separatist groups are vocally active in several different locales, including most prominently the far south of the country (Paraná, Santa Catarina, and Rio Grande do Sul), the state of São Paulo, and the Amazonian region. And in French Guiana on the northern coast of South America—technically an overseas territorial unit of France—several pressure groups agitate for a proposed Republic of Amazonia. Overall, the number of drexits in Latin America is not especially large, but they make their presence felt.

Europe

Europe, by contrast, is chock-full of drexits, from Scotland and Wales in the northwest to Bosnia's Serbs and Turkey's Kurds in the southeast. Perhaps best known among them is Scotland, which since 2007 has been ruled by its leading separatist force, the Scottish National Party (SNP). The SNP supported devolution in the 1990s—especially the creation of a Scottish Parliament, which it has persistently dominated. But that was hardly the full measure of its appetite. Devolution was seen mainly as one step in what the party hoped would be a persistent march toward some form of sovereignty, perhaps in the manner of former British Dominions like Australia, Canada, and New Zealand.

Progress was interrupted, however, when separatists failed to gain a majority in a referendum authorized by London in 2014. Asked if they favored independence, just 45 percent of Scotland's voters said "Yes." And further setbacks, including scandals involving financial improprieties, erupted in subsequent years, ultimately forcing a change of party leadership in early 2023. Popular support for the SNP dropped precipitously. Yet these reversals have not deterred many Scots from continuing to cherish their ultimate goal of full membership in the sovereignty club. Polling in 2023 suggested that support for independence remained steady at roughly 48 percent.[2] In the words of Alex Massie, a Scottish-based columnist for the Times of London, "The idea of Scottish independence will always have an emotional resonance."[3] Relations between the Scottish and British authorities, according to another commentary, now "oscillate between chilly and glacial."[4]

Also well known is the case of Catalonia, tucked into the northeastern corner of Spain. With a long and rich history, Catalonia stands out today as Spain's most important industrial and tourist area. Under the constitution adopted by the Spanish state after the end of the dictatorship of Francisco Franco in 1975, the Catalans gained a parliament for their provincial capital, Barcelona, and considerable self-government in internal affairs. For many in the province, however, that was simply not enough. Sovereignty remains the ultimate goal, though opinions vary on how to get there. No fewer than three separate pro-independence parties are represented in Catalonia's parliament.

Relations between Barcelona and the central government in Madrid remain frosty to this day. After a snap general election in 2012, which led to the first pro-secession majority ever in the Catalan parliament, a non-binding referendum in 2014 yielded a large majority in favor of independence but with a disappointingly low turnout. Three years later, after a second referendum that was declared illegal by Madrid, the Catalan parliament approved a motion proclaiming a sovereign republic. That, in turn, led to the arrest of many regional leaders on charges of sedition, although some were later granted amnesty.

Political fractures widened in 2023 following a general election at midyear, when additional amnesties were extended to some 300 activists as part of a controversial deal intended to keep Spain's ruling Socialist party in power. Opposition to the deal was widespread, polarizing the country's politics. Conservatives and nationalists insisted that separatists must pay for their sins, while more moderate elements stressed the virtues of clemency and compromise. Though the Socialists managed to win a regional election in May 2024, passions continued to run high. Many worried that Spain might be headed for a full-fledged constitutional crisis.

Nor is Catalonia Madrid's only secessionist nightmare. In fact, separatist movements are active in at least a half dozen regions around much of the country's periphery, from Valencia and the Basque country in the east to Galicia and Asturias in the far northwest. Dreams of exit can also be found in the Balearic Islands in the Mediterranean, centered on Majorca, and in the Canary Islands out in the Atlantic. Five regional separatist parties are represented in Spain's parliament in Madrid. And since mid-2023, three regional languages—Basque, Catalan, and Galician—have been given official status in parliamentary debate alongside Castilian Spanish. Spain is by no means the kind of "natural" homogeneous nation that is imagined by the Westphalian model. Rather, it is an apt example of just how heterogeneous an "imagined community" can be.

Nor is Spain alone in this regard. Across Europe, centrifugal forces are common. France faces avowed separatists in several of its peripheral regions, including Alsace, French Basque country, Savoy, and Corsica. In Belgium, the northern Dutch-speaking region of Flanders dreams of separation from French-speaking Wallonia to the south. A secessionist party named Vlaams Belang—"Flemish Interest"—currently ranks as Belgium's most popular party, with an average of 22 percent support in recent polling.[5] The leader of Vlaams Belang calls Belgium a "forced marriage." Denmark regularly experiences secessionist pressures from the Faroe Islands and Greenland, two long-standing overseas dependencies in the North Atlantic. Italy has to deal with would-be drexits in several of its provinces, including Sardinia, Sicily, Trieste, and Bolzano (known to many as South Tyrol or Alto Adige). For years, Rome has also been confronted with a campaign by one of its largest political parties, the Northern League, to carve out a new state in the affluent northern Po River basin to be called Padania. Romania copes with separatist sentiment in its historical region of Transylvania. Poland is faced with an autonomy movement in Silesia. Even tiny Kosovo in the Balkans must figure out how to manage the aspirations of its even tinier Serbian population, which is eager to abandon the Kosovars and join up with Serbia instead. Kosovo is another example of the "minorities-within-minorities" issue.

Lastly, there is Russia, that massive multinational federation covering some 6.6 million square miles, stretching some 6,000 miles from Europe to the Pacific, and incorporating almost 200 separate ethnic groups. Nearly one Russian citizen in five is a member of a minority—Chechens, Circassians, and Cossacks, to name just a few at the start of the alphabet. At the present time, of course, given Russia's authoritarian government, it is difficult to judge just how much separatist sentiment there might actually be across the country's eleven time zones. But it doesn't take much effort to imagine that it could be considerable. Given free expression, centrifugal forces could turn out to be massive. I will have more to say about Russia in a later chapter.

Africa

Africa, too, is chock-full of drexits, which is not at all surprising given the colonial heritage of most of the continent's fifty-four recognized states. In the nineteenth century, imperial powers like Britain, France, Portugal, and Spain were more interested in staking claims than in rationalizing frontiers. Territorial boundaries, for the most part, were drawn carelessly and largely without regard for the historical claims of indigenous populations. Traditional homelands were disregarded. It is hardly astonishing, therefore, to find many local minorities today that are acutely dissatisfied with the contours of the contemporary African map.

In the north, best known are the Berbers (or Imazighen), a collection of tribes and clans that consider themselves quite distinct from the Arab communities that rule over them and resent being treated as second-class citizens. Berbers are spread mostly across Algeria, Libya, Morocco, and

Tunisia, an area known collectively as the Maghreb. (Smaller numbers of Berbers can also be found in nearby countries like Burkina Faso and Mali.) In Algeria, separatism is promoted by the Kabylia people organized under the leadership of the Movement for the Self-Determination of Kabylie. In Morocco, pressure comes from the Rif Independence Movement, led by the Riffian ethnic group. And in Libya, the dream of sovereignty is kept alive by the Tuareg and Toubou peoples.

In the eastern Horn of Africa, separatists are especially active in Ethiopia and Somalia. Several regions in multiethnic Ethiopia have sizable secession movements, including, most notably, the Ogaden (with a predominantly Somali population), Oromia, and Tigray. In Somalia, we see not only Puntland (cited back in Chapter 1) but also English-speaking Somaliland, another breakaway area that was once a British protectorate. That is in contrast to the rest of Somalia, which in colonial days was a dependency of Italy. Upon receiving independence in 1960, British Somaliland and Italian Somaliland were formally united as a single sovereign federation, the Somali Republic, but subsequently broke apart again in the 1990s. For years, both Puntland and Somaliland have functioned as autonomous entities, quietly contesting the authority of the official Somali government in the capital city of Mogadishu.

Only occasionally are relations among the three competing pieces of the Somali puzzle disrupted by open controversy. The most recent was a dispute triggered in early 2024 when word leaked that Somaliland, acting on its own, had offered to lease a port on the Gulf of Aden to landlocked Ethiopia next door, along with a stretch of Somaliland's coastline that could have been used by the Ethiopians to build naval bases. In return, Ethiopia reportedly promised to consider extending diplomatic recognition to Somaliland. That would have made Ethiopia the first country to formally recognize the former British colony as an independent state. But Mogadishu reacted furiously, declaring the new agreement "null and void," and the plan was soon scuttled.

Secessionist movements also thrive further to Africa's south and west, where almost every government finds itself confronted by one group or another of determined separatists. The Democratic Republic of the Congo (once known as the Belgian Congo) contends with rebellious tribes in several of its eastern provinces, including, in particular, the province of Katanga. Nigeria struggles to contain the dreams of multiple minorities to carve out sovereign states of their own, particularly in the southern Niger Delta region and in the country's Yoruba-dominated eastern states. And

74   DREAM STATES

in Angola, a former Portuguese dependency, a challenge comes from the Bakongo people of Cabinda, Angola's oil-rich exclave just across the Congo River. Cabinda is separated from the rest of Angola by a narrow strip of territory belonging to the Democratic Republic of the Congo. The aim of the separatists is to gain recognition for a proposed Republic of Cabinda.

I could go on. It is the rare country in Africa that does not face centrifugal forces of some kind. Drexits are thick on the ground.

Asia

Much the same can be said of Asia as well. Here too we find many local minorities that are dissatisfied with today's map of their continent.

At the southwestern end of the continent, we, of course, have the Kurds, cited in the previous chapter. Secession movements have also emerged in many nearby countries, including Iran, Iraq, Syria, and Yemen. Conversely, at the eastern end of Asia, we have the troubled state of Papua New Guinea, where separatism is rife. More than 300 tribes are spread across the country, speaking more than 800 languages. Many local groups would prefer to secede if at all possible. In the words of one local researcher, "From the outside, it will look like they're one country.... But we really struggle with trying to live with each other, understand each other, given all the different diversities."[6] And in between the two ends of Asia, we have crowds of additional would-be separatists, all eager to shed their present national "sub-ness."

In Indonesia, for instance, we have the Free Papua Movement, coveting a proposed state of West Papua (or a merger with Papua New Guinea), as well as other active independence organizations in the Moluccan Islands and in the country's far-western province of Aceh. Malaysia has two major drexits to contend with in its peripheral areas of Sabah and Sarawak. The nearby Philippines have long had to deal with Muslim insurgents in the country's southern regions, while Myanmar faces more than a half dozen challenges from among its many ethnic groups, including the Chin people, the Kachin, the Karen, the Mon, and the Shan. Sri Lanka is rent by the aspirations of its Tamil minority, which has never abandoned the idea of its own separate state of Tamil Eelam. And in Iran, separatist sentiments keep bubbling to the surface among minorities all around the edges of the country, from the Kurds in the northwest to the Baluchis in the southeast and Arabs in the southwest. All resent being dominated by the majority Persian population at the center. In April 2024, Baluchi forces sought to take over two military bases run by Iran's Islamic Revolutionary Guards Corps. In battles lasting some seventeen hours, ten security officers and eighteen militants lost their lives.

Baluchi separatists are also active in Pakistan's southwestern region of Baluchistan, the country's largest province by area. For years, militants there have agitated noisily for sovereignty for themselves as well as for their brethren across the border in Iran. Many operate from clandestine bases inside Iran under the banner of the Baloch Liberation Army. As recently as December 2023, Baluchi separatists killed eleven people during an attack on a local Pakistani police station. A month later, Pakistan and Iran almost went to war after Iran attacked activist sites inside Pakistan. In retaliation, Pakistan carried out aerial strikes on some seven sites used by Baluchis on the Iranian side of the border.

Nor can we forget China and India, the two most populous nations in the world. Like Russia, both are huge countries with sizable and restless minority populations.

In China, the challenge is manifest mainly in two peripheral regions, Tibet and Xinjiang. Historically, China has always been informally divided between Inner China and Outer China. Inner China, where up to 90 percent of the country resides, is made up mostly of Han Chinese, considered the traditional core population of China, together with a scattering of more than fifty officially recognized small ethnic minorities. Outer China includes the more peripheral regions of Inner Mongolia (or South Mongolia), the northeast (which used to be known as Manchuria), Tibet, and Xinjiang. In Inner China today, any potential communal tensions are contained by a combination of repression in the name of "safeguarding ethnic solidarity" together with a range of accommodations from the center—for example, allowing classes in local languages or the celebration of traditional customs. In Outer China, by contrast, the dream of exit remains alive in both Tibet, which was forcibly annexed after the end of China's civil war in 1949, and Xinjiang, home of the mainly Turkic Uyghurs. In each of these two regions, despite intense pressures to assimilate, independence sentiment is nourished by long-standing governments-in-exile.

In India, by contrast, the challenges are almost endless. An abundance of separatists is hardly surprising, given the extreme ethnic diversity of the country. What other nation has as many as twenty-two officially recognized languages and over 720 dialects written in thirteen different scripts? (The

76 DREAM STATES

entire Western world uses only five scripts: Latin, Cyrillic, Greek, Arabic, and Hebrew.) What other country's bank notes spell out their value in fifteen different tongues? The central government in Delhi is beset with secession movements from all sides. Separatists are particularly active in the isolated northeast—in states like Assam, Manipur, and Nagaland—as well as in some of the less developed areas of eastern and central India and in the disputed area of Kashmir in the far north. As with Russia, I will have more to say about India in a later chapter.

Oceana

Finally, we arrive at the southern Pacific Ocean, otherwise known as Oceania. The Pacific, covering some one-third of the planet's surface, is home to nearly a score of the world's smallest microstates—collections of thinly populated islands and atolls with exotic names like Kiribati, Nauru, Palau, and Tuvalu. Even in some of these states, tiny as they are, we find instances of the recursive "minorities-within-minorities" pattern, where ostensibly homogeneous groups often splinter into thinner and thinner shards. Separatists are active in several of the Pacific microstates, seeking sovereignty for tinier island clusters or even for a single individual island.

Perhaps the most notable example in Papua New Guinea is the copper-rich island of Bougainville, where the population has made no secret of its desire to go its own way. Another is to be found in the Solomon Islands, where the poverty-stricken island of Malaita has long resented the dominance of the country's biggest island, Guadalcanal. A third case roils the waters in Vanuatu, where several of the country's 160 islands have called for referenda on secession. And a fourth simmers in Micronesia, where Chuuk state—the microstate's most populous island—has long campaigned for a vote on independence. Drexits are indeed ubiquitous.

Lessons

As in the last chapter, three lessons stand out. First, it is worth noting how *easy* it seems to be for a daydream to evolve into a drexit. Once a community starts to reflect at all seriously on its distinct cultural heritage—its history and homeland—it does not appear to require much of a leap for militants to begin organizing to gain more formal validation. To get started, separatists need hardly more than a name, a mailbox, and a bit of funding. Given the sheer number of secession movements that we find around the world, it seems that the transition from sentimental attachment to more radical identity-driven activism can be understood as something akin to a default setting: a more or less natural progression. One blends smoothly into the other. The process is typically gradual and may, for some, be agonizingly slow. But it could be said to have "inevitable" written all over it.

Second, there also seems to be no strict lower *limit* on the size of individual drexits. In theory, according to models of the optimal size of nations discussed back in Chapter 2, we should indeed expect to find a lower limit set by diseconomies of small scale, which raise transaction costs. In practice, however, it would seem that there are few barriers to the sort of recursive pattern that we have seen in Oceania and elsewhere. Progressive splintering of incumbent nationalisms into smaller and smaller sub-nationalisms also seems to be something of a default setting. The pull of identity trumps material interest.

Finally, the ubiquity of drexits would appear to reaffirm the final conclusion of the preceding chapter. Like the daydreams from which they evolve, drexits can become truly *disruptive*, whether that is their intention or not. Proponents may be quite sincere in their wish for an orderly separation, but if persistently frustrated in their ambitions, any number of them might well feel compelled to turn to a more overt threat of violence. The story may begin with moderate reform, but it can culminate in militant rebellion—at which point outsiders like the United States may feel that they have no choice but to become materially involved.

7

Rebels with a Cause

Separatist rebellions

Clearly, not every separatist movement is fated to turn violent. Wars of secession are not inevitable. Many communities in time grow reconciled to their sub-national status. Others may be successfully bought off with concessions and accommodations. And of course in more authoritarian states, minorities may simply be repressed, more or less indefinitely. But if frustration persists and grows, armed conflict may come to be seen as the only remaining option: the default choice. Moderate reformers may feel that they have no alternative but to become militant *Rebels with a Cause* (with apologies to James Dean, who became a Hollywood legend in a memorable 1955 film entitled *Rebel Without a Cause*[1]).

Overall, the number of rebels is bound to be fewer than the total universe of dream states. As one source observes, while there were more than seventy separatist movements around the globe in 2008, only seven of them were seriously violent.[2] Fewer, however, does not mean few. Recall, as noted back in Chapter 1, that there have been as many as fifteen wars of secession simmering in any given year during the period since World War II.[3] Fifteen is not as many as the dozens of daydreams and drexits that we know are out there. But neither is the number trivial. In reality, even a single separatist rebellion can be the cause of much pain and suffering. Fifteen rebel dream states at a time are more than enough to be truly nightmarish. And of course the longer the violence goes on, the greater will be the toll in terms of lives and matériel.

Notably, wars of secession hardly ever end quickly with a decisive victory for one side or the other. That too was noted in Chapter 1. A look at the record since World War II shows that outright winners or losers among separatist rebellions tend to be relatively rare. It is much more common to see secessionist struggles go on for years, even decades, frustrating all concerned without any clear resolution. Hot spots persist, ready to erupt in flames at any time.

Dream States. Benjamin J. Cohen, Oxford University Press. © Oxford University Press (2025).
DOI: 10.1093/9780197811672.003.0007

For the United States (US), separatist rebellions clearly pose more of a threat than do fantasy dream states, daydreams, or drexits. Washington may resist becoming directly involved. But the longer secessionist conflicts endure, the greater is the risk that they might spread to endanger vital US interests, pressuring Washington to intervene in one way or another. Here is where the external challenge becomes real—truly a nightmare for US policy makers.

Winners

At first glance, it might appear that wars of secession are remarkably successful. According to one count of some twenty-five large separatist conflicts since 1945, all but four ended with a rebel victory—a seeming near-sweep.[4] But those numbers are misleading, since they include many of the new states that emerged during the wave of decolonizations that swept through the global south after World War II. Properly speaking, these were imperial dependencies that gained their independence from a colonial power. They cannot be counted as secessions as conventionally defined. Separatist movements are understood as break-away communities located *within a state*. They are carved out from territory *inside* the established frontiers of an incumbent sovereign—not overseas colonies.

In plainest terms, a secessionist movement may be said to be a winner when it is admitted into the global sovereignty club as a full member. In principle, eligibility for the club is defined in terms of the four criteria for statehood set out in the Montevideo Convention. Have the separatists taken control of a defined territory? Do they have a permanent population? A government? A capacity to enter into relations with other states? We know, though, that exceptions to these four criteria are common. A simpler and more practical test is election to membership in the United Nations (UN). As I have suggested, that is the closest equivalent the club has to a formal admissions procedure. By that standard, the number of successful wars of secession since World War II can be counted on no more than the fingers of two hands.

Analytically, two groups of winners may be distinguished, depending on the consequences for the incumbent state. In one group, we have what we might call *classic* wars of secession—cases where a new state successfully gains recognition at the expense of an older state, but the older state remains

80   DREAM STATES

a member of the club (albeit shrunken in size). The incumbent continues to function despite losing a fraction of its territory. In a second group—what we might call *fatal* wars of secession—we have a more extreme outcome where the older state suffers not just amputation but demise. The incumbent is not merely reduced in area; it disintegrates and disappears. Since 1945, we can count just four classic wars that have been won outright by separatists. These were Bangladesh (carved out of Pakistan), Eritrea (from Ethiopia), South Sudan (from Sudan), and Timor-Leste (from Indonesia). During the same years, we also had one spectacular example of a fatal war of secession. That was Yugoslavia, whose six "republics" not only rebelled successfully but collectively *replaced* the previous Yugoslav federation. The old Yugoslavia didn't merely shrink. Following bitter hostilities, it vanished altogether.

Some might add the former Soviet Union to the category of fatalities. That federation too vanished after the end of the Cold War, to be replaced by its fifteen constituent "republics." But in the Soviet case, the process was relatively orderly (certainly as compared with Yugoslavia). Secessions by the fifteen were barely contested, with few lives lost, and it took less than two years to reach a final agreement in late 1991 formally dissolving the seventy-four-year-old Bolshevik experiment. Although there were some minor skirmishes over borders, there was nothing like the bitter series of conflicts that consumed Croatia and Bosnia in the early 1990s or the Kosovo War of 1998–1999. The only real wars of secession to erupt as the Soviet Union collapsed were fought *within* individual republics. Most noteworthy were two successive uprisings by Chechnya, a district in the northern Caucasus that was unhappy with its subordinate role inside the post–Soviet Russian federation. The rebellion was against Russia, not the Soviet Union. As we shall see, the pair of conflicts did not turn out well for the Chechens.

Bangladesh

Originally part of the historic region of Bengal in the Indian subcontinent, Bangladesh began its modern life as East Pakistan, one of the two geographically separate wings of the new state of Pakistan created by the partition of British India in 1947. Long dominated by the western wing of Pakistan centered on the provinces of Punjab and Sindh, East Pakistan finally revolted in March 1971, sparking an intense—but relatively brief—war of secession. With the aid of India's military, East Pakistan was quickly liberated from West Pakistani occupation. West Pakistan's troops surrendered to the Bangladesh–India Allied Forces in December 1971. By August 1972, the new state had been formally recognized by nearly 100 countries and was soon admitted to the United Nations.

Bangladesh's success could be attributed to three key factors. First was the unique geography of Pakistan, with two wings of one state physically separated by nearly 1,400 miles of sovereign Indian territory, which put Pakistani forces at a distinct logistical and strategic disadvantage. Second was the decisive intervention of India's army, providing needed aid for the Bangladeshi rebels. And third was the active support of prominent elements of civil society in Western nations, especially as news spread of massive atrocities by the Pakistan army. These included outright massacres of students, intellectuals, and political figures. Public appeals for assistance came from such foreign luminaries as Ted Kennedy, Bob Dylan, and André Malraux. Most memorable was the Concert for Bangladesh held in New York City in August 1971, a fund-raising appeal organized by George Harrison (one of the original Beatles) and Bengali sitarist Ravi Shankar. Great emphasis was placed on the awful human price that the Bangladeshis were being forced to pay for their independence.

Eritrea

The borders of the present-day state of Eritrea date from the infamous Scramble for Africa in the late nineteenth century, when European nations rushed to consolidate imperial claims over every available speck of the huge African continent. Italy laid claim to the new colony of Italian Eritrea in northeastern Africa in 1889, later combined during the Fascist period of the 1930s with a previously colonized portion of Somaliland (Italian Somaliland) and just-conquered Ethiopia to form a "new Roman Empire." But after Italy's defeat in World War II, Eritrea was joined together under the terms of a 1950 UN resolution with newly liberated Ethiopia in a loose federal structure. Effectively, Eritrea became a province of Ethiopia, ignoring the wishes of Eritreans for a state of their own. The result, soon enough, was a major disruption: a bloody war of secession, beginning in 1958, that lasted for more than three decades until a final victory for the rebels in 1991. Following a referendum in which the Eritrean people voted overwhelmingly for independence, Eritrea quickly gained international recognition and became

82 DREAM STATES

the 182nd member of the United Nations. Despite occasional eruptions of violence in the years since—including, in particular, a two-year war with Ethiopia at the turn of the century that cost the two combatants together as many as 100,000 deaths—Eritrean sovereignty is no longer in question.

Why did the Eritreans hang on for so long? The answer, it may be argued, had to do with the prior history of Eritrea, which for decades before Italy's Fascist period had already existed as a relatively homogeneous administrative unit of its own (albeit as an Italian dependency). The Eritrean people already had some sense of common identity. It seemed only natural, therefore, to fight on for recognition of their distinctive community.

But why, then, did success take so long? Above all, the delay could be attributed to the lack of an outside ally comparable to the role that the Indian army played in Bangladesh. Eritrea was small and poor, with few friends and even fewer resources. Ethiopia, by contrast, was the second most populous nation in Africa with numerous potential patrons. Essentially, Eritrea was on its own and could do little other than keep the pot simmering for years on end while waiting for a break. An opportunity finally presented itself in 1991 when Ethiopia's murderous Marxist–Leninist government known as the Derg, which had ruled in brutal fashion since 1974, was overthrown. In the climate of instability and political uncertainty that followed, the Eritreans were able to seize the advantage and soon prevailed militarily. A new sovereign state was born.

South Sudan

Bordering Ethiopia to the north and west is the nation of Sudan, for many decades ruled jointly by Britain and Egypt. The name Sudan comes from a vast swamp region known as the Sudd, which is formed in Sudan's east by the White Nile. The area of Anglo-Egyptian Sudan was huge—easily Africa's largest colonial dependency by land surface—and combined a mainly Muslim and Arabic population in the north with Black and animist peoples to the south. Sudan received its independence in 1956. But almost from its first day as a sovereign state, the country was beset by violent strife between its northern and southern halves. Literally hundreds of thousands of people, mostly innocent villagers, died as a result. The First Sudanese Civil War lasted for eleven years, from 1972 until 1983. After a brief pause for negotiation, a second separatist conflict soon followed, which lasted even longer until terminated in 2005 by a comprehensive peace agreement granting full autonomy to southern Sudan. Following an overwhelmingly favorable vote for independence in a referendum in early 2011, South Sudan became Africa's fifty-fourth sovereign state in July 2011 and soon became the 193rd and most recent new member of the United Nations.

As in the Eritrean experience, the same two questions might be asked. First, why did the southern Sudanese hang on for so long? In this case too, prior history mattered—but here it was a prior history of horrendous mal-treatment of southern civilians by a Sudanese government dominated by northerners. For many in the south, secession was literally a matter of life or death.

Second, why did it take so long? Partly it was because the two sides were relatively evenly matched. But mainly it was because there were vital material interests at stake. At the time, Sudan, within its original borders, was well on its way to becoming an important oil exporter. As it happened, however, virtually all of Sudan's petroleum resources were located in South Sudanese territory. A prominent American politician back when I was young liked to joke about the politics of the US federal budget: "A million dollars here, a million dollars there, and soon you're beginning to talk about real money." The northern and southern Sudanese were now talking about real money.

Timor-Leste

Located on the eastern end of the Indonesian archipelago (formerly the Dutch East Indies) and just a short distance across the Timor Sea from Aus-tralia, Timor-Leste occupies the eastern half of the small island of Timor. Colonized by Portugal in the sixteenth century, it was known as Portuguese Timor until 1975 when control was relinquished to an insurgent group, the Revolutionary Front for an Independent East Timor (Fretilin). Within a year, however, the island was invaded and occupied by the Indonesian mil-itary, which declared East Timor to be Indonesia's twenty-seventh province. Not surprisingly, the takeover then provoked an insurrection by Fretilin and other smaller separatist groups. Fighting lasted more than two decades and cost as many as 200,000 lives until intervention by the United Nations. In 1999, a UN-sponsored referendum produced a majority vote for indepen-dence. Three years later, following UN-sponsored negotiations, Timor-Leste became the twenty-first century's first new sovereign state and first new UN member.

84 DREAM STATES

Here, again, prior history mattered. Like Eritrea, East Timor had developed an identity of its own during centuries of Portuguese rule. Moreover, like the southern Sudanese, the Timorese were long subjected to a brutal occupation. Both factors help to explain why the rebellion persisted for so long. But here too, as in the Eritrean case, the Timorese faced a huge disparity between the two sides—a tiny obscure community of little more than a million, about which few cared, versus the fifth most populous nation on the planet. They too had little choice other than to keep the pot simmering and hope for a break. The opportunity finally arrived when it became clear how much oil and natural gas was to be found under the waters of the Timor Sea. Now the outside world did care. The UN intervention soon followed.

Yugoslavia

As noted back in Chapter 1, Yugoslavia first came into existence as a sovereign state at the end of World War I. Subsequently, it went through several different forms of government until emerging after World War II as a federation of six "republics" under the leadership of the communist leader Josip Broz Tito. In addition to the six republics (Bosnia, Croatia, Macedonia, Montenegro, Serbia, and Slovenia), there were also two autonomous provinces, Kosovo (with a mostly ethnic-Albanian population) and Vojvodina (mainly ethnic-Hungarian), both administered by Serbia. Bitter inter-ethnic tensions, however, fatally hampered Tito's efforts to mold a single unified nation. Once, many years ago, when I was visiting Yugoslavia for the first time, I was told how to understand the country. Yugoslavia had six republics, five languages, three religions, and two autonomous provinces, but only one Yugoslav—Tito! It was no surprise to anyone, therefore, that following the leader's death in 1980, the federation fell victim to mounting political and social fragmentation. Centrifugal forces intensified.

Matters came to a head with the fall of the infamous Berlin Wall in 1989. A wave of anti-communist revolutions swept through Eastern Europe, marking the end of the Cold War. Within three years, four of the six constituent republics of Yugoslavia—Bosnia, Croatia, Macedonia, and Slovenia—had seceded, each formally declaring its sovereign independence. That left just

Montenegro and Serbia in a rump Yugoslav federation, which in turn was formally dissolved in 2003 and replaced by a state union of the two holdouts. And that lasted just three years more, until Montenegro decided in 2006 to go its own way. In 2008, the former autonomous province of Kosovo also formally proclaimed its independence, although that initiative continues to be disputed by Serbia. With the emergence of this gaggle of successor states (and Tito in his grave), there was no longer even a single Yugoslav to be found.

The disintegration of Yugoslavia was by no means orderly. Vicious internecine conflicts were stubbornly fought over the decade of the 1990s. Before the dust settled, some 4 million people had fled their homes and 140,000 were dead. The first two republics to secede and gain international recognition were Croatia and Slovenia, both in 1991. Each was resisted by the armed forces of the federation, led by Serbia. The Slovenian War of Independence was brief and ended quickly. Today, it is recalled as the Ten-Day War. By contrast, the Croatian War of Independence—known to Croats as the Homeland War—was brutal and lasted some four years before the republic's dream of exit was accepted.

The bloodiest of the Balkan wars was fought in Bosnia where calm was not restored until the US-sponsored Dayton Agreement (or Dayton Accord) of 1995, negotiated and signed by the warring parties at Wright-Patterson Air Force Base outside Dayton, Ohio. The last active combat as Yugoslavia crumbled was in Kosovo, where in 1996 an aptly named Kosovo Liberation Army, drawn mainly from the province's majority Albanian population, began attacking federal security forces. That development triggered a massive campaign of repression by the forces of Serbia and Montenegro that killed upwards of 2,000 Kosovars. Hostilities were suspended three years later, in 1999, after the North Atlantic Treaty Organization (NATO) intervened with air strikes on Serbian targets, forcing the Serbs to allow UN peacekeepers into the province. As noted, Kosovo's independence was finally proclaimed in 2008.

In retrospect, it is clear that the Yugoslav federation was primed for failure. Inter-ethnic tensions were rife despite decades of effort to build a unified nation. The diverse southern Slavs simply disliked each other too much. Once the glue of Tito's leadership was removed, it was only a matter of time before the union would come unstuck. Multiple successful secessions were the result.

86 DREAM STATES

Losers

On the opposite side of the ledger are the losers—rebellious separatists who, despite their best efforts, have been denied membership in the sovereignty club. Their dream of drexit was quashed by superior military force. In practical terms, a war of secession may be said to be lost when defeat is formally acknowledged in some manner, whether by capitulation or negotiation. In diplomatic circles, this is known as "reintegration." In effect, vanquished rebels are compelled to reconcile themselves to sub-national status for the indefinite future.

Here too, again excluding imperial dependencies that have successfully campaigned for decolonization, the numbers are small. At most, we may count no more than a dozen classic secession struggles in the years since World War II that have ended in unconditional surrender.[5] Among these, seven quite diverse cases may be highlighted. These are Anjouan (an attempted secession from the Comoros Islands), Artsakh (from Azerbaijan), Azawad (from Mali), Basque Country (from Spain), Biafra (from Nigeria), Chechnya (from Russia), and Tamil Eelam (from Sri Lanka)—all, ultimately, lost causes. Today, they exist nowhere outside stamp albums.

Anjouan

Few observers other than professional cartographers are likely to have ever heard of Anjouan, one of a cluster of small islands in the southwestern Indian Ocean that make up the Union of the Comoros, a former French colony. The case of Anjouan is, to say the least, obscure. In July 2007, some three decades after France gave up control of the archipelago, Anjouan's local government declared itself to be independent of the Comoros. The secession, however, did not last long. Seven months later, in March 2008, Comoran forces—backed by reinforcements from the African Union—staged an armed invasion, meeting little resistance. By May 2008, the separatists were thoroughly vanquished. In the years since, residents of Anjouan seem to have fully reconciled themselves to sub-national status within the Comoros state.

Artsakh

Also quite obscure was a long-running stalemate over the status of Nagorno-Karabakh, a small landlocked enclave within the former Soviet Republic of Azerbaijan inhabited mainly by ethnic Armenians. The area was internationally recognized as part of Azerbaijan and was linked to Armenia by no more than a single mountain road through Azeri territory known as the Lachin Corridor. But while small in size, the territory has always loomed large in the eyes of both the Armenians, who are predominantly Eastern Orthodox Christians, and the Muslim Azeris. Once the Soviet Union started to fragment, the two sides took to contesting for control over the area.

During a first round of violence lasting from 1992 to 1994—today known as the First Nagorno-Karabakh War—the area, together with seven surrounding districts, was seized and occupied by Armenia. The enclave then declared its independence as the Republic of Artsakh (alternatively, the Nagorno-Karabakh Republic), though de facto it functioned as an integral part of Armenia. Years of low-intensity conflict ensued, leading eventually to a second round of hot combat in 2020 (the Second Nagorno-Karabakh War), which ended far more favorably for the Azeris. The Armenian military suffered heavy losses. Under the terms of a cease-fire agreement shepherded by Russia, Armenia was forced to abandon the surrounding districts it had occupied earlier.

Tensions lingered on, however, and in late 2023 once again briefly erupted in violence when Azerbaijan decided to tighten its grip on the narrow Lachin Corridor. This time the Azeris were even more successful, quickly consolidating control over the entire contested territory. In a battle that lasted less than a day, victory was absolute. The local Armenian authorities capitulated unconditionally, disbanding their governmental institutions, and in the following weeks most of the area's ethnic Armenian population—up to some 120,000 in all—fled to the relative safety of Armenia proper. The dream of Artsakh secession went up in smoke. Lamented one now-homeless refugee: "This is the end of the struggle."[6] The area was soon repopulated with a wave of Azeri settlers.

Azawad

A third case is the one-time dream state of Azawad, centered in the northern half of the former French colony of Mali in northwestern Africa. The region is populated mainly by Tuareg Berber people. It takes its name from the generic Tuareg name for all Tuareg Berber areas. Following a rebellion in 2012 that drove the Malian army from the Tuareg homeland, a sovereign state was declared unilaterally by the National Movement

88   DREAM STATES

for the Liberation of Azawad (MNLA). The MNLA was backed by the murderous forces of the Islamic State (ISIS) that were beginning to infiltrate the region, raising fears of intensifying Islamist terrorism. Little more than a year later, therefore, Mali's army returned and, aided by troops from France as well as the neighboring nation of Chad, decisively crushed the separatists. The amassed resistance to the secession was simply too overwhelming. In a quickly negotiated peace deal, the MNLA agreed to give up its dream of independence. Mali's national unity and territorial integrity were reaffirmed in return for a vague promise of greater local autonomy.

Basque Country

Among the oldest ethnic groups in Europe are the Basques, an ancient community with its own distinctive language, culture, and history. Basques are indigenous to an area traditionally known as Basque Country (Basque: Euskal Herria). Their homeland is located around the western end of the Pyrenees on the coast of the Bay of Biscay, straddling parts of north-central Spain and, to a lesser extent, southwestern France. Though the dream of sovereign statehood had long inspired Basque militancy, serious armed conflict did not break out until the creation in 1959 of a separatist organization known as Euskadi Ta Askatasuna ("Basque Homeland and Liberty": ETA). Combat took the form primarily of car-bombings, assassinations, and other terrorist-style attacks by ETA, followed in turn by iron-handed repression from government forces in repetitive cycles of violence. Assaults occurred mostly on Spanish soil, with France used by ETA primarily as a safe haven. Hostilities continued on and off for the next half century—resulting in the death of more than 800 Spanish security personnel, politicians, and judges, as well as a good number of civilians—until a weakened ETA, facing the combined forces of Spain and France, finally conceded defeat in 2011. Following an international peace conference in October 2011 aimed at promoting a permanent resolution of the Basque conflict, ETA announced a "definitive cessation of its armed activity." Seven years later, the group was formally dissolved, finally ending what had been called "Modern Europe's longest war."

Biafra

Nigeria, a former British dependency, is the most populous nation in Africa and among its most culturally diverse. The country gained its independence in 1960 but was almost immediately inundated by murderous ethnic and religious riots. Many attacks were aimed at the Igbo people whose traditional homeland is located in the easternmost region of the country. In September 1966 alone, some 30,000 Igbo civilians were killed during disturbances in the Muslim-dominated north. Six months later, in May 1967, the Igbo leadership unilaterally declared the independence of the Republic of Biafra in eastern Nigeria. The name of the newborn dream state recalled an ancient kingdom that had once dominated the area, variously referred to in early maps as Biafar, Biafara, Biafra, or Biafares. Rebels cited the many civilian deaths in preceding months as the main reason for their secession.

In reality, however, a more salient factor may have been the sizable oil reserves that had recently been discovered in the area. That made Biafra a prize worth fighting for. Outsiders took a strong interest, particularly after the federal authorities imposed a harsh blockade that in the next two years caused as many as two million Igbo deaths from disease and famine. Some aid came to the separatists from such countries as France, Spain, and Portugal. But even greater support was given to the Nigerian forces by the American and British governments, inspired at least in part by the key role played in the region by major US and UK oil companies. Nigeria's military soon prevailed. Biafra's insurgents surrendered in early 1970, formally abjuring any further claims to sovereign statehood—though half a century later there are still scattered groups of Igbo militants that would be happy to reignite the dream of an independent Biafra. Most prominent was a recent movement known as the Indigenous People of Biafra, headed by an activist named Nnamdi Kanu. Kanu was arrested by Interpol and handed over to Nigeria in 2021.

Chechnya

A long-time "republic" within the Russian Federation located in the North Caucasus, Chechnya declared independence for the Chechen Republic of

90   DREAM STATES

Ichkeria in the wake of the dissolution of the Soviet Union in 1991. Two successive uprisings followed. As a result of the First Chechen War, which lasted from 1994 to 1996, Chechnya gained de facto independence, although formally it remained a part of Russia under a peace treaty signed in 1997. But with unrest continuing, renewed hostilities broke out in 1999, lasting another four years until a referendum was held on a constitution that reintegrated Chechnya within Russia. The Second Chechen War was a particularly bloody affair, including massive bombing of the Chechen capital Grozny and many civilian deaths. Chechen rebels were no match for one of the world's biggest armed forces. Vladimir Putin had just come to power as Russian president. After a decade of political drift in Russia under his predecessor Boris Yeltsin, he was determined to demonstrate the virtues of firm, even ruthless, leadership. Since 2007, Chechnya has been ruled by Ramzan Kadyrov, a Chechen disciple of Putin. Kadyrov's regime has been characterized by widespread corruption, a poor human rights record, and a growing cult of personality. The dream of Chechen sovereignty was brutally extinguished.

Tamil Eelam

Tamil Eelam was the name given to a dream state sought by the Tamil minority in the island state of Sri Lanka (known as Ceylon in colonial days), just off the southern coast of India. The name is derived from the ancient Tamil term for the island. Even before Sri Lanka gained independence from Britain in 1948, historical tensions were rife between the Hindu Tamils and the majority Sinhalese, who are mostly Buddhists. Violent persecution of the Tamil minority periodically erupted in the form of murderous riots, often with state support. After years of mistreatment, a secessionist war was declared in 1983, led by the Liberation Tigers of Tamil Eelam, known to most simply as the Tamil Tigers. The aim was to gain recognition for a new sovereign state based in the Tamil homeland in the north and east of the island. In 1987, an Indian peacekeeping force sought to intervene, but after several costly battles with the rebels chose to withdraw again three years later. Fighting between the government and the Tigers then continued sporadically for another two decades until finally the separatists were decisively defeated in a cataclysmic battle in 2009. The cost of the rebellion was high, with upwards of 100,000 civilians and 50,000 fighters on both sides killed before the Tigers finally capitulated.

Stalemates

What about the rest? Do the math. In our age of secession, spanning the entire post–World War II period, separatist wars have numbered in the dozens. Yet we see that just a handful have ended decisively with either victory or defeat for secessionists. The rest of the wars, therefore, must fall somewhere in between—sporadic low-intensity conflicts that have yet to be sorted out, even after years of fitful combat. Despite a lack of success, rebels fight on. In a sense, they win simply by not losing. Struggles persist as armed stand-offs—unresolved *stalemates*.

Not many examples of armed stand-offs can be found in the Western Hemisphere where, as noted previously, most separatist movements in recent times have tended to take the form of more peaceable daydreams or drexits. There was one spectacular exception in 1954, when four members of the Puerto Rican Nationalist Party opened fire in the US House of Representatives in Washington, wounding five congressmen. But otherwise secessionist aspirations have been pursued typically by non-violent means. Whether we are talking of Puerto Rico, Hawaii, Quebec, or any of the lesser-known dream states to be found scattered across North and South America, bubbles have yet to pop.

Likewise in Europe, only a small handful of examples of ongoing stalemates are evident despite the plethora of daydreams and drexits cited in Chapters 5 and 6. Best known is the case of Northern Ireland, where tensions between Catholic separatists and Protestant unionists continue to fester despite the celebrated Good Friday Agreement of 1998. During the preceding Troubles, which lasted for some three decades, rebellion was led by the Provisional Irish Republican Army (Provisional IRA), a direct descendant of the IRA that led the fight for Irish independence nearly a century earlier. The Provisional IRA did not hesitate to resort to violence in pursuit of its ultimate goal: secession from the United Kingdom, to be followed as soon as possible by merger with the Irish Republic. Under the Good Friday Agreement, the Provisional IRA consented to lay down its arms and rely instead on political means to pursue its dream. But the accord did little to resolve the underlying existential issue. Should the six northern counties remain in union with Britain, or should they seek instead to join their Celtic brethren to the south? No one doubts that the tinder is still there, ready once again to burst into flames at the slightest spark.

92   DREAM STATES

And then there are Kosovo and Chechnya. In Kosovo's case, the province's former ruler—Serbia—has yet to accept the legitimacy of the Kosovar secession. Hostilities may have been suspended in the years since NATO's air strikes, but Serbian irredentism remains as adamant as ever. In late 2023, tensions were running particularly high after four people were killed in a shoot-out between Serbian gunmen and Kosovo police. Likewise, in Chechnya's case, dreams of independence may have been snuffed out for now as a result of Ramzan Kadyrov's brutal rule, but the embers of separatist rebellion could well be reignited if circumstances change. It's not beyond the realm of possibility that Kadyrov might one day die.

Across Africa and Asia, by contrast, armed stand-offs are far more common. From Morocco at the far western end of Africa, which has long fought an on-and-off war with indigenous rebels over the putative Sahrawi Arab Democratic Republic, to the Free Papua Movement at the eastern end of Indonesia that sporadically resorts to militant action, innumerable hot spots exist.

In many cases, conflicts tend to remain dormant for long periods of time, only occasionally erupting in violence. A degree of stability comes to prevail in what one scholar dubs a regime of "relational autonomy." Rebels come to occupy an anomalous position that is neither sovereign nor subordinate; neither formally separated from nor functionally incorporated into an incumbent state. A notable example is provided by the Wa people, a community of some 600,000 in Myanmar's remote northeast, who have long been ruled autonomously by the rebel United Wa State Army. The Wa State has sustained a durable, if ambiguous, relationship with the central government for decades.[7]

Other instances include Palestine, where firm control by Israel's occupation army long limited opportunities for rebellion prior to the outbreak of the Gaza war in October 2023; Somalia's separatist statelets of Puntland and Somaliland, where months or even years may go by without a serious incident; the Philippines, where a fragile peace agreement between the government and Muslim rebels presently reigns; and Senegal, in West Africa, where discontented secessionists roam the jungles of Casamance, an isolated region separated from Senegal's main territory by the finger-like state of Gambia. In other cases, low-intensity fighting boils along more or less continuously, as in places like Cameroon, the Congo, Ethiopia, and Yemen.

Either way, these hot spots are dangerous. At any moment, any one of them could explode in flames.

Lessons

Once again, three lessons stand out. First, it is clearly easier to start a separatist rebellion than to finish one. To get a fight going, you don't need much more than some rebels with a cause and a handful of weapons. But how will combat end? A rebellion may reach its denouement quickly, as in the cases of Anjouan, Bangladesh, and Biafra among others. But it may also set new records for longevity, as in "Modern Europe's longest war" in Basque Country. The record demonstrates that outright victory for either side may be quite elusive. Apart from the collapse of Yugoslavia, we have only four cases of rebellious dream states that managed to make it into the sovereignty club on nominally equal terms. Likewise, we have only a handful of instances of decisive defeat of militant separatists. The majority of struggles just go on and on. Long and painful stand-offs dot the world map, especially in Africa, the Caucasus, and Asia.

The underlying reason, we may conclude, is understandable stubbornness. It is easy to comprehend why secession movements might be reluctant to give up their dream of sovereignty. Conversely, we can sympathize with incumbent states that might resist the amputation of a significant chunk of their territory. Both sides, therefore, may be prepared to fight on indefinitely, accounting for the substantial number of unresolved stalemates and the high rates of casualties. In time, of course, some of today's stand-offs might join the list of winners or losers. It took Eritrea, South Sudan, and Timor-Leste decades to finally attain victory; similarly, rebels like the Basques, Chechens, and Tamils fought on for years before ultimately conceding defeat. The past duration of a stalemate is no predictor of its future outcome.

Second, it is also clear that much depends on what is at stake. In some cases, the prize may be a valuable natural resource. Timor Leste's rebellion, for instance, remained on a low boil for years, of little concern to the outside world, until the discovery of oil and gas deposits in the island's territorial waters. Then suddenly the former Portuguese dependency was in the spotlight. Biafra and South Sudan, too, attracted relatively little attention until the magnitude of their energy resources became known. In other cases, however, the issue may be more geopolitical. France made no secret of the fact that its intervention in Mali in opposition to the MNLA was driven first and foremost by fear of an Islamist threat in the region. Likewise, Russia's brutal suppression of the Chechens was motivated quite evidently by Vladimir Putin's desire to keep the shaky Russian Federation from disintegrating

94 DREAM STATES

like the Soviet Union before it. The higher the material stakes in a war of secession, the greater is the determination to force a definitive outcome.

Finally, it is evident that much depends as well on whether there is serious intervention from the outside. It is questionable whether the Bangladesh secession would have been so successful without the support of the Indian military. Likewise, we might ask whether Comoran forces could have suppressed the Anjouan separatists without help from the African Union. Conversely, we may wonder if the rebellions by Nigeria's Igbos or Mali's Tuaregs would have failed so quickly had Western powers not taken such a keen interest in opposing them. Would Eritrea have won its sovereignty earlier had it been able to line up a foreign patron? Would peace have come to Bosnia without the good offices of US diplomats? Would Kosovo have been able to resist Serbian pressure had NATO not intervened forcefully? Separatist rebellions typically begin as local affairs. Their outcomes, however, may well be decided on a much grander scale. Brush fires can spread in unexpected ways, pulling in outsiders from the neighborhood or beyond.

8

Clients

Co-opted secession movements

Finally, we come to potentially the most violent of all the categories in my list. Previous entries assumed that dream states were essentially endogenous, driven first and foremost by the preferences of the sub-national community directly involved. Outsiders at times also entered the story (as in the cases of Azawad and Bangladesh, among others), but mainly in a supportive role. In principle, priorities and strategies were decided by the separatists themselves. In practice, however, foreign intervention may occasionally become much more intrusive. Opportunistic outsiders might in effect try to appropriate secessionist sentiment to serve their own particular interests.

A sub-national community may hope to validate its identity, up to and including the possibility of secession. But suppose that separatists lack the material means needed to go much beyond daydreams or drexits. The solution, seemingly, might be to look for "a little help from my friends" (as the immortal Beatles might have put it). A trusted patron might be asked to step in, much like a Big Brother, to lend a hand. Aid from the outside could prove all-important in achieving separatist goals. But in the process, Big Brother could also end up hitching the dream state's aspirations to its own policy wagon. In return for promises to support a secession movement, by force if necessary, a degree of loyalty will naturally be expected. Separatists thus risk becoming little more than *clients* of their sponsor—essentially, cover for their benefactor's broader ambitions. Once the door is opened, the danger is that, in time, other outsiders could be drawn into the contest as well, on one side or the other. The degree of conflict risk is elevated to an even higher level. In the words of one astute observer: "Separatist movements are frequently manipulated by external powers as part of a geopolitical chess game that can become violent."[1]

Today, the most prominent example of such an opportunistic external power is Russia, which has backed separatist rebels in several former Soviet republics—most notably, Georgia, Moldova, and Ukraine. Other lesser

Dream States. Benjamin J. Cohen, Oxford University Press. © Oxford University Press (2025).
DOI: 10.1093/9780197811672.003.0008

96 DREAM STATES

known but nonetheless salient cases include Algeria and Turkey, both of which have also effectively co-opted secession movements in nearby states, converting separatists into clients. Not all would-be patrons are successful, however. Saudi Arabia and the United Arab Emirates, for example, failed spectacularly in the last decade in an attempt to exploit separatist rivalries in Yemen. But whether any of these Big Brothers eventually prevail or not, yet other potential sponsors might be tempted to imitate their behavior elsewhere. That could both increase the number of hot spots around the globe and intensify brush fires that are already smoldering.

As with rebels with a cause, the United States (US) may feel itself under pressure to intervene in some manner. But the pressure is apt to be all that much greater when clients are at issue, since in many cases Big Brother may be a direct geopolitical rival. In dealing with separatist movements around the world, America's external challenge is greatest when it provokes open confrontation with a powerful strategic adversary like Russia or a troublesome friend like Turkey. No other type of dream state is as dangerous.

Russia

If there were a contest for the contemporary world's most unapologetic sponsor of secessionist rebellions, the champion would surely be Russia. The reason is manifest. Russia today represents the heartland of what was once the sovereignty club's biggest overland empire, first under the czars and then under the Bolsheviks. Today, the empire is no more. But it is by no means easy for people to accept such a dramatic fall in status. Quite understandably, many Russians agree with Vladimir Putin that the disintegration of the Soviet Union in 1991 was "the greatest geopolitical catastrophe of the twentieth century." No opportunity is lost, therefore, to recapture Mother Russia's traditional sphere of influence wherever and whenever possible. As one expert has written: "It was always Putin's goal to restore Russia to the status of a great power .... The end goal was not to re-create the Soviet Union but to make Russia great again."[2]

One way to reach that goal, Putin seems to have decided, is to back secession movements that challenge the authority of neighbors that were once subordinate parts of the old empire. Perhaps they could be made subordinate again. Piece by piece, it might be possible to reconstruct a regional commonwealth led by an all-powerful Russia.

Moldova

The first piece was put into place as early as 1992 at the expense of Moldova, a post-Soviet republic in the far-southwestern corner of the lost empire, just north of Romania. Amid the chaos of the Soviet Union's disintegration, Moldova declared its formal independence. The démarche triggered a brief conflict with separatists in a long narrow strip of land squeezed between the Dniester River (which bisects Moldova from west to east) and Moldova's northern frontier. Long known as Transnistria ("beyond the Dniester River"), the area is ethnically closer to Ukraine and Russia than to the rest of Moldova. That cultural divide gave the Russians an excuse to intervene militarily on behalf of the rebels in March 1992. Under the terms of a cease-fire agreement concluded three months later, a Russian military garrison has occupied the territory ever since, ostensibly as a peacekeeping force. For close to a third of a century, the conflict with Moldova has been "frozen."

Using a tactic that has since become depressingly familiar, the Russians persistently override Moldovan protests about the occupation by burnishing Transnistria's credentials as an independent state. The rebel area now enjoys many of the trappings of sovereignty, including its own currency, flag, and postal system. In key respects, it meets the criteria for statehood laid out in the Montevideo Convention. Yet under international law, the breakaway statelet is still technically part of Moldova. In the eyes of most of the world, Transnistria is nothing more than an illegally occupied stretch of land under the tutelage of a foreign power; no current member of the UN, other than Russia itself, has offered any manner of diplomatic recognition. As we shall see, though, that has not stopped the Russians from using Transnistria's secession as a model for other chunks of the former empire. Separatist forces in states elsewhere on Russia's borders have been encouraged to follow much the same recipe.

Georgia

The next two pieces came at the expense of Georgia, another post-Soviet republic. The pattern in Georgia, which is located in the volatile Caucasian region between the Black Sea and the Caspian Sea, was similar. Here too, as in Moldova, the Soviet Union's disintegration resulted in a declaration of independence by the Georgian republic. Here too the new state's

98 DREAM STATES

government was opposed by ethnic separatists—not just in one breakaway area but in two, Abkhazia and South Ossetia (also known as Alania). And here too, Russian armed forces intervened successfully on behalf of the secessionists, though only after years of sporadic fighting between the rebels and the Georgian government. The climax came in the summer of 2008 in a brief conflict between Russia and Georgia, remembered today as the August War. The Georgians were decisively defeated, and occupation of the two areas by the Russian military was reaffirmed. Since 2008, these conflicts too have been "frozen."

De jure, Abkhazia and South Ossetia both remain international pariahs, recognized diplomatically by just a small handful of Russia's closest friends such as Nicaragua, Syria, and Venezuela. De facto, however, each of the two territories operates as an autonomous statelet much like Transnistria, though also obviously under firm Russian tutelage. Their usefulness as clients has been amply demonstrated by the role that South Ossetia has played in helping Russia obtain military hardware from North Korea. International sanctions on Russia and the North Koreans have been circumvented by routing transactions through banks in South Ossetia.[3]

Armenia/Azerbaijan

Yet another piece fell into place in late 2023 at the expense of the ethnic Armenian population of Nagorno-Karabakh, most of whom were driven out of the area following a lightning military strike by Azerbaijan (described in Chapter 7). In this case, Russian objectives were achieved not by action but by studied inaction. After the Second Nagorno-Karabakh War in 2020, Russia agreed to provide a neutral peacekeeping force meant to prevent renewed fighting between Armenia and Azerbaijan, both of whom could be described at the time as clients of Russia. But by 2023, Big Brother's strategic interests had tilted significantly toward Azerbaijan. In part, this was because of Moscow's growing reliance on trade with Turkey, Azerbaijan's principal ally; and in part because of Vladimir Putin's lingering anger over a popular uprising in Armenia in 2018 that had swept away a corrupt, Kremlin-backed regime. So this time the supposed peacekeepers stood aside, in effect giving the Azeris free rein. In the words of one informed observer, Azerbaijan "could not have done what it did without a green light from Russia .... Russia really needs Azerbaijan."[4]

Ukraine

The biggest pieces, of course, are to be found in Ukraine, formerly a cornerstone of the old Soviet Union—the second-most populous of the fifteen Soviet republics, a major agricultural producer, and home to much of the former empire's defense industries. Historical ties to Russia were strong, going back centuries to the Kievan Rus, the early Slavic state from which contemporary Russians and Ukrainians alike draw their lineage. Vladimir Putin was not alone in questioning Ukraine's qualifications to join the sovereignty club. Many others shared his skepticism. Representative were the comments of former West German chancellor Helmut Schmidt in an article published in 2014: "As late as 1990, nobody in the West doubted that Ukraine had for centuries belonged to Russia. Since then, Ukraine has become an independent state, but it is not a nation-state."[5]

Putin frequently expresses a yearning to return to *Novorossiya* (New Russia), a term dating back to eighteenth-century Russia when Ukraine's subordinate place in the empire was still unquestioned. In his mind, there appears to be no doubt that Ukraine belongs to Russia, as it did back in the good old days of the czars. It was only a matter of time before Russia's current ruler would take steps to act on his nostalgia.

The first step came in 2014, following the unexpected overthrow of Ukraine's then pro-Russian president Viktor Yanukovych. Under pressure from Moscow, Yanukovych had scrapped plans to formalize closer economic relations with the European Union. Very quickly, his decision triggered massive countrywide protests that came to be known as Euromaidan (after Maidan Square in the capital city of Kyiv, where the protests began). Within weeks, he was forced from power. In the ensuing tumult, President Putin saw an opportunity. Calling Euromaidan a "fascist coup" that endangered ethnic Russians in Ukraine's eastern and southern regions, he ordered a covert invasion, ostensibly a "rescue operation." In short order, battalions of soldiers appeared in camouflage khaki uniforms shorn of identifying insignias. Though derisively labeled Russia's "little green men," they were in fact notably effective against the unprepared Ukrainian military. Soon the strategic peninsula of Crimea was formally annexed by Russia, and pro-Russian separatist regimes were set up in the eastern Ukrainian provinces of Donetsk and Luhansk (together known as the Donbas). Another frozen conflict was born, stalemated, and unresolved. Both secessionist provinces claimed to represent independent states, not unlike Transnistria, Abkhazia,

100   DREAM STATES

and South Ossetia. But, in fact, it was clear that they too were no more than dependent clients under full Russian control. Between 2014 and 2021, more than 14,000 people died as a result of sporadic fighting in the Donbas, the bloodiest combat in Europe since the Balkan wars of the 1990s.

The next step came in February 2022, when President Putin ordered a full-scale invasion of Ukraine that he euphemistically labeled a "special military operation." Again the action was excused as a rescue mission to end an alleged fascist genocide of Russians in Ukraine. The ostensible aim was to "de-Nazify" Ukraine before it could become an existential threat to Russia itself (a bitter joke given the fact that Ukraine's president at the time was Volodymyr Zelenskyy, a Jew). But this time the Ukrainians were better prepared. Encountering unexpected resistance, the Russians were forced to backtrack, curtailing their ambitions considerably. The goal now was simply to protect the two secessionist regimes of Donetsk and Luhansk as well as two other neighboring provinces, Kherson and Zaporizhzhia. In September 2022, after quickly organized sham referendums, all four separatist entities were absorbed into the Russian Federation, even though only two of the four were then fully occupied by Russian forces.

I will have more to say about Ukraine in Chapter 12.

Turkey

Another unapologetic sponsor of secessionism is Turkey. Turks have always had a special interest in the nearby island of Cyprus—located in the Mediterranean Sea just to the south of Turkey's Anatolian mainland—owing to the ethnic makeup of the island's population. The Cypriot people have long been sharply divided between a majority (some 75 percent) who are ethnic Greeks and a minority (25 percent) of ethnic Turks. Turkish Cypriots live primarily on the northern side of the island and have always looked to Turkey as a protector—a role that Turkey has not been loath to assume.

Even before Cyprus gained its independence in 1960 after years of rule by Britain, tensions between its two ethnic communities ran high. As far back as the nineteenth century, when the island was still part of the Ottoman Empire, Greek Cypriots were already promoting the idea of *enosis*—secession from Cyprus to be followed by union with Greece. Contrarily, for their part, Turkish Cypriots increasingly called for a policy of *taksim*—partition of the island and creation of a Turkish polity in the north. Matters

came to a head in 1974 when a coup was staged by Greek Cypriot nationalists, who immediately sought to begin implementing *enosis* in the name of
the "Hellenic Republic of Cyprus." In retaliation, Turkey invaded Cyprus,
quickly taking charge of the northern half of the island (roughly 40 percent
of the total). As many as 200,000 Greek Cypriots were forcibly moved to
the south in exchange for some 40,000–50,000 Turkish Cypriots who relocated northward. (The numbers are disputed.) Nine years later, over the
protests of most of the world community, a separate Turkish Cypriot state
in the north was unilaterally declared: the Turkish Republic of Northern
Cyprus. Apart from Turkey itself, however, no other nation has ever offered
diplomatic recognition to the separatist state, which remains heavily dependent on Turkey for economic and military support. To this day, the Turkish
army maintains a large force in Northern Cyprus, giving Turkey a strategi-
cally advantageous position in the eastern Mediterranean. In security terms,
protecting Northern Cyprus clearly pays dividends to Turkey, too.

Algeria

A third example involves Algeria, which has long backed the indigenous
rebels fighting for the independence of the former Spanish-controlled Western Sahara. The separatists are led by the so-called Polisario Front, which has
never wavered from its dream of sovereignty for the putative Sahrawi Arab
Democratic Republic encompassing all of Western Sahara. Since Morocco
considers the area to be an integral part of the Moroccan kingdom, this
amounts to a war of secession. Morocco has sought to contain the rebellion by building an extensive sand-berm—known as the Border Wall or
Moroccan Wall—stretching the entire 1,700-mile length of the territory. The
Moroccan government maintains control of two-thirds of the territory on
the western side of the wall, bordering the Atlantic coast. Polisario occupies the eastern side, which is mostly low flat desert, under the protection of
Algeria next door. A government-in-exile operates from the nearby Algerian
town of Tindouf.

The Sahrawi dispute has been stalemated for years, interrupted from time
to time by brief armed clashes. Polisario has been successful in gaining formal recognition for Sahrawi from as many as four dozen states around the
world. But Morocco too has many backers, particularly in the Arab League
and other Muslim areas, though until very recently no other UN member

102 DREAM STATES

had officially recognized Moroccan sovereignty over any of Western Sahara. (That changed in 2020 when the United States, in the last days of Donald Trump's presidency, recognized Moroccan sovereignty over Western Sahara in exchange for Morocco's normalization of relations with Israel.) Polisario obviously would have hard time pursuing its cause without Algeria's support. But Algeria clearly gains as well. The country's relations with Morocco have long been strained over border disputes and other issues. In geopolitical terms, the two nations are natural rivals for a leading role in the North African region. Algeria's influence over Polisario gives it an extra pressure point to apply on the Moroccans—an extra arrow, as it were, in its foreign-policy quiver. Morocco, by contrast, has no comparable client that it can "unleash" against the Algerians when needed. Score one for Algeria.

Yemen

A final—and very different—example can be found in the rugged mountains of Yemen, where over the last decade as many as nine different warring factions have fought to control one fragment of the country or another. Fighting began in 2014 when Shiite insurgents—the Houthis—took control of Yemen's capital and largest city, Sana'a, with the backing of their co-religionists in Iran. In response, Saudi Arabia and the United Arab Emirates (UAE), two neighboring Sunni powers, commenced a campaign of air strikes on behalf of what was left of the country's officially recognized government, now relocated to the southern port city of Aden. The experience for both the Saudis and the UAE has been humbling, even humiliating. In the Sunni-Shiite proxy war that ensued, the Houthis managed to gain control over as much as one-third of Yemen's territory and some 70–80 percent of its population. They were even able to launch damaging missile and drone strikes across the border into Saudi Arabia, ultimately causing the Sunni coalition to splinter. Most recently, both Saudi Arabia and the UAE have been doing their best to extract themselves from Yemen in as face-saving a manner as possible.

Lessons

The major lesson here is aptly summarized by the popular warning: "Be careful what you wish for, you may just get it." Intervention in another country's war of secession may have its benefits, but there are risks, too. Just as it is easier to start a separatist rebellion than to finish one, it appears easier to start a client relationship than to finish one. Years, even decades, have gone by since Algeria, Russia, Saudi Arabia, Turkey, and the United Arab Emirates each chose to begin playing Big Brother in separatist struggles beyond their borders. Yet even now there is no sign that any of them feel that the time has yet come when they might be free to wash their hands and leave. All find themselves mired in prolonged standoffs that seem destined to go on and on without end. (The only exception is Russia's hot war with Ukraine, whose outcome is still unclear.) Words like quagmire or quicksand come to mind. One is reminded of the Tar-Baby featured in the old Uncle Remus stories, an insidious trap set by the villainous Br'er Fox to trap Br'er Rabbit. The more you struggle, the more entangled you become.

Can stalemates like these be broken? Options are limited. On the one hand, patrons like those highlighted here could redouble their efforts to win diplomatic recognition for their clients. But there is no assurance that in this respect they would be any more successful in the future than they have been in the past. Experience suggests that such a strategy would in most instances prove futile. On the other hand, they might decide simply to withdraw—much as the UAE tried to do in 2020—leaving their clients to continue the fight on their own. But that would be, to say the least, embarrassing, not to say seriously damaging to their geopolitical reputation. Many would see such a retreat as tantamount to abject surrender. The least costly choice might be just to hang on, hoping—like Mr. Micawber in Charles Dickens's 1850 novel *David Copperfield*—that eventually "something will turn up." With luck, the conflict could remain frozen indefinitely.

PART III
FUTURE HOT SPOTS

9

Familiar Faces

Combustion risks

We can now turn to prospects for the future. My guide to dream states, from Fantasies to Clients, demonstrates that there really are a lot of plausible threats to worry about. But how serious are they? How great is the risk that some of the world's many Daydreams or Drexits might in time breed deadly violence? In years to come, which of these smoldering hot spots are most likely to burst into flames? And among them, where are we likely to find the greatest dangers for the United States?

The most obvious combustion risks, clearly, lie in the many unresolved stalemates and "frozen" conflicts that we encountered in the previous two chapters—the now *familiar faces* of any number of stubborn rebels and clients. In these cases, time is the enemy. The longer underlying ambitions go unfulfilled—whether it is the separatist aspirations of Rebels or the geopolitical aims of a Big Brother—the greater is the risk of a build-up of explosive tensions, much like a pressure cooker that is left unattended. Costly conflagrations are not inevitable, of course. In time, as a result of reforms or repression, rebels could become reconciled to their sub-national status; their ardor for disruption might cool. Similarly, the attentions of a powerful patron may eventually turn elsewhere; pawns in the geopolitical chess game might well be sacrificed in order to pursue other prey elsewhere (as the Russians sacrificed the Armenians in Nagorno-Karabakh in 2023). But if our preceding discussion has taught us anything, it is that only a minority of secessionist struggles tend to be so obliging, fading quietly with the years. Most remain a conflict risk for decades. And as already noted, it doesn't take many brush fires to produce a cataclysmic inferno.

Which of the familiar faces should we worry about most? Plainly, given the many stalemates and frozen conflicts out there, each with its own unique story, it would be unrealistic to insist that there can be just one single narrative. As an old saying goes, prediction is difficult, particularly when it involves the future. Forecasts and scenarios, obviously, can vary. The best

Dream States. Benjamin J. Cohen, Oxford University Press. © Oxford University Press (2025).
DOI: 10.1093/9780197811672.003.0009

108 DREAM STATES

I can do is offer my own subjective judgment of where, among the many separatist threats cited in Chapters 7 and 8, the greatest dangers of armed combat would seem to lurk today. Here again, as in my classification of secession movements, I will focus on the degree of conflict risk involved, counting down from the least disruptive cases to what I fear could become the most violent. Ladies and gentlemen, I give you my Top Ten Combustibles.

Top Ten

In summary form, my Top Ten list includes the following:

10. Philippines
 9. Sahrawi
 8. Northern Ireland
 7. Katanga
 6. Georgia
 5. Yemen
 4. Myanmar
 3. Ethiopia
 2. Kurdistan
 1. Ukraine

As can be seen, the geographic spread is notable. Included are two cases in Europe (Northern Ireland, Ukraine), three in Africa (Ethiopia, Katanga, Sahrawi), two in the Middle East (Yemen, Kurdistan), one in the Caucasus region (Georgia), and two in East Asia (Myanmar, Philippines). Such dispersal is no accident; on the contrary, it illustrates just how ubiquitous dream states are in today's world. Only Latin America, for the moment, seems to be spared a serious threat of armed secession.

10. Philippines

In last place among my Top Ten—the least combustible case on my list—is the Philippines, where multiple groups of separatists have long been active in the country's south, mainly on the island of Mindanao and the adjacent Sulu Archipelago. The area is home to the Moro (or Bangsamoro) people, a mostly Muslim community that has a long history of resistance against rule by outsiders. The Moros comprise about 5 percent of the overall Filipino population, which is otherwise mostly Christian. Armed conflict began in 1968 following the so-called Jabidah massacre, when sixty Filipino Muslim commandos lost their lives in a failed attempt to reclaim a portion of territory from the Malaysian state of Sabah. Several competing separatist organizations—including most notably the Moro National Liberation Front, the Moro Islamic Liberation Front, the Bangsamoro Islamic Freedom Fighters, and the radical fundamentalist Abu Sayyaf—soon began fighting for some form of independence, resulting in thousands of combat deaths over the next four decades. Periodic negotiations to end hostilities went nowhere until 2014, when an agreement was reached with the Moro Islamic Liberation Front, the largest of the rebel groups, to establish a Bangsamoro Autonomous Region in Muslim Mindanao. A degree of self-rule was promised, including a regional parliament.

In the years since, while most of the insurgents have gradually disarmed, a degree of calm has prevailed—though many Moros continue to yearn for nothing less than full membership in the global sovereignty club. Explosive tensions have been contained but not eliminated. As recently as December 2023, four people were killed by a bomb attack on a Roman Catholic church that was attributed to a local Islamist faction. All sides concur that the conflict remains incendiary. For the United States (US), the danger is that its access to military sites in the Philippines could be jeopardized. Washington considers air and naval bases in the Philippines as essential to its increasingly tense confrontation with China in the South China Sea. Without these facilities, America's ability to project power in the region would be seriously diminished.

9. Sahrawi

Next, at Number 9, we have Sahrawi, the former Spanish colony of Western Sahara, which at present is informally partitioned between Morocco on one side of the Border Wall and the Polisario Front, backed by Big Brother Algeria, on the other side. Polisario's long-running insurgency, now nearly a half-century old, has been relatively quiet since a cease-fire under the auspices of the United Nations (UN) was agreed upon in 1991. Battles since then have been fought mostly on the diplomatic front, with each side seeking to reinforce its claims by competing for formal recognition

110   DREAM STATES

from the outside world. As previously noted, Polisario has managed to win accreditation for Sahrawi from nearly four dozen states; it has also been granted full membership in the African Union, the continent's main regional club. Morocco, meanwhile, has gained support from the Arab League and other Muslim countries. As noted in Chapter 8, Morocco also scored a diplomatic triumph in 2020 when the United States officially recognized Moroccan sovereignty over Western Sahara. Both sides have accepted the presence of a United Nations peacekeeping mission, backed by the African Union, which is deployed to control a buffer zone near the de facto frontier created by the Border Wall. Hostilities since the cease-fire have mostly taken the form of civilian demonstrations and protests.

No one doubts, however, that this conflict too—like the Moro conflict in the Philippines—remains incendiary. The pressure cooker continues to build up steam. From time to time, the Polisario Front threatens to resume fighting if Morocco continues to block implementation of a referendum that was promised at the time of the 1991 cease-fire. Armed clashes erupted in 2020 and again in 2022. As *The Economist* magazine suggested recently: "For several decades the rest of the world has looked away [The dispute] has been frozen in the baking desert, seemingly for ever. But of late the sands have been swirling."[1]

In part, the escalation is a measure of Polisario's stubborn tenacity in the face of Moroccan ambition. But even more importantly, it reflects a rising level of mutual animosity between Morocco and Polisario's patron, Algeria. To counter Moroccan military gains in Western Sahara in 2021, Algeria closed a key natural-gas pipeline that runs to Spain via Morocco. In turn, Morocco sought to embarrass the Algerians by going to the UN to call for self-determination in Kabylie, the restive Berber region of northern Algeria. Outside experts fear that if Polisario's dispute with Morocco intensifies, further alienating relations between Morocco and Algeria, armed combat between the two North African rivals cannot be excluded.[2] What began as a limited separatist rebellion could expand into outright war between two of Africa's largest military forces. The probability of such a lethal outcome may be low, but it is not zero.

Though the United States is not directly involved in the dispute, it has much at stake in both countries. Algeria is a major source of hydrocarbons; Morocco is one of just a handful of Arab nations that have extended diplomatic recognition to Israel. A regional war in northern Africa would clearly not be in America's interest.

8. Northern Ireland

At Number 8 is Northern Ireland, where the bad blood between largely Catholic secessionists and mostly Protestant unionists runs as deep as ever despite the Good Friday Agreement of 1998. According to that carefully negotiated accord, many governmental powers were to be devolved to a Northern Ireland Assembly in a manner similar to what was offered to Scotland and Wales. Executive authority, in turn, would be shared by parties representing both sides of the political divide based on their respective shares of votes for the assembly—a model of democracy called "consociational" by political scientists.[3] The leading party on one side would provide the first minister and the leading party on the other side the deputy. Key votes in the assembly would have to be passed by majorities representing both parties.

For two decades, the arrangement worked reasonably well. The Provisional Irish Republican Army (Provisional IRA) and unionist militias laid down their arms, and a considerable degree of order was restored. Border stations between the six northern counties and the Irish Republic to the south were removed for the first time in a century. But then, in 2022, came the shock of an electoral victory for Sinn Féin, the Provisional IRA's political wing, which horrified unionists. Within months, the government's power-sharing arrangement collapsed, sending Northern Ireland's future once again into limbo. Border stations were soon back in operation, and for two years, it was left to unelected civil servants to keep the government functioning until the terms of a new administration, headed by Catholic separatists, could be agreed.

The biggest danger in Northern Ireland today comes from the so-called Real (or New) Irish Republican Army, a dissident paramilitary group that split off from the Provisional IRA in 1997 and has continued to carry out periodic attacks on British security forces. In early 2023, the New IRA took responsibility for the shooting of an off-duty police officer, sparking fears of a fresh round of Troubles. In March 2023, Britain's domestic security agency, MI5, raised the threat level for Northern Ireland from "substantial" to "severe," meaning another attack was very likely. As one prominent resident put it, "Peace in Northern Ireland is a matchstick tower, and recently there has been a shifting of the ground below."[4] Once again, the British government might be distracted by an armed rebellion from some of its own citizens, limiting its ability to contribute to the common defense efforts of the US-led North Atlantic Treaty Organization.

112 DREAM STATES

7. Katanga

Number 7 is Katanga, a rebellious province in the Democratic Republic of the Congo (the former Belgian Congo, for a time known as Zaire). Ever since gaining its independence in 1960, the Republic has been faced with persistent uprisings across its lawless eastern provinces by literally dozens of local militias, each fighting for control of a piece of land or vital commodities. Among the most violent have been separatist groups in resource-rich Katanga, located in the far southeastern corner of the country adjoining Central Africa's Great Lakes. When the Democratic Republic of the Congo was born, many in the province dreamed of formal independence for their homeland, not unlike the Biafrans in Nigeria. The Katangese rebellion was supported by the Union Minière du Haut Katanga, a huge Belgian mining company with concession rights in the region, as well as by a contingent of Belgian military advisors and other foreign mercenaries. After the arrival of a United Nations peacekeeping force, the pace of combat appeared to ease, especially once Katanga's capital of Élisabethville was captured in late 1962. Most of the rebels either scattered or gave themselves up to the UN forces. Formal surrender came in January 1963.

Unlike what happened in the Biafra case, however, the insurrections never really stopped. Ever since, combat in the province has been sustained by an alphabet soup of liberation groups seeking some form of autonomy or sovereignty. As recently as January 2022, a new offensive was mounted by the best-known of the rebel forces, the Mai-Mai Kata Katanga, which briefly took control of a sizable chunk of provincial territory before being forced to retreat by the Congolese military. Katanga remains a potentially dangerous hot spot to this day because of its wealth of mineral riches, which could lure any number of interested outsiders to join the fray, including, of course, the United States. Explosive tensions remain strong.

6. Georgia

The next familiar face, Number 6, is Georgia, caught in a prolonged "frozen" dispute in the South Caucasian region with Russia. As noted previously, Georgia has not fared well in its resistance to ethnic separatists in the two breakaway areas of Abkhazia and South Ossetia. An initial round of fighting in the early 1990s, following the dissolution of the Soviet Union, resulted in the de facto secession of both regions under Russian protection, though very few other nations have extended diplomatic recognition to the pair. Subsequently, in 2004 and again in 2008, the Georgians tried to reclaim their lost territories but were soundly beaten each time. Tensions, however, linger on. Though the two conflicts have been frozen for years now, they remain a combustible powder keg. Both rebel territories would find it difficult to survive as sovereign states without massive political, economic, and security aid from Russia. Georgia still regards the two areas as legally part of its traditional homeland under occupation by the Russian military. No one doubts that given the opportunity, the Georgians would be prepared to try again to drive out the usurpers.

The risk is made especially threatening by the two rebels' client relationships with Russia. In the Caucasus region, geography favors the Russians—who are just next door—over other more distant powers like the United States. For the most part, Washington and its allies have avoided overt intervention in the area. Nonetheless, it is easy to imagine how swiftly a conflagration in either enclave could spread to pull in aid from outsiders, on the model of what we have seen in Ukraine since the start of Moscow's "special military operation" in 2022. The ice of these frozen conflicts could be melted in no time at all by the heat of battle.

5. Yemen

At Number 5 is Yemen, where separatist factions have been at each other's throats for at least the last decade. As noted in the previous chapter, the most successful of all the factions have been the Shiite Houthis, who now control the largest share of Yemen's territory and have managed to inflict embarrassing defeats on interventionist forces from Saudi Arabia and the United Arab Emirates (UAE), two Sunni powers. Ultimately, the Sunni coalition split apart.

In 2019 the UAE officially withdrew from Yemen, though it maintains a degree of influence and now backs secession for the southern half of Yemen, which before 1990 was a separate country known as the People's Democratic Republic of Yemen. (The model here would be the former British protectorate of British Somaliland, legally a part of the sovereign nation of Somalia, which, as mentioned earlier, operates quietly today on its own.) Saudi Arabia, by contrast, has backed a Presidential Leadership Council, which claims

114   DREAM STATES

to be the legitimate government of all of Yemen and has sought to mobilize
the country's many principalities and tribes against the Houthis.

Efforts to implement a series of UN-brokered cease-fires have proved
futile, and peace negotiations have been stalemated. As a result, low-intensity
warfare persists, punctuated periodically by violent flare-ups—most recently
in late 2023 during Israel's war in Gaza, when the Houthis began shelling
ships passing through the narrow Bab el-Mandeb Strait at the mouth of the
Red Sea. Given Yemen's strategic location controlling routes to and from
the Suez Canal, the stakes are clearly high. Despite the unfortunate experience of the Saudis and the UAE, there is always a danger of more outside
intervention. The theater of battle could widen at any time.

4. Myanmar

Number 4 is Myanmar, a multiethnic country known in British colonial
days as Burma. Almost since its first day as an independent state back in
1948, the southeast Asian nation of some 55 million inhabitants has been
racked by multiple separatist insurrections in what some have called the
world's longest ongoing civil war. Motivated by resentment of the dominant Bamar people (after whom colonial Burma was named), diverse ethnic
groups around the country's rugged periphery have campaigned ceaselessly
for independence or self-rule. These include Myanmar's second and third
largest ethnic groups, the Shan and Karen peoples, as well as smaller communities like the Chin, the Kachin, and the Mon. Perhaps most notorious is
the Wa region, which, as noted earlier (Chapter 7), has long distanced itself
from the authority of Myanmar's central government. Wa State has been
nicknamed *Narcotopia* because of its importance as a source of illegal drugs
like heroin and methamphetamine.[5]

As recently as the 2010s, hostilities in Myanmar seemed to be on the wane
as a result of a series of negotiated cease-fires and the introduction of a
new civilian government to partially replace the previous military regime.
But when a sudden coup d'état brought the military back to full control
in early 2021, the tempo of fighting picked up again, rekindling hot spots
in every corner of the land. It is estimated that as many as 50,000 people
have been killed since the coup, including at least some 8,000 civilians. In a
typical episode in 2023, some twenty-nine civilians—including children—
were killed during a bombing of a displaced persons camp controlled by

the Kachin Independence Army. In a significant development, the Kachins were then joined by Chin and Shan forces in a new Brotherhood Alliance, which kicked off a massive offensive in northern and western Myanmar in late 2023 ("Operation 1027," named after the date the offensive started). And the Alliance soon inspired fighting elsewhere as well, most notably in Kayin state in the southeast and in Rakhine state in the southwest. (The Kayins are also known as the Karen people.) Even some Bamars now chose to make common cause with the minority militias (known as people's defense forces) in opposition to military rule. As a result, according to one observer, "Myanmar's conflict has for the first time moved from the country's periphery deep into the Bamar heartland."[6] By the end of 2023, armed opposition groups claimed to control more than half of the state's fragmented territory. Toward the end of the year, a provisional cease-fire was negotiated but immediately broken by both sides. By mid-2024, the Brotherhood Alliance was poised to capture Mandalay, the country's second-largest city.

The intense combat in Myanmar not only jeopardizes the lives of many civilians, thousands of whom have already been killed by fighting over the decades. Here too, as in the Congo, there is also a risk of intervention by interested outsiders who might further fan separatist flames. The Indian government, for instance, worries about historical ties between the rebellious Chin people in Myanmar's northwest and restless separatist groups just across the frontier in India's isolated northeast. In early 2024, a decades-old policy of visa-free travel for local residents was suspended, and plans were announced by India for the construction of a fence along the entire length of the border with Myanmar. The Chinese government, meanwhile, is attracted by Myanmar's strategic position linking China's southern provinces to outlets on the Indian Ocean. And with two such giant rivals potentially involved, could the United States afford to remain aloof? Myanmar's long-running domestic conflicts could easily turn the country into a nasty geopolitical battlefield.

3. Ethiopia

At Number 3 we have Ethiopia, another multiethnic pressure cooker. Like Myanmar, Ethiopia has been racked for decades by multiple separatist insurrections. Here too is a central government that is traditionally dominated by one ethnic group—in this case, the Amhara people, constituting

116   DREAM STATES

roughly one-quarter of the country's population. And here too, around the state's edges, are a number of resentful minority communities that dream of self-rule or more for themselves. These include, most notably, the Tigray people in the north, Oromia in the southwest, and the Ogaden region in the southeast (with a largely Somali population closely related to the people of Somalia next door). Repeatedly, efforts have been made to find some manner of reform that would meet rebel objectives. In 1994, for instance, a new state constitution was promulgated, offering different communities some degree of cultural, linguistic, and economic autonomy. But after a time, fighting nevertheless began to recur in one part of the country after another. More recent was a brief but intense conflict that broke out in 2020, pitting the principal Tigrayan separatist army, the Tigrayan People's Liberation Front, against the central government allied with forces from Eritrea. By the time a truce was signed in late 2022, hundreds of thousands of civilians were thought to have died from war-induced hunger or disease.

No one, however, saw the cease-fire as the end of the tale. The situation remains combustible, seemingly even more so than in Myanmar. Most observers fear that, as in the past, a temporary pause in Ethiopian brush fires will be followed by yet more costly armed combat in years to come. No more than nine months after the truce in Tigray, new fighting broke out in the Amhara heartland, threatening even more death and destruction. One informed commentary warns, "the [most] likely outcome is a bloody and chaotic disintegration of the country along the lines of the former Yugoslavia."[7] Tribal animosities have already long troubled some of Ethiopia's neighbors, including Somalia to the south and Sudan to the north. The entire region is a tinderbox of ethnic hatreds and rivalries. To date, the United States has largely managed to keep out of the direct line of fire, relying primarily on diplomacy behind the scenes to dampen the risk of combustion as much as possible. But if the flames of combat continue to spread, bringing something like the Balkan wars to East Africa, Washington may feel it has no choice but to become more openly involved.

2. Kurdistan

Number 2 on my list is Kurdistan, one of the world's saddest dream states. Most dream states fall within the borders of a single sovereign country, or perhaps two. The Kurdish people, as noted earlier, are divided among no fewer than four established states—Iran (known to Kurds as Eastern Kurdistan), Iraq (Southern Kurdistan), Syria (Western Kurdistan), and Turkey (Northern Kurdistan). In principle, the populations of all four fragments share the same aspiration for validation as a single nation. But the fate of each community, in practice, has been dictated separately by the distinctive circumstances of their respective host countries as well as by their own internal divisions, making any form of common action difficult.

While Iranian Kurds, for instance, are denied any pretense of self-rule, Iraqi Kurdistan has enjoyed a degree of autonomous status since a 1970 agreement with the Iraqi government in Baghdad. The accord was subsequently enforced by a Western-imposed no-fly zone following the Desert Storm war of 1991 and then reaffirmed in 2005 in a new Iraqi constitution after the downfall of Saddam Hussein. Yet in more recent years, the Kurdish regional government has been losing strength, in large part because of persistent squabbling between its two leading families, the Barzanis and the Talabanis. Syrian Kurds also enjoy a degree of autonomy in sections of northern Syria where they were able to seize control during the prolonged Syrian civil war, but without the benefit of foreign recognition. Turkey's Kurdish area, meanwhile—the largest of the four fragments—has long put up resistance to the authority of the Turkish government under the leadership of the Kurdistan Workers' Party (PKK). In Turkey, the PKK is officially considered to be little more than a bunch of barbarous terrorists. The mere mention of the word "Kurdistan," whether written or spoken, can lead to detention and prosecution.

Because of all this complex fragmentation among such a large cast of mutually antagonistic actors, the puzzle is especially fragile. On occasion, leaders of the four Kurdish fragments may find themselves working at cross-purposes, weakening their ability to promote their common cause peaceably. Worse, the Kurdish cause may be subverted by heightened cooperation between two or more of the four host countries. A case in point could be seen in early 2024 when the Iraqi government in Baghdad suddenly banned the PKK from its territory, evidently as part of an effort to increase business ties with Turkey.

Worst of all, the four host countries may on occasion step on each other's toes, provoking even more serious tensions. One can only imagine what might follow if some anti-Kurdish initiatives were accidentally to do harm to local civilians or infrastructure. From time to time, the Turks

118   DREAM STATES

have rained rockets down on rebel sanctuaries in Iraq and Syria—most recently in late 2023, ostensibly in retaliation for a Kurdish attack that resulted in the death of a dozen Turkish soldiers. According to Turkey's defense ministry, at least twenty-six militants in Southern and Western Kurdistan paid for the incident with their lives. Similarly, the Iranian government has been known to attack bases of Kurdish opposition groups located across the border in Iraq (just as they have attacked Baluchi bases inside Pakistan, as noted in Chapter 6). Most prominent among the Kurdish insurgents in Iran is Komala, a militant group that has a history of secessionist ambitions. The danger of combustion is certainly not negligible.

For the United States, calculations are especially tricky. Support for Iran's Kurds would seem a natural choice, considering the level of antagonism between Washington and Tehran since the Islamic Revolution in 1979. But would America also opt to give succor to the PKK in Turkey, a member of the NATO alliance, or to autonomous Kurdistan in Iraq, which does everything it can to resist the authority of the Arab-dominated government in Baghdad? The Middle East is already a heated cauldron. In a region where alliances and coalitions are constantly shifting, Kurdish aspirations could easily have the effect of turning up the flames.

1. Ukraine

Finally, with a sad fanfare, we come to Number 1: Ukraine. As noted in the previous chapter, the Ukrainians have suffered the loss of several key provinces to secessionist forces backed by the Russian military. These include not only the vital Crimean Peninsula, which was annexed by Russia in 2014 immediately following a brief so-called rescue operation. Additional territorial losses came as a result of Vladimir Putin's "special military operation," when four more provinces were formally absorbed into the Russian Federation despite Ukrainian resistance. These episodes demonstrate what can happen when the pressure cooker is allowed to heat up uncontrollably. Inter alia, the "special military operation" has acted as a magnet to draw in the United States and its European allies, who have provided unprecedented amounts of aid to the Ukrainians. America's Council on Foreign Relations recently rated the Ukraine conflict as one of the seven most dangerous hot spots in the world today, alongside such hardy perennials as Taiwan, Iran, and North Korea.

In practical terms, there is little that differentiates Russia's client relationships in Ukraine from those that still simmer in Moldova or Georgia, or for that matter, in other parallel cases like northern Cyprus or Western Sahara. In all of these instances, opportunistic external powers have sought to take advantage of local separatist aspirations. The main difference is that in the Ukrainian case, the risk of violence actually became a tragic reality and could easily spread—hence the honor of being designated Number 1 among my Top Ten Combustibles.

The honor is dubious, of course. One is reminded of what Abraham Lincoln said about the presidency: "I feel like the man who was tarred and feathered and ridden out of town on a rail. To the man who asked him how he liked it, he said: 'If it wasn't for the honor of the thing, I'd rather walk.'" The Ukrainians, I am sure, would have preferred to walk.

Fragility

One final question: Am I exaggerating? Skeptics may concede that the risks I have highlighted are genuine, yet might well ask: Are the risks really big enough to worry about? It could be that the probabilities involved are simply too small to warrant much concern.

There is, of course, no easy way to quantify the kinds of dangers that my Top Ten represent. Direct comparative analysis seems an insurmountable challenge. But indirectly, a measure of risk may be inferred courtesy of the Fund for Peace, an independent non-partisan organization based in Washington, DC, and Abuja, Nigeria. Every year the Fund publishes a Fragile States Index for some 179 countries, based on an analysis of a dozen economic, political, and social indicators. The higher the score as calculated by the Fund for Peace, the greater is a country's fragility. According to the Fund's estimates for the year 2023, Somalia ranks as the most fragile state in the world (1st place). Norway, in 179th place, is said to be the least fragile.

Arguably, it would be fair to assume that the greater a country's fragility, the more vulnerable it is to an outbreak of armed conflict as a result of unresolved stalemates or "frozen" conflicts. Not surprisingly, many of the familiar

120　DREAM STATES

faces in my Top Ten list rank among the most fragile polities anywhere. These include Yemen (2nd most fragile), the Congo (4th place), Ethiopia (11th place), Myanmar (12th place), Ukraine (18th place), the Philippines (61st), Georgia (79th), Algeria (83rd), and Morocco (90th). From those numbers, it seems reasonable to conclude that in most, if not all, of my Top Ten, the risk of violence is indeed substantial. Secession movements are not a fringe phenomenon.

10
Special Cases

Unusual hot spots

The Top Ten Combustibles, as well as other familiar faces, are all in the mold of what I have called *classic* wars of secession. The scenario is straightforward. A minority community located within the recognized frontiers of an established state (or states) seeks to break off on its own, either to gain validation for its homeland as a sovereign nation (e.g., Katanga or Kurdistan) or as a step toward merger with another sovereign nation (e.g., Northern Ireland or Ukraine's Donbas). The key is territorial control. The incumbent formally governs the territory in question. The secessionists dream of supplanting the incumbent.

But that is not the only possible paradigm. As we look around the world, we see a number of other more unusual hot spots that must be noted as well—*special cases* that may also carry with them a high degree of conflict risk. These cases too are all about separation: a community that dreams of gaining its own unique place under the sun. But they are exceptional because in one key respect or another, they diverge significantly from the classic model. These days, four such cases stand out: Palestine, Kosovo, Taiwan, and the Islamic State (otherwise known as ISIS). Each of these is about secession in some form; each of them is at least as incendiary as the more conventional dream states that we have encountered in previous chapters; and each of them is of particular salience for the foreign policy of the United States (US).

Palestine

I begin with the Israel–Palestine dispute, a battle that has been high on the US policy agenda ever since the founding of the Jewish state in 1948. Some might wonder why the long-running conflict between Israelis and Palestinians should be included here as a secession struggle. In fact, it is more than

Dream States. Benjamin J. Cohen, Oxford University Press. © Oxford University Press (2025).
DOI: 10.1093/9780197811672.003.0010

122   DREAM STATES

that. It is a *double* secession struggle. What makes it atypical is that each side, Arabs and Jews, regards the other side as the true usurper. At issue for both communities is the same piece of land. Both sides cherish a singular territory, known to the world as the Holy Land, as their own ancient homeland. Both see themselves as the legitimate occupant and historical heir. And both see themselves as an aggrieved victim.

An apt image of the Palestinian–Jewish struggle is a double helix—two intertwined and congruent strands of history, each shaped like a corkscrew or spiral staircase, conjoined forever. The image of the double helix was made familiar by two veteran scientists, James Watson (a biologist) and Francis Crick (a physicist), who together were awarded a Nobel Prize for their discovery of the double-helical structure of DNA molecules. Like the twin strands that make up our DNA, the Palestinian and Jewish communities warily circle each other in a kind of twisted ladder to nowhere, seemingly without end.

Origins

How can two separate communities both claim the same territory as their historical homeland? It all depends on where we begin the story. If we go back far enough—say to the time of Abraham, the founding father of Judaism some four thousand years ago—the Jewish side would appear to be the usurpers. In the Book of Genesis, according to Jewish tradition, God promised that he would multiply Abraham's descendants "as the stars in the sky" and would give them a specific piece of land forever (Genesis 12:1–3). That turned out to be the land of Canaan. Abraham lived out the rest of his life in Canaan; and following his descendants' long sojourn in Egypt and then forty years of trailing behind Moses in the wilderness, God's prophecy was finally fulfilled sometime around 1300 BCE (Before the Common Era). That was when Joshua, following the death of Moses, led the twelve tribes of Israel across the Jordan River into the proverbial "land of milk and honey." Soon the conquest of Canaan was complete, and the area remained the home of the Israelites for another 1,300 years. That was the first twist of the double helix.

Along the way, there were misfortunes, as we well know. These included the disappearance of the Ten Lost Tribes, the destruction of not one but two temples in Jerusalem (586 BCE and 69 CE), and, finally, in 134 CE, a total ban on the practice of Judaism anywhere in the Holy Land after a failed revolt against the Romans. For the Jewish people, that defeat was the beginning of nearly two millennia of exile, first to areas around the Mediterranean and then later to the wider world. Effectively, the usurpers were expelled, although small numbers of Jews, mostly devout religious scholars, did manage to continue living in the area. But throughout the worldwide diaspora, the dream of a return one day never died. The Holy Land was still, in Jewish tradition, the community's homeland. Every year, at the end of the ceremonial Seder meal of the Passover holiday celebrating the Exodus from Egypt, Jews around the globe would repeat the mantra: "Next year in Jerusalem."

But what if we go back only as far as the seventh century of the Common Era? That was when the dynamic new religion of Islam began to spread from its origins in the Arabian Peninsula to encompass much of the known world, including the Holy Land. The double helix took a new twist. Now it was the Muslim Arabs who could be considered the usurpers, displacing earlier inhabitants. Jews were mostly gone by the end of the eleventh century. Henceforth, Palestine was to become a key part of the Arab world's own historical homeland. The Arabs too had their misfortunes, of course—not least the Crusades, which occupied parts of the Holy Land for as long as a century, and later the arrival of the Ottoman Turks. But they too retained their dream of Jerusalem, the place where, according to legend, the prophet Muhammad ascended to the heavens on a strange winged creature named Buraq, half-horse and half-mule. In their tradition too, as for Jews, the Holy Land was home.

Thus, by the time we arrive at the modern era, the stage was already set for conflict. Appealing to different historical eras, both sides feel that they have a genuinely legitimate claim. Sadly, both have a case.

Partition

If we move our starting point to the final decades of the nineteenth century, we find yet another twist of the double helix. This time, the turn was inspired by the new Zionist movement, which aimed to bring fresh life to the old idea of a Jewish homeland in the Holy Land. Large-scale immigration began in the 1880s, mostly Jews from Europe and Russia, and continued in waves through the first half of the twentieth century. By the end of World War II, the Jewish population of Palestine had grown to more than 650,000, half the

124 DREAM STATES

size of the Arab population. For the Zionists, this was a return to their ancient home. Arabs were seen as an alien presence, illegitimate squatters on land that had long ago been promised by God to the Jews. Holding aloft a copy of the Old Testament before the General Assembly of the United Nations (UN) in 2019, Israel's ambassador declared, "This is the deed to our land." As Benjamin Netanyahu, Israel's longest-serving prime minister, put it in his memoir, "It is not the Jews who usurp the land from the Arabs, but the Arabs who usurp the land from the Jews ... The Jews are the original natives, the Arabs the colonialists."[1]

For the Arabs, however, this was nothing less than an invasion. It was the Zionists who were the usurpers—the alien presence. In Arab eyes, Jews were seen as secessionists, intruders determined to carve out for themselves a piece of the land on which Palestinians had lived for centuries. The true story was just the reverse of the Zionist narrative. Arabs were the original natives, and it was the Jews who were the invading foreigners. In contemporary parlance, Palestinians were the victims of "settler colonialism."

Not surprisingly, therefore, tensions between the two communities steadily increased. Arab uprisings in 1929 and again in the late 1930s caused many deaths on both sides. In response, the British government—which had taken charge of Palestine after World War I as a League of Nations mandate— issued a White Paper in 1939 aiming to restrict future Jewish immigration. But following the tragedy of the Holocaust, which caused the demise of some six million European Jews, immigration resumed on a sizable scale, much of it clandestine. By 1947, an Arab–Jewish conflict seemed unavoidable.

Called upon to resolve the dispute, the newborn United Nations— nominally responsible to preserve peace in the post–World War II period— did its best. Understandably reluctant to assign historical blame to one side or the other, the organization's General Assembly took a Solomon-like approach, voting in November 1947 for a neutral compromise solution: *partition*. In effect, the baby would be cut in half. While the contested city of Jerusalem was to be internationalized, the rest of the Holy Land would be divided more or less equally between Arabs and Jews, each community awarded control of pieces of territory where its people happened to be in the majority. It was almost as if the UN had taken its cue from the poet Robert Frost, who famously wrote that "Good fences make good neighbors." The resulting map of the Holy Land, full of fences, was hardly elegant, but it did hold out some hope of calm between the quarreling neighbors.

SPECIAL CASES 125

Unfortunately, it didn't work. Immediately after the UN vote, Palestinians began attacking Jewish settlements, backed by the collective military might of six Arab governments. These included, in particular, neighboring Egypt, Jordan, and Syria, who attacked from three sides. Putting up a spirited defense, the Jewish community proclaimed independence for a newborn state of Israel in May 1948; a year later, after a formal cease-fire between the combatants, the fledgling Jewish state was elected the fifty-ninth member of the United Nations—the world's first sovereign Jewish government in over two thousand years. For the Israelis, this represented a miraculous vindication of their ancient claims. Many of the Arab "squatters" had been evicted. The remaining Palestinian territories, meanwhile, were divided up between Egypt, which took charge of Gaza, and Jordan, which absorbed the West Bank and the Old City of Jerusalem. For the Palestinians, the outcome could not have been more disappointing. The despised Zionist secessionists had prevailed. The defeat has been remembered ever since as *al-Nakba*—the "catastrophe."

Another twist

The story since then is well known—and incendiary. Three more wars with Israel's neighbors were fought in 1956, 1967, and 1973, all ultimately victorious for the "Zionist entity." The most impactful was the Six-Day War in 1967, which in less than a week resulted in Israeli occupation of Gaza, the Old City, the West Bank, and even Syria's Golan Heights. With those unexpected triumphs, the double helix took one more twist. Now Israel became the incumbent formally governing the territories in question. The indigenous Palestinians became the secessionists who dreamed of supplanting the incumbent.

Over the years after Israel's stunning victories, attitudes toward the Jewish state across much of the larger Arab world seemingly began to mellow—if only a bit. A few regional governments even came to accept the Jewish state as a member in good standing of the sovereignty club, albeit at arm's length. In 1994, peace treaties were signed with Egypt and Jordan, removing two of the most serious military threats to Israel; in 2020, normal diplomatic relations were established with four more Arab regimes in Bahrain, Morocco, Sudan, and the United Arab Emirates—all part of the so-called Abraham Accords promoted by the US government. Israel's presence in the heart of

126 DREAM STATES

the Muslim world may not have been welcomed with open arms. But for a growing number of Arab countries, it seemed, the Jewish state was coming to be tolerated.

Not so, however, for the Palestinians, whose attitude toward Israel largely remained as hostile as ever. Understandably, the Israeli occupation of so much Palestinian territory did not sit well with the occupied. For the Palestinians as well as for nearby sympathizers such as the Hezbollah militia in Lebanon and Hamas in the Gaza Strip, the Six-Day War was not a triumph but a disaster—a second *Nakba*. Resistance to the "Zionist entity" grew exponentially, led by the Palestine Liberation Organization (PLO), which in late 1988 proclaimed an independent state of Palestine in Jerusalem, the West Bank, and Gaza. Since the PLO lacked any effective control in any of these areas, the declaration rang somewhat hollow. But it was enough to gain Palestine status as a permanent non-member observer at the United Nations (as noted in Chapter 2). For the Palestinians, the dream of sovereignty, eclipsing Israeli incumbency, burns as brightly as ever.

Should anyone be surprised, therefore, that the dispute between Israel and the Palestinians has remained highly combustible? Periodically, noisy disruptions have erupted in the occupied West Bank or across the borders with Gaza or Lebanon, resulting in widespread death and destruction. For years, luckily, most of these brush fires were successfully contained before they could spread very far. But the prolonged and devastating war that erupted in late 2023, triggered by a murderous attack across the Gaza border by Hamas, proved that the risk of a major conflagration in the region remains sadly ever-present. Pressure cookers can be left unattended for only so long before they blow up in someone's face.

Kosovo

Another special case is found in Kosovo, which, as we know, formally seceded from Serbian jurisdiction in 2008 after forceful intervention by NATO (North Atlantic Treaty Organization). Back before the disintegration of Yugoslavia in the early 1990s, Kosovo—though populated mostly by ethnic Albanians—was ruled as an autonomous province by Serbia, an Orthodox Christian "republic." Kosovo's proclamation of independence could be regarded as consistent with the classic model of secession except for one atypical feature. In subsequent years, centrifugal forces continued

SPECIAL CASES 127

to pull the province apart. Soon, new separatist demands emerged from Kosovo's small Serbian population—some 40,000 in all—which is concentrated mainly in municipalities in the former province's north, adjacent to Serbia. In effect, inside one secession (Kosovo), a fresh secession movement was born in northern Kosovo—another example of the "minorities-within-minorities" issue. If the double helix is an apt image for the Israel-Palestinian dispute, a suitable image for the Kosovo case is a Matryoshka doll, the familiar toy from Russia. Matryoshka dolls, also known as stacking dolls or nesting dolls, consist of a set of wooden dolls of decreasing size, placed one inside another. The Serbian separatist movement in the north fits neatly inside Albanian Kosovo's larger drexit.

The result is yet another incendiary hot spot. Serbs consider northern Kosovo to be the cradle of Serbian civilization. It was the site of a critical battle in 1389 and is home to several historically significant monasteries and churches. The dream of the Kosovar Serbs is a return to Serbian rule, much as Northern Ireland's Catholics yearn for a reunion with their cousins in the Irish Republic. Serbia has yet to concede Kosovo's sovereignty, despite the fact that the former province has received diplomatic recognition from more than a hundred other countries and is supposed to be safeguarded by the presence of a UN peacekeeping force drawn mainly from NATO countries. The European Union (EU) has tried to get the two sides to agree to a deal that would trade Serbian acceptance of the status quo for Kosovo in exchange for a grant of autonomy to Serb-dominated municipalities, but negotiations remain stalled.

Meanwhile, though calm has more or less reigned in the area since the end of NATO air strikes in 1999, there are periodic moments of unrest. The latest began toward the end of 2022 when the Kosovar government formally submitted an application to join the EU. Kosovo's Serbs clashed violently with police over a mandate to replace their Serbian vehicle number plates with those of Kosovo, leading the Serbian community's representatives to withdraw from Kosovo's governmental institutions. At year's end, amid the escalating tensions, Serbia's army warned that it was at its "highest level of combat readiness." In May 2023, some twenty-five UN peacekeepers and fifty Serbs were injured in clashes sparked by the election of several ethnic Albanian mayors in Serb-majority areas. (Ironically, the Albanian candidates won only because the election was boycotted by the Serbian population.) Over the following months, Serbian troops massed on Kosovo's border until persuaded by the United States to stand down. And then in

128   DREAM STATES

late 2023, a Serbian plot was uncovered aiming to seize control of Kosovo's north using a proxy force modeled on the "little green men" that Russia had deployed so successfully in Ukraine in 2014. In one incident, a shoot-out claimed the lives of three Serbs and one Kosovar police officer.

In all, it is clear that it would not take much of a provocation to light the fuse again. The threat of violence on a wider scale is real. In the words of *The Economist*, "An incident in which either Serbs or Albanians die could spark a conflagration."[2]

Taiwan

A third special case is Taiwan, an island of some 24 million people located off the coast of China at the junction of the East and South China Seas. Taiwan is of undoubted importance to US security policy in East Asia. Long known as Formosa, the island has had a checkered history. Annexed by imperial China in 1683, the island was lost to Japan following China's defeat in the Sino-Japanese War of 1895. Taiwan then remained a colonial dependency of Japan until the end of World War II, when nominal control was temporarily transferred back to the Chinese government by the victorious allies. Four years later, however, the "nationalist" government was forced to flee to Taiwan after suffering defeat in the Chinese Civil War at the hands of their Communist foes. Ever since, the political status of Taiwan has been hotly disputed. Some describe it as "the most dangerous place in the world."[3]

At issue is the island's relationship to the mainland. What makes the case unusual is that it is not at all evident who plays what role. In the classic separatist model, it is usually unmistakably clear who formally governs the territory in dispute. We know who the incumbent is and who the challenger is. But that is by no means true of the Taiwan dispute. For the communist authorities in Beijing, of course, there is—or should be—no debate. In their eyes, Taiwan is simply a renegade province, intent on secession, which must sooner or later revert to China. But the Taiwanese and many others object, pointing to the fact that, in reality, the issue of sovereignty after World War II was never fully settled. The defeated Japanese agreed at the war's conclusion to surrender all claim to the island, but never indicated to whom. No official "successor state" was ever named, either in 1945 or later in the Treaty of San Francisco, signed in 1951, that brought the Pacific War to a formal conclusion. Hence, most Taiwanese, citing the principle of self-determination, believe that they—and only they—should have the right to decide their island's future. They consider themselves not renegades but a free people entitled to decide their own fate. In their eyes, they are the staunch defenders of a homeland, and it is the mainland regime that is the disruptive troublemaker. According to a 2022 poll, less than 3 percent of the island's population identify as exclusively Chinese. Three out of five identify exclusively as Taiwanese.[4]

No wonder, then, that Taiwan has become one of the hottest of hot spots on the globe. Mainland China, now a nuclear-armed superpower, never ceases to issue martial threats in response to the slightest provocation. Few issues seem to matter more to the country's sense of *amour propre*. Following a brief visit to Taiwan in late 2022 by America's then Speaker of the House of Representatives (second in line of succession for the US Presidency), Beijing spent ten days openly rehearsing blockade and invasion maneuvers. Over and over, the Chinese send a message to Taiwan that amounts to declaring "Love me or I'll kill you!" In response, Washington repeats its pledges of support to the island and sends ships of the US Seventh Fleet steaming through the Taiwan Strait to demonstrate US resolve. The armed confrontation between China and the US is obviously flammable. Observers agree that sparks could fly at any time.

Islamic State

Finally, we have the Islamic State, a militant Islamist organization, which is perhaps the most novel case of all. The Israelis and Palestinians may twist around each other like a double helix. Kosovo's troubles with Serbia may resemble a Matryoshka doll, one secession fitting snugly within another. Taiwan's relationship with the mainland may be clouded in ambiguity about roles. But in all three cases, there is no doubt that the crux of the issue is the same: territorial control. The contest, ultimately, is about a piece of land that is coveted by both sides. With ISIS, however, we have a secession movement that does not imagine territory to be the quintessence of sovereignty. Authority is spiritual, a matter of faith, rather than temporal or material in nature.

In effect, ISIS rejects the Westphalian model of political geography, which centers on the territorial state as the world's basic unit of governance. Like Benedict Anderson, ISIS thinks in terms of "imagined communities." But

130   DREAM STATES

harking back to a much earlier era well before Westphalia, the most important "imagined community" is thought to be not the conventional territorial
state but, rather, a much broader conception of a supranational community
of believers—the *oomah* (Arabic for community or commonwealth) following the commands of Allah. The notion of a Muslim *oomah* emerged in the
Koran (*Qur'an*) from the teachings of the Prophet Muhammad, who was
said to have been sent to transmit Allah's divine message. Following Muhammad's death, authority was to be exercised by a caliph (literally, "successor
of the prophet"), though in time the caliphate system came to be seriously
eroded by civil wars and prolonged dynastic struggles. The last officially
recognized caliphate, based in Istanbul, was abolished in 1924 during the
secularization of Turkey under the rule of Kemal Atatürk. ISIS believes that
its mission is to revive the institution of the caliphate and to govern through
the implementation of a strict interpretation of Islamic law (sharia). In effect,
it wants to secede not from a single state but from the state *system*—the
sovereignty club as we know it.

Founded in 1999, ISIS gained international prominence in 2014 when it
drove Iraq's security forces out of much of the country's northwest, including Mosul, Iraq's second-largest city. ISIS then proclaimed itself to be a
worldwide caliphate, claiming religious, political, and military authority
over Muslims everywhere. Its leader, Abu Bakr al-Baghdadi, named himself as caliph. At its high point in late 2015, ISIS controlled about one-third
of Syria and 40 percent of Iraq, together home to an estimated 8–12 million
people. Almost all of the group's military gains, however, were soon lost as a
result of effective counteroffensives by a mix of foreign troops, including US
special forces. By 2017, the so-called caliphate appeared to be on the wane.
Abu Bakr al-Baghdadi himself died at the hands of American soldiers in
2019. What was once regarded as one of the world's most fearsome Islamist
networks seemed reduced to not much more than a low-level insurgency,
struggling to retain its relevance.

But that does not mean that any threat of violence is now over. Quite the
contrary, in fact. The United States and other foreign governments have not
found it easy to extract themselves from the fight. Despite its setbacks, ISIS
appears determined to carry on its separatist campaign, and to do so wherever observant Muslims can be found. In a particularly spectacular operation
in early 2024, more than 130 Russians were slain by armed ISIS militants at
an entertainment complex outside of Moscow. Russia was targeted because
of its support of the government in Syria, a long-time ISIS foe. In addition to

SPECIAL CASES 131

Iraq and Syria, nearly a dozen ISIS "provinces" have been declared across the globe to carry on the fight. These include Afghanistan and Pakistan (Khorasan Province), Algeria, the south Caucasus states (Caucasus Province), Central Africa, Egypt, Libya, Philippines (East Asia Province), Saudi Arabia, West Africa, and Yemen. With each new province, the global total of potentially explosive hot spots is increased. ISIS's war on the Westphalian model is by no means over.

Quite the opposite, in fact. In rejecting the Westphalian model, ISIS might seem to many to be archaic, even primitive in nature. In reality, however, it may in fact be quite the opposite—a harbinger of more special cases to come. The essence of the Islamic *oomah* is a *network*—a social space defined not by political frontiers but, rather, by shared relationships; a "space-of-flows," to recall a popular expression, rather than a territorially defined "space-of-places."[5] Prior to Westphalia, spaces-of-flows were not easy to build or sustain. But in the contemporary era, with its revolutionary developments in information technology, networks of all kinds have sprouted like mushrooms after a rainstorm. For astute observers, it seems only a matter of time before many more spaces-of-flows—what have been called "network states"[6]—will join ISIS in challenging the authority of the traditional sovereignty club. A network state has been defined as "a highly aligned online community with a capacity for collective action." That certainly seems to describe ISIS.

Theme and variations

Though Palestine, Kosovo, Taiwan, and ISIS may, at first glance, seem to share little in common, it is evident that they are in fact closely related— each, in effect, a distinct variation on our central theme of secession. All four may fairly be considered "special cases," since they are each unique in one way or another. Yet at their core, they are more alike than different. All are separatist Rebels with a Cause. All aspire to their own unique version of a dream state. And all are prepared to be disruptive troublemakers—to challenge the existing order, by force if necessary. Whatever we think of the legitimacy of their ambitions, the risks to the larger world cannot be denied. Each case adds to the lurking nightmare of armed conflict somewhere on our contentious planet.

11

Fragile Federations

Large multiethnic unions

Many of us, at one time or another, have spent a sleepless night or two watching old movies on television. If that includes you, it is likely that you will remember the kind of loud commercial advertisement that often appears in the wee hours of the morning, climaxing with the seductive words "But wait, there's more!" Here I can say the same. The Top Ten Combustibles and four Special Cases certainly add up to a formidable litany of lurking nightmares. But not even all these possibilities, taken together, fully exhaust the list of separatist hot spots to be found across the globe. But wait, there's more!

Recall the body of political economy theory, encountered back in Chapter 2, that aims to specify the optimal size of nations. Central to most models, I noted, was the degree of domestic heterogeneity. The bigger the state, the more likely it is that a multiplicity of ethnic communities will be found gathered together under one roof. Hence, the more likely it is that social preferences will diverge significantly; and that possibility in turn suggests a higher risk of identity-driven disputes that could spawn disruptive secession movements. In principle, political science teaches us, such tensions may be moderated by a *federal* form of government that divides and shares powers, delegating a portion of authority to administrative units below the top national level. Minority populations are thus able to sustain a degree of control over their lives despite their sub-national status. In practice, however, the approach doesn't always work out as theory supposes. Some federations, particularly large multiethnic unions, are brittle and suffer persistently from the threat of centrifugal forces. These *fragile federations* add substantially to the risk of conflict around the globe, both within countries and between them.

As it happens, formal federations are relatively scarce. Of the 193 members of the United Nations, only some twenty-five are legally structured on federalist principles.[1] But among these are most of the biggest members of today's sovereignty club, as well as some of the most brittle. All but one of the planet's

---

Dream States. Benjamin J. Cohen, Oxford University Press. © Oxford University Press (2025).
DOI: 10.1093/9780197811672.003.0011

eight largest countries by area—occupying nearly 40 percent of the world's dry land—are constitutional federations. These are Russia (11 percent of the total), the United States (6.1 percent), Canada (6.1 percent), Brazil (5.6 percent), Australia (5.2 percent), India (2.0 percent), and Argentina (1.8 percent). The sole exception among the top eight is China (6.3 percent), a nation that is highly centralized under the rule of the Chinese Communist Party. Other notable federations include Austria, Belgium, Ethiopia, Germany, Malaysia, Mexico, Nigeria, Pakistan, Spain, Switzerland, and, of course, the United States (US). A brief review of this mixed collection illustrates well the dangers posed by large and fragile multiethnic federations.

Federalism

In simplest terms, federalism represents a compound mode of governance formally combining a general government at the national level (the central or "federal" government) with sub-national governmental units (variously labeled, depending on where you are, as cantons, oblasts, provinces, regions, republics, states, or territories) in a single political system, with powers divided by some constitutional formula among the separate levels. Federal systems are less centralized than so-called "unitary" states, which concentrate political authority at the top. But they are not as decentralized as "confederations," which reserve most powers to lower-level units. If we can imagine a political spectrum running the gamut from loose confederation to tight unitary state, federal systems are to be found somewhere in the middle.

Federalism is meant to allow sovereign states to be both sizable and diverse. The core logic rests on the notion of *subsidiarity*, a principle of social organization that holds that public policy issues should be dealt with at the most immediate or local level that is consistent with their resolution. Translated into plain English, this means that a central authority should have a *subsidiary* function, performing only those tasks that cannot be handled effectively at a lower level. The concept has roots in the natural law philosophy of Saint Thomas Aquinas and since his time has become a central feature of Catholic social teaching. In Europe, it has been formally adopted as a general principle of European Union (EU) law. EU institutions are assigned responsibilities only if the job cannot be handled efficiently at the level of the union's member states or below.

134   DREAM STATES

Compromises

In effect, federal systems offer a compromise solution to the critical trade-off at the center of theoretical models of optimal state size. While aiming to ensure sufficient hierarchy to preserve most of the advantages of large size, they also seek to provide enough practical leeway to accommodate divergent social preferences. Each lower-level unit retains some degree of control over its own internal affairs even while remaining part of a broader sovereign state.

As with most compromises, of course, specifics may vary considerably. As the old adage goes, there are many ways to skin a cat. In federations, there are many ways to implement the notion of subsidiarity. At one extreme is the Tenth Amendment of the US Constitution, which holds that "The Powers not delegated to the United States by the Constitution, nor prohibited by it to the States, are reserved to the States respectively, or to the people." At the other extreme is a country like Canada, America's northern neighbor, whose constitution declares that powers not explicitly granted to provincial authorities are retained exclusively by the federal government. No two federal systems are quite alike in how they provide for the division and sharing of powers at different levels.

Whatever their differences, however, the central question for all federations is the same: Can they achieve their aim? The challenge is tricky. Will minority communities in a multiethnic framework be content with their allotted degree of autonomy? Or will the unstable equilibrium of a daydream threaten to mutate into a drexit or, worse, a resort to armed rebellion? A federation may be regarded as reasonably successful in this regard if it manages to reconcile the trade-off between size and diversity in a manner that is broadly acceptable to the majority of those involved. It is nearer to failure if the bubble threatens to pop.

Classes

Given the trickiness of the challenge, it is obvious that any attempt to generalize about the performance of diverse federal systems is bound to be difficult. But the risks involved in federations—especially large multiethnic federations—are surely clear. In their effort to implement the notion of subsidiarity effectively, federal systems may manage to get the compromise

FRAGILE FEDERATIONS   135

right, successfully balancing the trade-off between size and diversity. But then again, they may not. The danger of a descent into violence cannot be excluded.

Much like airline seating, we can distinguish roughly among three classes of federations: premier, business, and coach. Once again, alternatives may be ranked by the degree of conflict risk they pose. Premier class, up front, includes federal systems that are manifestly successful in finding a workable formula for sharing political authority in a multiethnic framework. The degree of conflict risk is minimal. Business class, a few rows back, seeks to emulate premier class but is less effective at gaining consensus. While these federations go about their business, the menace of drexits hangs over them. The degree of conflict risk is correspondingly greater. And then there is coach class, further to the rear, where dissatisfaction is rampant and fighting could break out at any time. Conflict risk is highest. Examples of all three classes can be found among today's federal systems.

Premier class

Premier class is for the high achievers—federal systems that have managed to hit the sweet spot in the size-diversity trade-off. If prizes were to be given for historical performance, top honors would have to go to Switzerland, which formally adopted a federal constitution as long ago as 1848 following a brief civil war. The Swiss are by no means a homogeneous society. They are divided into twenty-six administrative units, formally known as "cantons," and speak as many as four separate languages in different parts of the country—French, German, Italian, and Romansh (a Gallo-Romance language). Yet they all live comfortably together under the flag of one federal system. The roots of the Swiss federation actually go as far back as the fourteenth century, when eight cantons joined together in what historians call the Old Swiss Confederacy, later expanded incrementally. The 1848 constitution (updated in 1999) represented the first time that the Swiss had a central government (a federation) rather than merely a collection of autonomous units bound by treaties (a confederation). Over time, the federal system has worked impressively well. Nowhere in Switzerland's heterogeneous collection of cantons do we find any sign of serious separatist sentiment. Armed rebellion by any of the twenty-six cantons seems unimaginable.

136 DREAM STATES

Other high-achievers can also be found in neighboring Austria and Germany, as well as further afield in Australia. Each of these countries has also found a way to divide political authority between the central government and sub-national units to more or less general satisfaction. Few disruptive complaints are ever raised about reigning constitutional structures. Voices may be heard from time to time promoting the idea of secession for some minority area, such as Frisia or Silesia in Germany or Tasmania in Australia. But for the most part, these amount to whispers rather than shouts. While there may be some conversation about rearranging borders, separatism as such is rarely mentioned. Federations like these would seem to suggest that workable compromises are in fact possible. No matter how tricky it may be to design a successful federal system, the challenge can ultimately be met.

Business class

The task, however, is not easy and at times fails utterly. That brings us to business class, where federations may be undermined by persistent dissatisfaction with the prevailing rules. The sweet spot is missed. Understandably, national authorities would like to move their country forward to premier class. They may do all they can to engage with the aspirations of separatist forces, whether by way of reforms or repression, in hopes of reconciling discontented minorities to their status of "sub-ness" within the broader multiethnic state. Yet tensions endure in the form of stubborn drexits. The dream of secession will not die.

Among the most familiar countries in business class are Britain, with its Celtic separatists, and Canada, with its *Québécois*. In both cases, the central government has tried to allay secessionist pressures via strategies of administrative decentralization. In Britain, this has meant a devolution of powers to regional assemblies in Northern Ireland, Scotland, and Wales. In Canada, this has meant formal recognition of Quebec as a distinct nation within the broader Canadian state. In neither case, however, have tensions been fully allayed. In Scotland and Wales, as noted earlier, support for separatist parties remains considerable. In Northern Ireland, the recent collapse of joint governance under the Good Friday Agreement again put the area's future in doubt. And in Canada, few citizens are persuaded that the Parti Québécois's recent electoral setbacks are necessarily irreversible.

Other federations that would appear to belong in business class have been mentioned previously. In Europe, we have Spain, with its several separatist movements (including, most notably, Catalonia), and Belgium, with its mutually antagonistic Flemings and Walloons. And in South America, we have Mendoexit and Patagonia in Argentina as well as vocal secessionists in Brazil's southern and Amazonian regions. At first glance, sub-national communities as diverse as the Scots, *Québécois*, Catalans, and other activist minorities might seem to have rather little in common. But they all share a marked distaste for the prevailing division of powers, which they believe fails to validate their own long-standing dreams. Though drexits are, by and large, loath to resort to violence, they do not easily surrender their ambition for membership in the sovereignty club. The specter of rebellion hovers menacingly in the background.

Coach class

Finally, moving yet further back, we arrive in coach class where, by contrast with business class, the risk of violence is rather more ominous. That is the big difference between these two models. Like business-class federations, coach class starts with a daydream—a bubble that pops. But whereas in business class a more peaceable path to change tends to be preferred, relying primarily on negotiation and compromise, in coach there is a much greater appetite for armed struggle should the central government resist major reform. Business-class federations face drexits. Coach class must cope with the threat of militant rebels with a cause.

Violence in coach class is not inevitable, of course. Consider Mexico, a federation that historically was long beset with powerful centrifugal forces. Today, secession hardly gains mention. Regional rebellions flared frequently in the nineteenth century, following Mexico's independence from Spain in 1821, but tapered off in the twentieth century. The last separatist uprising of any significance occurred in Chiapas, Mexico's southernmost state, in early 1994, led by the so-called Zapatista Army of National Liberation. But fighting lasted only twelve days before a cease-fire was signed and hostilities in the area gradually faded. Today separatist violence in Mexico is a distant memory, and the country seems poised to move up to business class.

Or consider Malaysia, a union of former British dependencies in Southeast Asia that joins together the mainland Malay Peninsula (also known as

138   DREAM STATES

Peninsular Malaysia) with the two states of Sabah and Sarawak (also known as East Malaysia) located across the South China Sea on the island of Borneo. (The rest of Borneo belongs to Indonesia.) Ethnically and religiously distinct from Peninsular Malaysia, Sabah and Sarawak long campaigned for a high degree of autonomy. Conflict, however, remained low-intensity. Separatists only occasionally resorted to outright violence. In 2021, their efforts were rewarded when the Malaysian constitution was amended to reconfirm rights that were first promised to the two states when the union was initially agreed upon back in 1963. Today, any danger of militant rebellion seems to have largely receded.

Even if not inevitable, however, violence nonetheless does loom as a serious possibility in many federations so long as the size-diversity trade-off remains unresolved. Recall the failed federal systems of Yugoslavia and the Soviet Union, neither of which was ever able to overcome deep internal divisions. As soon as the opportunity presented itself at the end of the Cold War, their disparate components chose to go their separate ways, leaving a considerable amount of death and desolation in their wake. Numerous hot spots burst into flames as the two brittle federations disintegrated.

Today, there are other federal systems that, in time, could follow the same route. Ethiopia, a multiethnic pressure cooker if there ever was one, seems well on the road toward an African version of the Balkan wars. The situation there is particularly incendiary. And much the same can be said of both Nigeria and Pakistan, where low-intensity combat has long been a fact of life in several rebellious regions. As recently as March 2024, Baluchi separatists attacked the Pakistani port of Gwadar, the centerpiece of a key economic corridor linking China to the Arabian Sea. Ethiopia, Nigeria, and Pakistan all demonstrate just how serious is the danger of spontaneous combustion in large fragile federations. Coach class clearly is not a comfortable way to travel.

The Big Three

But wait, there's more! Coach-class countries like Ethiopia, Nigeria, and Pakistan may be potentially disruptive. But as threats to world order, they would seem to be eclipsed by three of the biggest federations of all: India, Russia, and the United States. Call these the Big Three.

Current fragilities in the increasingly Disunited States of America have already been highlighted in Chapter 3. How do India and Russia compare? Both India and Russia play a major role on the global stage, and both consider themselves worthy rivals of the United States. One (India) recently became the most populous country in the world, surpassing China. The other (Russia) encompasses more landmass by far than any other member of the sovereignty club and has amassed the largest stockpile of nuclear weapons anywhere. The geopolitical importance of both federations is undeniable. Yet each is far more fragile than most people appear to realize. Both are giants—but, arguably, giants with feet of clay, beset with a wide range of powerful centrifugal forces that could seriously disrupt the international system. Each deserves a chapter of its own to assess just how big a danger they pose.

12

Russia

Like a Matryoshka doll?

Consider Russia first, far and away the sovereignty club's biggest member by area. Everyone knows that, in practical terms, power in Russia is highly concentrated at the top in Moscow. In constitutional terms, however, the country is nominally a federation, with many governmental responsibilities delegated to lower tiers of authority. The federal structure is even enshrined in the country's formal name: not Russia, but the Russian Federation.

Not surprisingly, with its enormous size and variety, Russia shows many signs of fragility. It is way back in coach class. According to the Fragile States Index of the Fund for Peace, where a higher score means greater fragility, Russia ranks as number 53, well above the median among the 179 countries included in the calculation. The Russian Federation is clearly vulnerable to the disruptive aspirations of domestic dream states.

Of course, the true extent of separatist sentiment across the country's vast expanse is difficult to judge given Moscow's tight grip on political expression. But there seems little doubt that thoughts of drexit lurk in the minds of many of the federation's restive minorities. Here too, as in the case of Kosovo, one is reminded of a Matryoshka doll: minorities within minorities. Today's Russia emerged from a disintegrating Soviet Union; in turn, any number of potential secessions could be quietly nested inside Russia. Several questions suggest themselves. Can the Russian Federation survive despite its brittleness? Or might Russia, too, be fated soon to unravel? And if so, where does that leave the United States (US), Russia's greatest geopolitical adversary?

Federal structure

In one form or another, Russia has been around for more than a millennium. Its origins go back to the so-called Kyivan Rus, a medieval federation of Slavic princedoms that first emerged in Eastern Europe in the late ninth

Dream States. Benjamin J. Cohen, Oxford University Press. © Oxford University Press (2025).
DOI: 10.1093/9780197811672.003.0012

century centered on the city of Kiev (known today as Kyiv, Ukraine's capital). The modern states of Belarus, Russia, and Ukraine all claim the Kyivan Rus as their cultural ancestor. Together they comprised a refined European civilization with roots in the Byzantine Empire and its Orthodox Christian religion.

The Kyivan Rus reached its zenith in the eleventh century before gradually fragmenting into various rival regional powers. In later centuries, borders and rulers changed repeatedly until the emergence of the Romanov dynasty in the early 1600s. Within decades, under the leadership of powerful czars like Peter the Great and Catherine the Great, the Russian Empire expanded incrementally, stretching overland from the Baltic Sea bordering Europe to the Sea of Japan in the Far East. The Soviet Union, which grew out of the Bolshevik Revolution of 1917, essentially replicated the physical dimensions of the Czarist Empire until it too, in turn, disintegrated in 1991. Russia, one of fifteen successor states, was reduced to the federation that we know today, shrunken but by no means inconspicuous. Many describe today's Russia as an "imperial state"—like the Czarist Empire and the Soviet Union before it, a centralized empire-like form of sovereignty.

Given Russia's still exceptional size and the wide range of its ethnic minorities, some delegation of authority from the center to lower-level sub-nationalisms would seem to be only natural. And given the country's long and eventful history, which has seen so many political changes over time, it is hardly surprising to find a federal structure today that is anything but simple. Vestiges of regime after regime have piled up like so many Siberian snowflakes, freezing many complexities in place.

Today's structure is defined by the latest constitution of Russia, which was adopted by national referendum in December 1993, shortly after the end of the Cold War. At the top of the structure, of course, is the central government in Moscow, exercising its powers from behind the ramparts of the ancient citadel known as the Kremlin. Below are what Russia's constitution describes as the "constituent entities" or (depending on the translation) "subjects" of the Russian Federation. As of the end of 2022, the official count of constituent entities was 89. That includes the city of Sevastopol and the Republic of Crimea, added in 2014 as the eighty-fourth and eighty-fifth federal subjects of Russia. It also includes four separatist entities taken from Ukraine during Vladimir Putin's "special military operation," which were annexed as Russia's eighty-sixth, eighty-seventh, eighty-eighth, and eighty-ninth federal

142   DREAM STATES

subjects. None of these last six acquisitions, however, have been recognized internationally. All six entities are considered by most of the world to remain legally part of Ukraine.

Each federal subject is allowed its own separate parliament and courts and has equal rights in relation to the central government. Each has two delegates apiece in the Federation Council, the upper house of the Federal Assembly (technically equivalent to the Senate in the Congress of the United States). But constituent entities are by no means equal in terms of the degree of autonomy they enjoy. In the division of powers that has emerged under the 1993 constitution, some are offered much greater authority than others. George Orwell would say that some are more equal than others.

Under the constitution, as many as six different types of federal subjects operate side by side, variously named oblasts, republics, krais (singular: krai or kray), autonomous okrugs, federal cities, and autonomous oblasts. Each type is distinguished by the way powers are shared or divided with Moscow.

1. *Oblasts.* These are by far the most common type of constituent entity. Presently, there are some forty-eight oblasts in all, each with its own chief executive (governor) and locally elected legislature. There is no universal translation of oblast, which is variously rendered as "area," "province," or "region." The designation dates back to czarist days. Oblasts were created as purely administrative units and are commonly named after their governing centers.

2. *Republics.* Republics are granted more powers than oblasts. Each is nominally independent with its own constitution and language, though represented by Moscow in international affairs. Typically, each is home to a specific minority or group of minorities. Originally created in the early days of the Bolshevik Revolution, republics were meant to give representation to areas of non-Russian ethnicity that had been absorbed earlier through imperial conquest. At the time labeled "autonomous republics," they were placed one step below the fifteen "union republics" that mutated into sovereign successor states when the Soviet Union dissolved in 1991. In today's Russia, yesterday's autonomous republics are now simply republics (without an adjective), the equivalent of what in Soviet days were called union republics. Under Russia's 1993 constitution, there are twenty-four republics sprinkled across the map of the federation.

3. *Krais.* For most purposes, krais are legally identical to oblasts. The title "kray" ("frontier" or "territory") is historic, relating to a geographic

position that existed at some time in the past. These days, krais are scarce: only nine of them remain. None is any longer related to a frontier. The term is a historical vestige.

4. *Autonomous okrugs.* These are even more scarce than krais. Only four okrugs exist at present. Occasionally referred to as an "autonomous district" or "autonomous region," each okrug has a substantial or predominant ethnic minority. Confusingly, most okrugs are legally part of an oblast even while simultaneously also federal subjects in their own right.

5. *Federal cities.* These are major cities that function as the equivalent of separate regions. Traditionally, there were only two cities considered weighty enough to warrant the designation: Moscow and Saint Petersburg. After annexation in 2014, Sevastopol was added as a third federal city.

6. *Autonomous oblast.* There is just one entity in this category, the unique Jewish Autonomous Oblast, which was first proclaimed in 1928 in an effort to deflect the flow of Zionist migrants then heading to Palestine. Located in the Russian Far East on a piece of land seized from China in the mid-nineteenth century, it never proved successful as a magnet for Jewish settlement. At its peak in the late 1940s, Jews numbered no more than 40,000–50,000, just 25 percent of the overall local population. Today, the Jewish share of the population is a bit more than 1,600, less than 1 percent of the total.

Finally, in an initiative begun by Vladimir Putin when he first came to power at the turn of the century, a new layer of authority was interposed between the central government and the country's many constituent entities in the form of eight so-called federal districts. Ostensibly, these are meant to improve the quality of governance across Russia's eleven time zones. Each district gathers together a cluster of federal subjects and is administered by an envoy appointed by the President of Russia. Federal districts are not mentioned in the country's constitution, nor do they have any direct policy responsibilities of their own. They do not manage regional affairs. Rather, it seems that they exist mainly to provide oversight. Officially, their purpose is to monitor consistency between federal and regional bodies of law. Unofficially, they would appear to offer help in maintaining central control over courts, the civil service, and other public institutions throughout the federation. In bluntest terms, they are instruments of autocracy.

144   DREAM STATES

The past

Complexity, of course, does not necessarily mean fragility. What really matters is how much real separatist sentiment there might be out there among the country's many minorities and regions. Are there a lot of unhappy communities harboring daydreams of sovereignty, just waiting for an opportunity to go their own way? Or are they all more or less reconciled to remaining sub-nationalisms within the multiethnic Russian state? Admittedly, these are not easy questions to answer. Possibly the most trusted source on such matters is the Levada Center, a non-governmental research organization founded in 2003 that does its best to monitor Russian public opinion on a regular basis. According to the center's long-time director, Lev Gudkov, latent separatist sentiments still simmer in several parts of the giant federation.[1] But even Gudkov admits that we truly have little hard evidence to go on. In a country where polls are taken infrequently and never really trusted, it is difficult to gauge public sentiment with any degree of precision. That applies in particular to thoughts about a topic as touchy as sovereignty.

History, however, allows us to make some educated guesses. Suggestive clues are provided if we look at past experience.

Revolution

Begin with the Bolshevik Revolution in 1917. During the next few years, the former Czarist Empire was rent with political and military strife. At the broad national level, there was a bitter civil war between the communist Red Army and the monarchist Whites, battling for control of the central government in Moscow. In many locales, there was also an explosion of separatist uprisings by discontented minorities. Pretenders to sovereignty seemed to crop up all over the place. Many were quite violent.

As it happens, relatively few of them managed to achieve their dream state. There were really only three true success stories—the Baltic trio of Estonia, Latvia, and Lithuania. In 1918, all three took advantage of the collapse of the imperial monarchy to declare their independence. Over the next two years, they successfully defended their newborn freedom, repelling invasion by Russia's Bolsheviks and gaining widespread diplomatic recognition. By the end of 1920, they had become full members in the global sovereignty club, though as noted earlier their independence was lost again when they were occupied and annexed by the Soviet Union near the end of World War II.

Most uprisings blossomed only briefly before ending in failure. Examples abound. One was the Don Republic, a self-proclaimed anti-Bolshevik republic formed in the traditional homeland of the Don Cossacks, who had long lived along the middle and lower Don River in western Russia. A provisional government that was formed in early 1918 soon went out of existence after the Don Cossacks, who had formed an essential part of the White Russian army in the civil war, were soundly vanquished by the Red Army. A subsequent policy of repressive "Decossackization" aimed to eliminate the Cossacks altogether as a distinct minority community. And another example was the Idel-Ural State (alternatively, the Volga-Ural State), a short-lived republic that aimed to unite Tatars and several other nearby minorities. Proclaimed in March 1918, the republic was defeated and disbanded a month later by the Bolsheviks. As a consolation prize, Tatarstan was given the status of an autonomous republic within the Russian Federation.

The most prolonged rebellion was the awkwardly named "United Mountain Dwellers of the North Caucasus" (or "Mountainous Republic of the Northern Caucasus"), formed in late 1917 by several neighboring communities in the anarchic northern Caucasus region, including Chechnya, Dagestan, Ingushetia, and Kabardino-Balkaria. Here too the Red Army ultimately prevailed, though only after three years of bitter combat. Like Tatarstan, each of the defeated Caucasian communities was made an autonomous republic within Russia.

In the face of these multiple rebellions, the strategy of the Bolshevik government was in effect a combination of Repression and Reconciliation. First and foremost, military means were used—often quite ruthlessly—to put down bids for secession. The cost in terms of blood and treasure was high. But, in addition, the new category of autonomous republics was added to the former empire's federal structure in an overt effort to win over hearts and minds. Minorities, it was hoped, would be content to remain within the new Soviet Union if they had a sub-national political unit that they could call their own.

The point, however, is not whether these diverse rebellions could be beaten or seduced into submission. The moral of the story lies in the fact that they happened at all. Before 1917, the Czarist Empire may have given the impression of political solidarity and long-term durability. But the reality, as we know, turned out to be quite different. Lurking throughout that

146   DREAM STATES

sprawling multiethnic regime, stretching from Europe to the Pacific, were a host of latent secession movements just waiting for a chance to pursue their dreams. The key was the unexpected breakdown of central authority. The sudden fall of the Romanov dynasty opened the door to suppressed ambitions. A wave of avid separatists then flooded through. The empire was stable—but only until it wasn't!

Dissolution

Flash forward some three-quarters of a century to the conclusion of the Cold War, and the story is similar. Following the fall of the Berlin Wall in 1989 and the tsunami of anti-communist revolutions that then swept through Eastern Europe, the Soviet Union met its ignominious end. Once again, there was an unexpected breakdown of central authority as one union republic after another, led by the Baltic trio and the southern Caucasus republic of Georgia, declared their independence from Moscow. And once again, there were more than a few minorities and regions that, seeing the door suddenly thrown open, sought to barrel their way through.

One example was in Gagauzia, a region in the south of the former union republic of Moldova, where the locally dominant Gagauz people declared independence in 1990 as the Gagauz Republic. After prolonged negotiations, the area was reintegrated into newly independent Moldova in 1994 as a "national-territorial autonomous unit." Another example was the short-lived Ural Republic, a territory in the southern Ural Mountains, which declared its independence after an unauthorized referendum in April 1993. The republic lasted only seven months until it was declared unconstitutional and returned to Moscow's authority. And a third example once more involved the Tatars, who again attempted to secede from the Russian Federation (just as they had tried after the Bolshevik Revolution) in order to establish Tatarstan as a sovereign state in its own right. In 1994, after a three-year stand-off, a bilateral treaty was signed delegating a substantial range of powers to the Tatars, who in turn agreed to remain formally part of the Russian Federation. Here too there was a referendum that heavily favored independence. But here too the bid for secession was ultimately declared unconstitutional, and in 1997 the power-sharing treaty was rescinded. Since then, Tatarstan has remained a republic within the Russian Federation.

By far the most violent episode involved Chechnya, as described previously. In the old Soviet federal structure, Chechnya had been an autonomous republic. After the Soviet Union disintegrated, the Chechens hoped for more. Their aim was to join the global sovereignty club as a member in their own right. It took the Russians years—not one but two prolonged and savage wars—to subdue the Chechen rebels, who were determined to achieve their dream of independence at almost any cost. During the Second Chechen War, which started in 1999, Russia's massive bombing campaigns left the region's capital Grozny looking like Berlin in 1945. Hardly a single building remained undamaged. Though the insurgency was declared officially over in 2003, low-level violence continued for years. Today, Chechnya ranks as one of Russia's twenty-four republics. Under the brutal rule of Ramzan Kadyrov, Vladimir Putin's eager disciple, the area remains as far from full sovereignty as ever.

Again, the moral of the story is clear. Like the Czarist Empire before 1917, the Soviet Union before 1991 gave the impression of solidarity and long-term durability. But here too the reality turned out to be quite different. Once again, a sudden breakdown of central authority revealed the presence of many latent secession movements—all eager to seize the day, by violence if necessary. For the second time in less than a century, declarations of independence sprouted like mushrooms. Separatists, it turned out, were plentiful across the federation. Below the surface, there were a lot of bubbles ready to pop.

The future?

Could it happen again? As an old saying goes: "Once is an accident; twice is a coincidence; three times is a pattern." Is there a pattern here, or just a coincidence? The topic is hotly debated by academics, journalists, and even government officials.[2]

Discontent

On the whole, the evidence suggests that there really is a pattern. Certainly there is more than enough tinder scattered around Russia to set many hot spots aflame, just as there was in 1917 and again in 1991. In the words of

148 DREAM STATES

one veteran observer, the Russian Federation is "a ticking time bomb spread across 11 time zones."[3]

From Eastern Europe to the Far East, there are close to 200 distinct ethnic minorities included in the Russian Federation, with populations that add up to more than 27 million people—nearly one citizen in five. As many as 20 million are Muslims, clustered in areas that are cherished as ancient homelands. Many of the minorities are resentful of their sub-national status in a huge lumpy stew cooked up by people who do not speak their language and may not share their religion or customs.

In such a muddle of clashing ethnicities, discontent is almost certain to flourish. It should hardly come as a surprise that across the Russian landscape today, we find as many as fifty publicly acknowledged separatist movements. Inter alia, these range from the Komi People's Congress representing the hopes of the Komi people in the northwest to the Free Cossack Movement in the south, the Ural Democratic Foundation in the Ural Mountains, and the Alliance of the Pacific Peoples in the Far East.

Admittedly, most of these movements appear to amount to little more than sentimental daydreams. At least that is the impression they have chosen to project, especially since the arrival of Vladimir Putin in the Kremlin. Within limits set by Moscow, they have restricted themselves mostly to celebrating their distinct communal identities, concentrating more on cultural heritage than public policy. Like so many other minorities around the world, they would appear to be reconciled to their sub-national status. All they want, seemingly, is some degree of validation of their distinctive sense of self. Even erstwhile rebels like the Tatars and the Chechens show little appetite these days for another round of violent conflict.

But is that out of an abundance of affection or fear? Knowing what we do about Russia's history over the last century, it is hard to argue that the glue that holds the Russian Federation together is unalloyed devotion. Minorities keenly remember the ill-treatment they often received from the Czars or the Bolsheviks in the past. Stories of repression and abuse are handed down from one generation to the next. Descendants of the Don Cossacks have still not forgotten the vicious Decossackization campaign undertaken by the Bolsheviks after the Red–White Civil War. The painful deportations of most of Crimea's Tatars to Central Asia at the end of World War II are still fresh in that community's memory, softened only slightly by the restoration of a right of return to Crimea years later. Since Russia's takeover of Crimea in 2014, the Tatars have once again become an object of persecution because of alleged Ukrainian sympathies. The Chechens too are unlikely soon to forgive the many munitions that rained down on them during the Second Chechen War. As Russia's brutal "special military operation" in Ukraine has amply demonstrated most recently, the dominant Russians do not seem to go out of their way to curry the favor of the many sub-nationalisms within their borders—strict autocracy rules.

In turn, the strikingly high number of Russian minorities—Chechens, Crimean Tatars, and others—who have volunteered to fight alongside the Ukrainians since the "special military operation" began amply demonstrates how raw those historical grievances remain. The Ukrainian cause allows them to seek a form of revenge against Russia; indirectly, it also enables them to fight for their own separatist dreams back home. Says one Chechen fighter: "Our aim is the liberation of the Chechen Republic of Ichkeria."[4]

The depth of minority discontent across the federation has perhaps been best illustrated by the angry reaction to a series of conscription drives launched by Moscow starting in September 2022. The government's aim has been to mobilize massive numbers of new recruits to bolster Russia's stalled offensive in Ukraine. In response, thousands of draft-eligible young men have taken flight by car, train, or plane in order to escape military service— many coming from isolated ethnic communities far from the country's main urban areas, who are repelled by the openly racist attitudes of Russian officers. Typical is a member of the Sakha ethnic group who deserted after repeatedly being called a "reindeer herder" because of his origins in the Siberian region of Yakutia.[5]

One of the most poignant stories of the Ukraine operation involved two courageous fishermen in Russia's remote Far East, both of the indigenous Chukchi people, who undertook a dangerous journey in a small boat across the stormy Bering Sea in order to win political asylum in the US state of Alaska.[6] Though neither of the escapees was likely to have ever heard of another US state, New Hampshire, they would surely have endorsed New Hampshire's famous motto: "Live free or die."

Breakdown?

A plentiful supply of tinder, however, is not enough to establish a pattern. The presence of restless minorities is a necessary condition. But on its own, it is hardly sufficient. In addition, there must also be some kind of trigger

150   DREAM STATES

to cause bubbles to pop. The key to past conflagrations was a sudden unexpected breakdown of central authority. In 1917, the trigger was the Bolshevik Revolution. In 1991, it was the fall of the Berlin Wall. Is there another such trigger on the horizon for Russia's imperial state today?

Russian nationalists would say "No." An imperial state, many in Russia insist, has long been the country's natural form of government. Only a strong centralized regime can efficiently govern such a vast expanse of territory. Absolutist rule binds the federation together as a single polity under Russian leadership—a distinct "Eurasian" civilization where identity is based not on narrow ethnicity but on a broader common culture. That ancient viewpoint, however, prioritizes economies of scale at the expense of divergent social preferences and invites widespread dissent by minorities. Autocracy may rule, of course. Indeed, so long as the impression of durability can be sustained, it is unlikely that many peaceable daydreams would dare consider mutating into disruptive drexits or rebels with a cause. But if Russia's history teaches us anything, it is that the risk of regime decay is ever-present. Sooner or later, a loss of effective control may be triggered, opening the door for separatists.

The lurking danger of separatism is acknowledged by many in Russia[7]—not least by Vladimir Putin himself. More than a decade ago, speaking of the possibility of secession by one or more of the republics of the northern Caucasus, Putin declared that "If this happens, then, at the same moment—not even an hour, but a second—there will be those who want to do the same with other territorial entities of Russia."[8] Echoes a former speech writer for Putin: "The Kremlin is afraid of nationalism and separatism .... Putin and his circle were traumatized by the collapse of the Soviet Union and are worried that Russia will repeat its fate."[9] The irony is that Putin himself may have now supplied the trigger for such a scenario: his disastrous invasion of Ukraine. Many analysts see Ukraine as "Putin's last stand," the beginning of the end of his long term in power.[10] One satirical commentary, looking back from late in the twenty-first century, even put a precise date to the final dissolution of Putin's empire: May 16, 2023.[11] That date may have passed without incident, but the danger remains.

Since coming to office more than two decades ago, Putin has gone to great lengths to keep up the appearance of power—scoring hockey goals, diving for antiquities, riding horseback shirtless. He has even compared himself to Peter the Great, one of the most revered rulers in Russian history. His aim, obviously, has been to sustain the illusion of his regime as muscular, even invincible. But his setback in Ukraine has revealed a Hercules gone to seed; his army turned out to be not much more than a military version of a Potemkin village. Rumor has it that when Russian forces first invaded Ukraine in February 2022, they were instructed to bring along dress uniforms for a victory parade that was expected after a swift occupation of Kyiv. Instead, after some initial advances, they found themselves thrown backward, suffering massive casualties and mired in a glacial stand-off with the Ukrainians. The blow to Moscow's prestige could hardly be greater.

At a minimum, Putin's failure in Ukraine could lead to a change of leadership in Moscow. As a prominent historian of Putin's Russia has noted,

> The gods of Russian history are extremely unforgiving of military defeat .... When a Russian leader ends a war in a clear defeat—or with no win—usually there is a change of regime. We saw that after the first Crimean War, after the Russo-Japanese war, after Russia's setbacks in World War I, after Khrushchev's retreat from Cuba in 1962 and after Brezhnev and company's Afghanistan quagmire, which hastened Gorbachev's perestroika-and-glasnost revolution. The Russian people, for all their renowned patience, will forgive a lot of things—but not military defeat.[12]

Worse, failure in Ukraine could produce yet another round of political disarray comparable to 1917 and 1991—another fatal breakdown of central authority. Russia briefly came close to civil strife in June 2023 when the mercenary Wagner Group, led by Yevgeny Prigozhin, a former confidant of Putin's, seized control of the headquarters of the Russian army's southern command and launched a march on Moscow. Troops were less than a day's drive from the Kremlin when a fragile accommodation was negotiated with the rebels. Putin's government survived but seemed fatally weakened.

Once more, therefore, the stage seems set for a possible regime collapse. Yet again, the door could be thrown open to latent separatists, tempted to seize the moment. Bubbles could pop all over the territory of the federation. In the words of another authoritative observer:

> Mr. Putin's war is turning Russia into a failed state, with uncontrolled borders, private military formations, a fleeing population, moral decay and the possibility of civil conflict .... There is growing concern about Russia's own ability to survive the war. It could become ungovernable and descend into chaos .... Russia's own restive regions ... are likely to head for the exits.[13]

152 DREAM STATES

It is unlikely that most or all of those exits would be orderly. Moscow cannot be counted upon to accede quietly to the dismemberment of its realm. Quite the contrary, resistance must be expected. Warns another informed commentator, we "should assume that further fragmentation of Russia will be more like Chechnya in 1994 (brutal conflict) than Estonia in 1991 (peaceful and straightforward)."[14] Once again the vast imperial state could be consumed with multiple wars of secession, from the Urals and the Caucasus to Siberia and the Pacific. Worse, it is possible that, in many instances, outsiders could be drawn in as well, at the risk of spreading violence well beyond Russia's existing borders.

A chaotic breakup is not inevitable, of course. As an old adage advises us, Russia is never as strong as it looks or as weak as it looks. Putin (or some successor) could yet pull a rabbit out of a hat. But the longer Russian forces remain bogged down in Ukrainian mud, the greater will be the stain on the country's reputation. At the moment, it is hard to see how Moscow can extricate itself from its embarrassing "special military operation" without serious new challenges to its traditional authority at home. Fear, the glue holding the state together, is losing its grip. Once again, therefore, secessionists are feeling emboldened. Could armed violence be far behind? As a pair of well-informed observers warn us:

> Though Russia's defeat would have many benefits, [we] should prepare for the regional and global disorder it would produce .... Disorder could take the form of separatism and renewed conflicts in and around Russia .... A disorderly Russian defeat would leave a dangerous hole in the international system.[15]

Another round?

In short, there does indeed appear to be a recurrent pattern in Russian history, and it really could soon prove to be calamitous. Russia's fragile federation is threatened by yet another round of fracture, for the third time in little more than a century. And as a result, a new wave of wars of secession seems possible, which could leave chaotic destruction in its wake, in Russia and perhaps even beyond it. The hole in the international system could turn out to be like the black holes at the heart of distant galaxies, with a gravitational pull so strong that not even light can escape. The most obvious beneficiaries would be the United States and its allies in NATO, who would now have one less giant geopolitical adversary to worry about.

Russia's fate is not written in stone, of course. More peaceable outcomes are possible. But past experience suggests that more attractive scenarios are just not very likely. Mark Twain is reputed to have said that "History doesn't repeat itself, but it often rhymes." Russian history seems particularly prone to rhyming with its own sad past.

13

India

Can the federation be sustained?

The other Big Three country is India, estimated to have surpassed China to become the world's most populous nation sometime during 2023. No one doubts the fragility of the giant Indian federation. Few members of the global sovereignty club are as ethnically diverse. On the Fragile State Index of the Fund for Peace, India ranks as number 73, only marginally better than Russia. Like the Russians, India is back in coach class. Many think that the Indian union is just too vast and variegated to be governed effectively. Separatist demands come from all sides. In the words of one expert observer, "India is one of the most secessionist-prone countries in the world."[1]

Yet for more than three-quarters of a century, since its emergence as a sovereign state in 1947, the republic has managed to hold itself together. Indeed, India has thrived, recently surpassing Britain, its former colonial master, to become the fifth largest national economy on the planet. Again, as with Russia, several questions suggest themselves. Can India's record of success be sustained? Can the federation continue to hold together despite its brittleness? Or is it fated at some point to succumb to persistent centrifugal forces—to become, in effect, another Yugoslavia? And if it does come apart, what would that mean for the level of violence in India's neighborhood or beyond, and what might it mean for the United States?

Federal structure

The Indian subcontinent, which encompasses today's states of Pakistan and Bangladesh in addition to the Republic of India, is home to one of the world's oldest and most influential civilizations. Since earliest times, the area has provided an attractive habitat for human occupation. To a large extent, it has been sheltered from outside threats by wide expanses of ocean and the massive ranges of the Himalayas. Settled life emerged as early as 9,000 years ago,

Dream States. Benjamin J. Cohen, Oxford University Press. © Oxford University Press (2025).
DOI: 10.1093/9780197811672.003.0013

gradually evolving into the Indus Valley Civilization of the third millennium BCE. Subsequent centuries saw the rise and fall of numerous warring empires and kingdoms, including an invasion by Alexander the Great in 327 BCE and later intermittent occupations by Muslim armies from Central Asia. A period of relative calm was ushered in by the Mughal Empire in 1526 CE, lasting a bit more than two centuries until India's Muslim rulers were displaced by the subcontinent's last foreign invader—Great Britain.

The story of modern India really begins with the arrival of the British East India Company, a joint stock company founded in 1600 that, in its day, was the largest corporation in the world. It even boasted a powerful army of its own totaling some 260,000 soldiers, twice the size of the British government's armed forces at the time. Beginning in 1757, the company gradually came to rule over large areas of India, exercising military power and assuming most governmental functions. Its reign lasted for a century until the bloody Indian Rebellion of 1857, which led a year later to the company's dissolution. In its place, under the Government of India Act, the British Crown assumed direct control of India, widely considered to be the jewel of the British Empire. Rule by the new British Raj, in turn, lasted for close to another century until independence came to the subcontinent in 1947. Amid widespread unrest, the area was partitioned between the new Republic of India, mostly Hindu, and the Muslim state of Pakistan (later divided, as we know, into the separate states of Pakistan and Bangladesh).

Even before the British sailed into the sunset, it was understood that self-rule of an area as fissiparous as India would be a challenge. Like Russia, India is extremely diverse, home to some 1.4 billion people crowded elbow-to-elbow into an area one-fifth of Russia's size. Under the British Raj, power was mostly exercised indirectly through preexisting kingdoms, commonly referred to as "princely states." Amazingly, at the time of independence, there were as many as 565 princely states in all, each of which opted ultimately to join either the new Indian state or Pakistan. The question was: How could self-rule work in such an extreme multiethnic setting?

The answer, India's new leaders decided, would have to be some form of federalism. As in Russia, some delegation of administrative responsibility from the center to lower-level units seemed the only natural course. The principle of subsidiarity was thus placed firmly at the heart of the union's constitution, which came into effect in January 1950. Though subsequently amended more than ninety times, the constitution's basic formula remains

156 DREAM STATES

the same. In the constitution's very first article, the Republic of India is declared to be a union. The institutions of government are then organized as a multilevel federation, which legally cannot be altered or dissolved without strict judicial review by the country's Supreme Court.

Executive and legislative powers under the constitution are carefully divided between the union government in Delhi and the governing authorities of lower-tier units. Immediately below the central government, two types of sub-national entities are recognized: states and union territories. As in America, *states* are the core constituents of the union. Many hark back to earlier princely kingdoms. Each state has its own elected government, though unlike in Russia (but as in the United States) a principle of symmetry prevails. All states enjoy the same rights and privileges and the same degree of autonomy. *Union territories*, by contrast, are with two exceptions directly ruled by the central government through appointed administrators. One of the two exceptions is the National Capital Territory of Delhi (similar to America's District of Columbia); the other is the special case of Puducherry, a former French colonial settlement in southeastern India that did not join the Indian union until 1954. Today's India comprises twenty-eight states and eight union territories.

Secession was ruled out from the start. As Jawaharlal Nehru, the Indian union's first prime minister, insisted: "We can give you complete autonomy, but never independence. You can never hope to be independent. No state, big or small, in India will be allowed to remain independent. We will use all our influence and power to suppress such tendencies."[2] In the history of the union, only one exception has been permitted. That was the special case of Bhutan, a politically external unit that had enjoyed separate protectorate status under the British Raj. The protectorate arrangement was extended under a treaty with India in 1949 in which both countries recognized each other's sovereignty. Though informally this was equivalent to secession from the union, it was acceptable to India because the Bhutanese monarchy tacitly reaffirmed India's de facto hegemony even post-independence.[3] Bhutan's separation from India was formally completed when the country joined the United Nations in 1971.

State borders, however, could be changed. Under the constitution, adjustments may be imposed by the central government, existing states can be combined, and new states can be carved out of old states. In this sense, India, it has been said, is an "indestructible union of destructible states." Many of the constitution's amendments over the years have involved just such border revisions. Since the passage of the States Reorganization Act in 1956, states have been defined mostly along linguistic lines.

The formal division of powers between the center and the states is laid out by the constitution in three lists. First is the *Union List*, which currently consists of one hundred items (earlier ninety-seven items) on which the Delhi parliament has exclusive authority, including such matters as defense, currency, and foreign trade. Second is the *State List*, covering some sixty-one items (earlier sixty-six items) where uniformity is considered desirable but not essential. Included here are such matters as maintaining law and order, healthcare, and transport. On these subjects, state governments have exclusive authority. And third is the *Concurrent List* of some fifty-two items (earlier forty-seven items) where law-making powers are shared. These include such matters as marriage and divorce, education, and contracts.

In principle, the three lists were meant to establish an enduring foundation for the country's federal structure—a delicate balancing of political rights and obligations. In practice, however, the effective pattern of governance has been more fluid, with the predominant locus of authority shifting back and forth over time as political circumstances have evolved. When it first came into effect, the constitution leaned toward a strong central government, which many Indians felt would be needed to hold such a heterogeneous population together. Beginning in the 1980s, however, power swung more toward the states, driven by the emergence of many strong regional parties. The power of the Congress Party, a secularist force that had ruled since independence, was eclipsed, and coalition politics at the national level now became the norm. And then after the turn of the century, the tide moved once again back toward the center with the rise of the Bharatiya Janata Party (BJP), a strong proponent of right-wing Hindu nationalism. The BJP's guiding principle is *Hindutva*, which calls for Hindu cultural hegemony over the country's many minorities, including India's 190 million Muslims (14 percent of the population). The party has controlled the government in Delhi since 2014 under the leadership of Narendra Modi, a former chief minister of the western state of Gujarat.

Secession movements

Like Russia, India can be described as an imperial state, an empire-like form of sovereignty. The biggest difference has to do with who built the empire

158 DREAM STATES

in the first place. In the case of the Russian Federation, it was the Russians themselves who over time managed to subdue and incorporate the expanding empire's many component parts. The imperial state had an inside leader—Russia—that was in a position to exercise authority over subordinate neighbors. In the case of India, by contrast, it was Britain, an outside power from half-way across the globe. When the Raj abruptly handed over formal control in 1947, there was no obvious inside leader to replace it. Instead, the Indians had to learn very quickly how to govern collectively on their own. India's constitution represents a valiant effort to meet the challenge of self-rule in a large multiethnic setting.

Sadly, the regime has not been entirely successful. As the renowned Scottish poet Robert Burns wrote some two and a half centuries ago, "The best laid schemes o' mice an' men gang aft a-gley." ("The best-laid plans of mice and men often go awry.") And so it has been in India, almost from the republic's first days as a member of the sovereignty club. Hopes for an orderly federal union have been repeatedly disrupted by militant separatist forces, driven by differences of caste, language, or religion. Despite the constitution's ban on secession, dream states have repeatedly emerged. In total, the country has faced as many as eleven secession movements since independence in 1947. Responses by the central government have varied considerably and have included elements of both harsh repression and accommodative reform.[4]

Some of India's dream states popped up almost immediately after the British departed and then, as quickly, tended to fade away. Others have been more enduring and even today may be considered potential threats. The most notable include Khalistan in the central Punjab region, the so-called Naxalite-Maoist insurgency in several eastern and southern states, a jumble of smaller states in the country's isolated northeast, and—the thorniest of all—Kashmir in the far north.

Khalistan

The Punjab region, encompassing today's state of Punjab adjacent to the Capital Territory of Delhi along with parts of other nearby states, is the traditional homeland of India's Sikh population. Sikhism is a monotheistic religion that evolved out of Hinduism around the end of the fifteenth century. The aggregate number of Sikhs in India today is not large—at last count only some 21 million, amounting to less than 2 percent of India's total population. But Sikhs have long played an outsized role in domestic Indian politics, particularly in Punjab where they amount to nearly 60 percent of the population. Even before independence came to the subcontinent in 1947, many Sikhs in Punjab had begun crusading for a separate and sovereign state to be called Khalistan (Land of the Khalsa, the "pure"). After years of agitation, the Khalistan movement crested in the 1980s before going relatively quiescent in more recent years.

The movement began around 1940 as what could be described as a drexit—a political campaign seeking a path to secession by relatively peaceable means. But after decades of frustrating negotiations, first with the British Raj and then with the new Indian government, the cause eventually evolved into a more militarized rebellion, abetted by financial and political support from the sizable Sikh diaspora. Sikhs were particularly provoked by the Punjab Reorganization Act of 1966, which divided the Punjab region into the separate states of Punjab and Haryana while requiring the two states to share a common capital in the city of Chandigarh (today a centrally administered union territory). By the late 1970s, violence was clearly on the rise. From 1982 to 1984, more than 1,200 armed incidents were recorded resulting in the death of more than 400 people. Emergency rule was imposed on Punjab in 1983, mandating direct control by Delhi, and continued for more than a decade. Promotion of the Khalistan cause was outlawed.

Violence reached its peak in mid-1984 when militants occupied the famous Golden Temple in the city of Amritsar—the most sacred site in Sikhism. After negotiations with the rebels stalled, the Indian Army launched Operation Blue Star, surrounding and ultimately capturing the temple complex at the cost of nearly 500 casualties. Three months later, in a shocking act of revenge, Indira Gandhi—the prime minister who had ordered Operation Blue Star—was assassinated by her two personal security guards, both Sikhs. That in turn triggered anti-Sikh riots across northern India that resulted in yet countless more casualties before the cycle of violence faded.

By the early 1990s, India's security forces managed largely to suppress the Sikh insurgency. Some Sikh political groups have continued to pursue the goal of an independent Khalistan, mostly by more peaceable means. Among the most prominent today is a popular movement called Waris Punjab De ("Heirs of Punjab"), led by a self-styled preacher named Amritpal Singh who was arrested in April 2023 following an attack on a police station.[5] Later, in September 2023, an all-out diplomatic war broke out between

160   DREAM STATES

India and Canada when another well-known separatist, a Canadian Sikh activist named Hardeep Singh Nijjar, was assassinated outside a Sikh temple in the city of Surrey on Canada's west coast—allegedly at the hands of agents of the Indian government, according to Canadian prime minister Justin Trudeau.[6] And not more than two months later, a second assassination plot was reported aiming at another vocal separatist, Gurpatwant Singh Pannun, a dual US–Canadian citizen resident in the United States.[7] For the most part, however, violent incidents have become relatively rare. Separatist sentiment seems stronger outside of India, among Sikh émigrés in places like Canada and Australia, than in the putative state of Khalistan.

At the moment, therefore, it would appear that what began as a non-violent drexit and then mutated into an armed rebellion has now been largely reduced inside India to a comforting daydream. But appearances can be misleading. A critical question remains. Is the waning of tensions due to reconciliation or repression? Has the Sikh population of India fully accepted its "sub-ness" within the broader Indian federation? Or does the dream of a sovereign Khalistan still live on, subdued but not extinguished? Today, warns a prominent Sikh academic, "there is no Khalistan movement as such ... But there is a sense that somehow justice is not done to us."[8] Are groups like Waris Punjab De simply waiting, like a good number of Russian minorities, for an opportunity to revive a dormant rebellion? Much rides on the answer.

Naxalite–Maoist insurgency

Now more than fifty years old, the Naxalite–Maoist insurgency offers a prime example of the sort of stalemate pattern that I described back in Chapter 7. The conflict pits radical separatist groups known as Naxalites or Naxals against the central Indian government. Taking their inspiration from the teachings of China's Mao Zedong, the Naxalites's battle for secession is driven by a particularly virulent form of communist ideology. Try as they might, India's armed forces have never been able to fully suppress the rebellion. The result is a frozen conflict that remains a persistent menace. One former prime minister has called the Naxalites the country's "biggest threat to internal security."[9]

The insurgency dates back to a 1967 incident in Naxalbari, a tiny village in the state of West Bengal, where local police opened fire on a group of farmers demonstrating for access to a disputed piece of land. The protests that followed quickly blossomed into a full-scale peasant revolt that spread like wildfire across much of eastern and southern India and has continued, on and off, to this day. Militants are most active in remote forest areas cutting across a stretch of states from Bihar and Odisha in the north to Andhra Pradesh and Telangana in the south—an area often called the tribal belt or Red Corridor. Support comes mainly from the indigenous communities of India known as the Adivasi (or, more formally, "scheduled tribes"). These are tribal people who feel neglected or even disrespected by the politicians in Delhi. The Adivasi are thought to be descended from the original inhabitants of the Indian subcontinent and make up some 8–9 percent of the country's population, just over 100 million persons in all. Additional support comes from India's Dalits (formerly labeled Untouchables) occupying the lowest rung of the caste hierarchy. Dalits make up another 25 percent of the country's population (350 million).

Conflict over the years has followed a familiar pattern—extended periods of low-intensity stalemate interrupted from time to time by more intense eruptions of violence. Occasionally, the government launches a counterinsurgency initiative intended to dispose of the rebellion once and for all, only to end in frustration. Two apt examples were the notorious Operation Steeplechase in 1971 and Operation Green Hunt in 2009, each of which left many Naxalites dead or behind bars but also encouraged new waves of rebel enlistments that left the militants more numerous—and more disruptive—than ever. We can add the Naxalite–Maoist insurgency to the already long list of armed separatist stand-offs that dot the world map. India has its own home-bred frozen conflicts.

The northeast

To that list we can also add the seven small states of India's remote northeast, a regional cluster that is also home to a variety of low-intensity frozen conflicts. These are the poverty-stricken "Seven Sister" states of Arunachal Pradesh, Assam, Manipur, Meghalaya, Mizoram, Nagaland, and Tripura, with a total population of roughly 45 million. The Seven Sisters are connected to the rest of India—at best tenuously—by a narrow strip of land called the Siliguri Corridor (or "Chicken's Neck"), with Nepal and China to the north and Bangladesh to the south. At one point, the Corridor is no

162 DREAM STATES

more than 15 miles (23 kilometers) wide. In the northeast too, we find restless tribal communities that feel neglected or disrespected. And here too we see the familiar pattern of prolonged stalemate interrupted by occasional upheavals.

The number and variety of separatist groups in the northeast are bewildering. Some movements call for outright independence for one or another of the Seven Sisters. Most notable are secessionists in Manipur, a state that had a long tradition of independence going back nearly a thousand years before its conquest by Britain in 1891. Manipur's incorporation into the newborn Indian Union in 1949 has been persistently contested, even after the area was formally made a separate state of the republic in 1972. Parallel examples include rebel insurgencies in the states of Mizoram and Nagaland.

Other groups, by contrast, are more concerned—in Matryoshka-doll fashion—with promoting the rights of one or more small tribal populations inside states created to satisfy the aspirations of bigger rival communities. The prime victim of the area's "minorities-within-minorities" scenario has been Assam, an older state where ethnic Assamese are the dominant population. No fewer than four newer states—Arunachal Pradesh, Meghalaya, Mizoram, and Nagaland—were carved out of Assam in the 1960s and 1970s in efforts to accommodate the demands of various smaller local tribes. In turn, some of these freshly minted states have themselves been beset with separatist pressures from even smaller local communities, such as the Bodo people in the northwestern corner of Nagaland. The Bodos started a separatist campaign of their own that ultimately resulted in the creation of a Bodoland autonomous region.

A particularly ironic example is found back in Manipur, where the majority Hindu community, known as the Meitei people, has long been at odds with the minority Kukis, who are mostly Christian, in what has been described as one of Asia's longest-running ethnic conflicts. At one and the same time, the Meiteis dream of independence from India even as they resist Kuki aspirations for a state of their own. Periodically, mob clashes break out causing fatalities—for example, in early 2023 when two Kuki women were paraded naked by Hindu demonstrators and later sexually assaulted.[10] Very quickly, nearly 5,000 houses and hundreds of temples and churches were burned. By mid-2024, some 200 people had been reported killed. The Matryoshka doll sits uneasily under a persistent threat of violence.

Apart from Manipur, recent years have been relatively quiet in most of the northeast. Sustained armed conflict has been confined mainly to an area at the juncture of Arunachal Pradesh, Assam, and Nagaland. But a close look suggests that the calm is fragile, more a product of repression than reconciliation. Most of the northeastern region remains officially classified as an "area of disturbance" under the terms of the Armed Forces (Special Powers) Act of 1958, which gives the country's security forces ample leeway to crack down on any outbreak of violence. Who knows what could follow if Delhi's grip were to loosen? Multiple hot spots remain in the area that could once again burst into flames at any time.

Kashmir

Finally, we come to what seems to be the most intractable of all of India's dream states—the northernmost region of the Indian subcontinent known broadly as Kashmir. Until the nineteenth century, that simple label was enough. Kashmir denoted the serene "Vale" of Kashmir, nestled between the Great Himalayas and the nearby Pir Panjal mountain range. Today, however, the region's geography is more complicated. Aside from some glacial border areas disputed with China, the area is now sharply split into two main zones, one occupied and administered by India and the other by nearby Pakistan. Both India and Pakistan claim the entire northern area as rightfully theirs. Local militants can be considered to be clients of Pakistan.

The juridical status of the zone administered by India has long been disputed. Until recently, the area was granted limited autonomy under a special provision of the Indian Constitution. In 2019, however, it was formally divided into two separate union territories—one to be called Jammu and Kashmir, and the other labeled Ladakh—with most authority reverting to the central government in Delhi. Despite repeated calls from India's Supreme Court to restore the area's statehood, Delhi has procrastinated, claiming that it can comply only when the situation in the region becomes "normal." But little clarity has been provided on what normality means or when it might come to pass.

My own personal instruction in the importance attached to Kashmir began back in 1965, when I visited India for the first time. Seated one day in a government office, I could not help noticing a huge map of the Indian union hung on one wall, with what looked like a suspiciously inaccurate representation of the country's northern border. I was sure that the bulge I saw was a

164   DREAM STATES

mistake until I realized that it included not only Indian-administered Kashmir but also the part of the area occupied by Pakistan. In effect, the map was aspirational rather than accurate—the government's own version of a dream state!

The Kashmir dispute goes back to the partition of the subcontinent in 1947. Since the princely state of Kashmir had a Muslim majority (77 percent Muslims by the last previous census in 1941), it was naturally expected to join the new state of Pakistan. But the reigning monarch, a Hindu, chose instead to join India, triggering a year-long war between Pakistan and India. A cease-fire was finally agreed upon under United Nations (UN) auspices in late 1948. Ever since, the area has been divided along the so-called Line of Control separating the two armed forces. Full-scale wars were triggered in 1965 and 1999.

In essence, the dispute over Kashmir has much in common with the Israel–Palestine conflict highlighted in Chapter 9. Like that bitter quarrel, it can be described as akin to a double helix—a twinned (and twisted) secession struggle. Both sides cherish the same piece of land; each regards the other's claim as illegitimate. Pakistanis consider India a usurper since the area's population has always been predominantly Muslim (some 68 percent according to the most recent census). Indians, meanwhile, see Pakistan as the real outlaw because of its refusal to accept the choice of Kashmir's rightful ruler at the time of partition. Like the Israelis and Palestinians, both sides see themselves as aggrieved victims.

The result, accordingly, is a stand-off that appears to have no end in sight. Hostilities keep erupting from time to time—most recently, in late 2022 when deadly attacks by Muslim militants began targeting Hindu families. In response, the Indian government has revived once dormant local militias, arming thousands of Hindu civilians who are not above taking the law into their own hands.[11] There seems little doubt that further violence is possible so long as the long-running dispute remains unresolved.

The future?

What, then, does the future hold? The risks to India's fragile federation are undeniable. As in Russia, there is more than enough tinder scattered around the country to set hot spots aflame—stubborn separatists in the Red Corridor and Seven Sisters; discontented Muslims, backed by Pakistan, in

Kashmir; and possibly even a revived Khalistan movement in the Punjab region. But as we know, the presence of restless minorities, by itself, is not enough to cause bubbles to pop. There must also be some kind of trigger to get things started.

Disintegration?

In the case of Russia, we have seen, the trigger was a sudden unexpected breakdown of central authority (twice!). Conceivably the same could happen in India, opening the door to powerful centrifugal forces. There is, after all, nothing truly "natural" about a union as variegated as the Indian republic. Individuals in the country's twenty-eight states may share common roots going back to the early Indus Valley Civilization. But, today, they can barely communicate with one another without the intervention of English, the language of their former colonial master. People in thriving southern states like Karnataka, Kerala, or Tamil Nadu have little in common, linguistically or culturally, with the poorer, more populous Hindi-speaking states of the northern Indo-Gangetic Plain. The Seven Sisters of the northeast have even less in common with anyone on the western side of the Chicken's Neck. Even cuisines differ greatly from region to region. The specialties of northern India, which rely heavily on vegetable oil and roti, contrast sharply with the tropical flavors of the south, which rely more on coconut oil and rice. Given such immense diversities, it is not difficult to imagine the possibility of a messy disintegration at some point in the future.

Doubts about the union's durability go back a long way—indeed, even to colonial days, when the union was just a dream and the British Raj was still in charge. Not without a touch of arrogance, most of Britain's imperialists took for granted that their presence was needed to hold things together. Representative were the words of no less an authority than Winston Churchill, speaking in London in 1931. The man whom many Indians called the "angry British bulldog" famously predicted that should Britain abandon the subcontinent, "the whole efficiency of the services, defensive, administrative, medical, hygienic, judicial; railway, irrigation, public works and famine prevention, upon which the Indian masses depend for their culture and progress, will perish with it." The local lads simply were not up to the job.

Churchill turned out to be wrong, of course. So far, despite multiple separatist threats, the union has managed reasonably well to hold centrifugal

166 DREAM STATES

forces in check. The federal government may not have been wholly successful to date in maintaining domestic order; separatist forces have not been
fully eradicated. But neither can it be said that the constitutional scheme
has gone completely awry; the federation as such is far from disintegration. Apart from Kashmir, where militants can count on the support of Big
Brother Pakistan next door, the tide of threats to the government in Delhi
has receded significantly over time. For three-quarters of a century, the center has held. Were grades being handed out, the Indians would deserve
something like a B or B–, certainly not an F.

As the years have gone by, therefore, a breakdown of authority of the sort
that brought down the czars and then the Soviets has come to seem less and
less likely. Partly, this is because India continues to live by the democratic
principles laid out in its constitution, which provide ample outlets for the
expression of local or regional grievances. That is a huge difference from
the Russian case. Indians take great pride in being known as "the world's
largest democracy." Dissatisfied minorities know that armed rebellion is not
the only option available to them to pursue their dreams. But partly also the
system endures because of key elements of culture that are shared by most, if
not all, of India's many sub-nationalisms. For all their differences and occasional outbursts of violence, most Indians are alike in valuing a high degree
of tolerance, an inclination that is seemingly integral to their historical DNA.
Over the centuries, Indians have learned that civilization in their crowded
subcontinent is best based on the idea of more or less peaceful cohabitation
and acceptance of each other's cultures. In principle (if not always in practice), mutual respect has ruled. In the words of one astute observer, writing
two decades ago:

> India is, overall, a highly accommodating society, and its politicians are
> skilled at the art of compromise. Historically, Hinduism has absorbed and
> incorporated outside ideologies and cultures, even as it has helped spawn
> other faiths, including Jainism, Sikhism, and Buddhism .... [Policy makers]
> have demonstrated a flexibility that has been absent in other complex, mul-
> tiethnic, multinational states such as Pakistan, Yugoslavia, and the former
> Soviet Union.[12]

In short, the union is arguably rather more resilient than it looks—certainly
more resilient than today's Russia would appear to be. The risk of a major
breakdown of central authority is considerably more limited than in the

much more fragile Russian Federation. India does not appear to be poised to become the world's next Yugoslavia.

Concentration?

But what about the opposite possibility—not a risk of disintegration but rather the possibility of an excessive *concentration* of central political authority? Since the BJP took control in 2014, constitutional power has steadily moved back toward Delhi at the expense of a divided and increasingly frustrated opposition. The BJP practices a particularly aggressive version of the politics of polarization. Its hard line on *Hindutva*—and particularly its often shrill animosity toward Islam—runs directly counter to the norms of tolerance and flexibility that have worked so well in the past. The irony is that the more the BJP succeeds in consolidating its dominance at the center, the greater is the risk of discontent around the country's periphery.

As already noted, the BJP is a strong proponent of right-wing Hindu supremacy. The party advocates social conservatism at home and a foreign policy based on nation-first principles (not unlike Donald Trump's "America First" slogan in the United States). Close links are maintained with the Rashtriya Swayamsevak Sangh (RSS), the progenitor and leader of a large body of organizations called the Sangh Parivar ("Sangh Family") that promotes the concept of Hindutva across the country. For the BJP and RSS, India is first and foremost a *Hindu* nation: the country's dominant culture is its traditional Hindu culture, and all other religious traditions are marginalized, at best of secondary importance.

Islam, in particular, is demonized. At the BJP's behest, school textbooks have been revised to erase prominent Muslim contributions to Indian history and politics.[13] Likewise, in early 2024, a controversial law was implemented offering an accelerated route to Indian citizenship for persecuted minorities in neighboring countries. Muslims were pointedly excluded. During India's national election in the spring of 2024, Prime Minister Modi took to calling the country's indigenous Muslim population "infiltrators," as if they were no more than recent immigrants who would grab India's wealth for themselves if given the chance.

Emblematic of the BJP's hard-line ideology was its handling of a long-running dispute over a temple site in the legendary city of Ayodhya, located in the north-central state of Uttar Pradesh. Ayodhya is believed to be the birthplace of a key Hindu deity, Lord Ram. As the setting for one of the religion's greatest epics, the *Ramayana*, it is one of the seven most important pilgrimage sites for all Hindus. A temple thought to mark the spot of Ram's birth was demolished on the orders of a Mughal emperor in the early sixteenth century and replaced by a mosque, which in its turn was destroyed in 1992 by Hindu demonstrators who aimed to rebuild a grand temple of Ram on the site. After nearly three decades of judicial proceedings, India's Supreme Court finally ordered the property to be handed over to a trust to build a Hindu temple, which was formally consecrated in early 2024 after an expenditure of some $220 million. A separate site some distance away was set aside, as a sort of consolation prize, for the construction of a replacement mosque. During all the years of the dispute, the BJP loudly supported the Hindu side of the fight and dismissed all counterclaims from the Muslim community. The rights of Hindus were privileged over the country's largest religious minority, and activists were given free rein to repeat their predations elsewhere.

Across the country, anti-Muslim actions—up to and including lynchings—have risen noticeably. In the words of a Human Rights Watch report, "the B.J.P.'s ideology of Hindu primacy has [empowered] party supporters to threaten, harass, and attack religious minorities, particularly Muslims, with impunity."[14] Extrajudicial killings have become increasingly common, often accompanied by chants of "Jai Shri Ram" (victory to Ram). Some mob attacks even occur in real time on television.[15] Laments a popular Indian journalist: "The world's most populous country is slowly degenerating into a conflict zone of sectarian violence."[16]

For the BJP, the advantages of an ideology of Hindu hegemony are plain. Religion is one of the most important of the symbols that Benedict Anderson had in mind when he spoke of states as "imagined communities." A common faith, with all of its rituals and festivals, can aid greatly in cultivating a sense of national identity. In a large multiethnic federation like India, it is much easier to centralize political authority when citizens feel themselves bound together as members of a single social unit. By promoting Hindu primacy, the BJP may believe that it is doing much to advance Indian patriotism—to build a genuine *amor patriae* (love of country) in a diverse population of some 1.4 billion individuals.

But what if minorities object? What if they are unwilling to settle for second-class citizenship in an avowedly Hindu state? Signs of growing discontent were evident during the 2024 election campaign, which saw the BJP lose its parliamentary majority. The principal disadvantage of the BJP's hard line is the risk that it could in time meet with widespread resistance—rebellion rather than reconciliation—precisely the opposite of what the party ostensibly hopes to achieve. Non-Hindu minorities make up as much as 30 percent of India's overall population. Not all of them can be expected to reconcile themselves comfortably to permanent sub-national status. At a minimum, older rebellions like the Naxalite–Maoist insurgency might be reinvigorated. Worse, dormant drexits such as the Khalistan movement might be resurrected. And worst of all, elements of the country's Muslim community might be provoked to rise in armed revolt, much as has occurred in Kashmir from time to time. It bears repeating that India is home to more than 170 million Muslims, making it the third largest Muslim community in the world (exceeded only by Indonesia with 280 million and Pakistan with 240 million). It is not difficult to imagine how quickly violence could spread throughout the country if the BJP pushes *Hindutva* too vigorously.

Nor would violence necessarily be confined within India's frontiers. I have already alluded to the ties between some separatist groups in the isolated Indian northeast and ethnically related rebels next door in Myanmar (Chapter 9). Renewed struggle on the Indian side could easily spill over the border between the two countries. Even more serious is the risk of renewed rebellion in Kashmir, which could draw Pakistan into yet another full-scale war with its detested Indian neighbor. Few disputes seem more dangerous in today's world than the long-running stand-off between South Asia's two nuclear powers.

For the United States, the stakes could not be higher. America's security strategy in the entire Indo-Pacific region would be affected. In the face of China's ascending ambitions in the area, Washington has sought to promote a counterbalancing coalition of local powers known as the Quad—a loose arrangement including India along with America, Australia, and Japan. Nothing would be more damaging for US interests in the region than destabilizing violence, either inside India or with Pakistan, that might impede the construction of defenses against China. What happens in India does not necessarily stay in India.

India's fate?

Overall, then, it would appear that India's fate is very much in its own hands. Threats to the fragile federation may be numerous. But the union's record since independence suggests more resilience than many—including

170   DREAM STATES

Winston Churchill—had ever anticipated. If there is a risk of fragmentation today, it comes from the present trend of the country's politics driven by the BJP's intolerant brand of Hindu-first ideology. The more the center promotes a hard-line ideology of Hindu primacy, the more animosity it is likely to stir up among India's many long-suppressed minorities. Rather than building patriotism, the BJP could end up simply reinvigorating centrifugal forces. The risk of nightmarish violence will be heightened, not dampened.

PART IV
SOLUTIONS?

14

The Challenge

Incompatible imperatives

What, then, is to be done? Pretenders to sovereignty can be found every-where. The risk is that in one place or another, separatist ambitions could turn out to be the spark for prolonged and bloody conflict. As we have seen, violence is a ubiquitous threat, whether we are talking about familiar faces like my Top Ten Combustibles, special cases like Palestine or Tai-wan, fragile multiethnic federations like Russia or India—or (yes!) even the United States (US). Halcyon dream states can easily mutate into fiery night-mares. Can anything be done to dampen the danger of ever more destructive conflagrations?

The challenge is daunting. At issue are a pair of seemingly incompatible imperatives. On the one hand, we should pay due respect to the aspira-tions of would-be separatists. That is only fair. We cannot simply dismiss all secession movements as frivolous or unreasonable. The sincerity of identity-driven discontent in many places cannot be denied. But on the other hand, we are also restrained by the norms of the Westphalian system, which put great emphasis on the territorial integrity of incumbent states. Undisputed control of a defined piece of landscape—what one expert calls "deep ter-ritoriality"[1]—is a cardinal principle of the global sovereignty club. The constraint of the "territorial integrity norm"[2] cannot be ignored, either. The twin imperatives of secession and deep territoriality are naturally in con-flict, since successful secession violates territorial integrity while successful defense of territorial integrity bars the way to secession. There is a natural trade-off between the two.[3]

The challenge is to find some way to reconcile the twin imperatives to the mutual satisfaction of all concerned. In theory, the easiest way to reconcile the two would be simply to magically rule one of them out by assumption. Either disallow secession under all circumstances, insisting on the absolute permanence of existing national borders, or else abandon completely the norm of deep territoriality, opening the door wide to amputating parts of

Dream States. Benjamin J. Cohen, Oxford University Press. © Oxford University Press (2025).
DOI: 10.1093/9780197811672.003.0014

174   DREAM STATES

many members of the sovereignty club. In practice, however, neither path offers a realistic choice. They are implausible—in a word, non-solutions. In the real world, can we truly imagine all pretenders to sovereignty willingly surrendering their dreams? Or, alternatively, is it really likely that many existing states might voluntarily submit to wholesale dismemberment? Either option would be truly magical.

Secession

Of the two imperatives, it is easier to conceive of the delegitimization of secession. The reason is simple. The option has never been formally *legitimized*. In international law, there is no such thing as a generally recognized right to secede.[4] In a sense, therefore, we might say that secession is *already* effectively disbarred. Its lack of legitimacy just has never been made official. Secession, as such, has no formal standing under the club's membership rules.

Over the years, our understanding of national sovereignty has been built up in a succession of treaties, covenants, and declarations going back to the Peace of Westphalia in 1648. Especially important in the twentieth century were the Montevideo Convention of 1933 and the Founding Charter of the United Nations (UN) in 1945, succeeded by a series of clarifying resolutions formulated and adopted by the UN General Assembly.[5] It is striking that in most of those documentary sources, the word "secession" never makes so much as a cameo appearance. Instead, we find what one scholar describes as "a widely accepted and continuing negative attitude towards secession."[6] For obvious political reasons, denial prevails. States are understandably disinclined to contemplate the loss of any portion of their territory. The secession option is like an eccentric uncle or aunt long hidden away in the attic. No one in the family wants to acknowledge that the embarrassing relative even exists.

But of course a hard line like that is not very realistic. From extensive experience, amply described in previous chapters, we know better. Secession may be dismissed as little more than a ghost at the banquet. But try telling that to the many separatist movements around the world that doggedly persist in their pursuit of a state to call their own. Tell that to the Bangladeshis or Eritreans or South Sudanese, who have actually managed to win membership in the sovereignty club. Or tell it to the many other pretenders to

THE CHALLENGE   175

sovereignty who refuse to forfeit their dreams despite years, even decades, of frustrating stalemate. Like America's slave states in the antebellum era, secessionists today preach some version of the compact theory of union, which concedes that in the real world, statehood may in all likelihood be settled ultimately as an "extralegal" matter by political or military means. That is how the Confederacy's bid for separation finally was resolved—not in a courtroom but on the battlefield. The US Supreme Court's *Texas v. White* decision merely ratified what had already been achieved by force.

Besides, even as a matter of international law, some exceptions are reluctantly admitted—most importantly under the rubric of *remedial* secession, which suggests the possibility of exit for a minority whose members have been persistently denied equal rights on account of, for instance, racial, religious, or linguistic differences.[7] Effectively, the notion of remedial secession encompasses the first three of the seven arguments identified in Chapter 3 that might potentially be used to justify secession in selected circumstances. These are political morality, economic self-interest, and cultural integrity. Other possible loopholes include origins, centrifugal forces, mutual suspicion, and dysfunction.

Admittedly, tight limits are placed on the use of any of these possible exceptions. A particularly important role is played by a key resolution adopted by the UN General Assembly in 1970, known familiarly as the Friendly Relations Declaration.[8] The essential purpose of the Friendly Relations Declaration was to provide support for the waves of decolonization then sweeping across the global South. In the Declaration's words: "By virtue of the principle of equal rights ... enshrined in the Charter of the United Nations, all peoples have the right freely to determine, without external interference, their political status and to pursue their economic, social and cultural development."[9] But the Declaration's support was quickly qualified by a supplementary stipulation that has come to be known as the "saving clause" (alternatively: "safeguard clause"). Under that notorious provision, text was added specifying that "Nothing in the foregoing paragraphs shall be construed as authorizing or encouraging any action which would dismember or impair, totally or in part, the territorial integrity or political unity of sovereign and independent states."[10] In other words, secession is excluded.

Even within the narrow constraint of the saving clause, however, some room is left to legitimize a bid for secession. The hard line is not necessarily inaccurate. But as a characterization of reality, it is simply *too* hard. Exceptions *are* possible. Of course, potential justifications for a dream state may be

176   DREAM STATES

subjective, resting ultimately on qualitative judgments. That point must be conceded, as noted previously. The case for separation may not always be persuasive. But that does not rule out the possibility that secession may be a genuine material challenge, despite its limited standing under international law. It just means that in practical terms, the option cannot be blithely ignored. It is tempting to think that the twin imperatives might be reconciled simply by ruling out secession by assumption. But that would be a mistake. Disreputable or not, the embarrassing relative in the attic must be acknowledged. The trick cannot be managed by mere sleight of hand.

Self-determination

The absence of a formal right of secession is of course easy to understand. The danger posed by separatism is manifest. Even without the sanction of international law, the world is flooded with secession movements pushing hard to open the door to membership in the sovereignty club. Just imagine how many more dream states might be encouraged if secession were to be elevated formally to the status of a legitimate policy option. Today's dozens might soon become scores, even hundreds. The figure of 8,000 potential nations suggested by Ernst Gellner[11] might no longer seem quite so astounding. Violent wars of secession could break out everywhere—not a pretty picture.

As a practical matter, the possibility of secession, however remote, can hardly be denied. To pretend otherwise would expose the sovereignty club to ridicule as naive or worse. In the real world, the dreams of drexits and rebels with a cause will not be snuffed out so easily. So how does the global community acknowledge the possibility of secession without actually encouraging it? The answer is: by inventing an ambiguous new term that allows for a range of plausible interpretations. In a manner of speaking, governments hope to have their cake and eat it, too.

An old jibe explains the contrast between scholars and diplomats. Scholars use words to clarify disagreements. Diplomats use words to camouflage disagreements—in short, to obfuscate. A classic example from the world of international finance came up in 1944 when World War II's allied nations, led by the United States, met at Bretton Woods, New Hampshire, to hammer out the details of a proposed International Monetary Fund. One key issue had to do with when a government with an external payments problem might be authorized to devalue its currency. Unable to agree on specific conditions, delegates instead resorted to the amorphous phrase "fundamental disequilibrium." Negotiators were unsure of the phrase's practical meaning but were happy to kick the can down the road for others to worry about in the future. To this day, no one is quite sure how to define fundamental disequilibrium. But most policy makers are confident that they will know one when they see it.

In debates about dream states, the conveniently ambiguous term that has come to provide a substitute for secession is *self-determination*. In the legal literature, as many as six different meanings have been attributed to the idea of self-determination.[12] As one commentary wryly observes, "international law is not 'univocal' on the subject."[13] Most relevant for our purposes, among the six, is the notion of *external* self-determination, which relates to choices about an entity's status in relation to others. The connection of external self-determination to secession is obvious; the two plainly have a lot in common. Yet the nature of the connection remains indeterminate. Formal secession is neither implicitly encouraged, nor is it categorically excluded. Instead, room is left for negotiation. The ambiguity of the term is its virtue.

The idea of external self-determination has a long history, going back centuries, though it did not achieve widespread application until well into the twentieth century. Its rise to prominence in the contemporary era may be said to have begun with US President Woodrow Wilson's historic "Fourteen Points" speech in January 1918, which highlighted the idea of self-determination without actually using the term explicitly. It was only a month later, in an address to a joint session of America's Congress, that Wilson formally consecrated the right of self-determination as a moral cornerstone of the global community. Self-determination, he declared, was an "imperative principle" that would be key to making the world "safe for democracy." Since then, the idea of external self-determination has become firmly enshrined as an integral part of customary international law—in the words of one noted scholar, "a defining principle of modern politics, of people's efforts to appropriate authority."[14] The notion was affirmed in the first article of the UN Charter, which—anticipating the later Friendly Relations Declaration—declared that a central purpose of the new United Nations was "to develop friendly relations among nations based on respect for the principle of equal rights and self-determination of peoples." The pledge has been repeatedly reaffirmed ever since.[15] Today, in most formal settings where we might

178   DREAM STATES

expect to see the word "secession," we more often find "self-determination" instead. Drexits and rebels call for self-determination when they really mean secession.

Territoriality

Whether we use the language of secession or self-determination, the challenge is the same. The twin imperatives of secession and deep territoriality seem irreconcilable. But if we cannot rule out separatism by assumption, what about the reverse? To find a workable solution, could we instead rule out deep territoriality?

In principle, the answer might be thought to be "Yes." After all, there is nothing particularly sacred about the lines that separate most countries from one another. There are exceptions, of course, such as the Israel–Palestine dispute over the Temple Mount in Jerusalem or the Hindu–Muslim dispute over the historic Rama temple site in Ayodhya. But these instances are relatively rare, as I noted back in Chapter 1. We may live in a Westphalian world, where the world map is nominally carved up into a pastiche of "neatly divided spatial packages." But in reality, there is nothing at all "natural" about the map's separate constituent units that we call sovereign states. Most are the "imagined communities" that Benedict Anderson wrote about: entities that were deliberately created and must be cultivated if they are to succeed in nurturing a sense of national identity. Most state borders are pliable at best and often quite random—"artificial, arbitrary, and accidental," to quote one informed observer.[16]

Examples abound. Recall again the waves of decolonization that swept through Africa and Asia after World War II, leaving in their wake literally dozens of new states whose borders in most cases followed lines casually laid down earlier by their colonial masters. Historical claims of indigenous populations were cavalierly ignored. Northern Africa's Berber population was divided among as many as six newly independent states. The Middle East's Kurds were split among four countries. Singapore was temporarily forced into a federation with its Malay neighbors before going its own way. Tibet was absorbed against its will into the People's Republic of China. Could anything have been more arbitrary than developments like these?

Or consider Europe, which most of us are inclined to think of as a relatively stable collection of historical communities. In fact, no continent in modern times has redefined sovereign territory more frequently. Following the defeat of Nazi Germany in 1945, many borders in East-Central Europe moved westward. Poland, for instance, lost parts of its eastern domains to the Soviet Union while absorbing Germany's Silesia region further to the west. The coal-rich Saarland, meanwhile, was claimed by the victorious French, only to be returned to German rule in 1957. Germany itself was cut in half after the Iron Curtain descended, and then reunited forty years later when the Cold War ended. In 1954, the Free Territory of Trieste was dissolved and divided between Italy and Yugoslavia. In the early 1960s, both Cyprus and Malta became independent states. The Czech Republic and Slovakia divorced amicably in 1992. Following the disintegration of both Yugoslavia and the Soviet Union in the 1990s, more than a score of newly sovereign successor states appeared in their place. And most recently, starting with Crimea in 2014, we have witnessed blatant land grabs by Russia from its neighbor Ukraine.

Or consider some of the large multiethnic federations discussed in Chapters 11–13, some of which—like Ethiopia, Nigeria, or Pakistan—have sought to jam together a mare's nest of mutually antagonistic ethnic communities. "Imperial" states like Russia or India are particularly vulnerable to relentless centrifugal forces. And, of course, we cannot ignore the increasingly disunited US, with its growing polarization between red and blue states.

In practice, however, the answer to our question is surely "No." Throughout most of human history, land was a commodity that could be exchanged routinely between sovereign rulers—sometimes as a commercial transaction; at other times, as a valued prize of war. Few countries illustrate the process better than the United States, which in two and a half centuries has expanded from its early precarious foothold on the Atlantic seaboard to something in excess of 3 million square miles today. Partly, this was the result of peaceful acquisitions—most notably the Louisiana Purchase in 1803 and the Alaska Purchase ("Seward's Folly") in 1867—and partly as a result of victories in conflicts like the Mexican–American War of 1846–1848 and the Spanish–American War of 1898. Other striking examples were provided by Czarist Russia, which spread eastward through the Ural Mountains and across the Siberian steppes by way of conquest over one indigenous population after another.

Those days, however, are long gone. Today, the Westphalian model of political geography prevails almost everywhere. (The one significant

180 DREAM STATES

exception is the continent of Antarctica, where competing territorial claims remain frozen—pardon the pun—under the terms of the Antarctic Treaty of 1959.) Deep territoriality is not merely an incidental feature of the international system. Since the Peace of Westphalia was signed in 1648, the idea has come to be one of the system's core foundational principles: the "territorial integrity norm," as noted back in Chapter 1. Borders, no matter how artificial they may seem, are treated now as inviolable. To consider surrendering part of a country's land mass is, in effect, to tolerate a compromise of sovereignty itself.

For most policy makers, therefore, the principle of territorial integrity trumps the very thought of secession. Any bid to exit from an already existing state is held to be *verboten*—an inadmissible violation of Max Weber's famous dictum, which puts control of territory at the core of the notion of sovereignty. The tone was set by the UN Charter, which formally prohibits members of the global club from threatening or using force "against the territorial integrity or political independence of any state" (Article 2), and has been reiterated repeatedly ever since. Only a small handful of national constitutions set out procedures that might legitimize secession. The vast majority are either silent on the matter or explicitly opposed. Most states prefer to regard themselves, in practical terms, as indissoluble. As a general rule, they will brook no compromise with such a fundamental attribute of sovereignty. For them, there is only one true imperative, not two. The dominant imperative is the preservation of authority within existing frontiers.

A binding constraint

In short, the constraint is binding. Governments today are no more likely to abandon the norm of deep territoriality than would-be secessionists can be expected to give up their dream states. Neither of the twin imperatives, secession or deep territoriality, can be conveniently ruled out by mere assumption. There is no magic solution.

15

A Modest Proposal

Reconsidering the twin imperatives

Though magic may be out of the question, all is not lost. Against the odds, there is a workable path forward should decision-makers be receptive to some form of constructive compromise. In 1729, the satirist Jonathan Swift offered a "modest proposal" to ease starvation among the impoverished Irish by encouraging them to sell their children to the wealthy classes as food. Here I too offer a modest proposal—though not one that requires devouring infants.

In a nutshell, I propose that we take a new look at the dichotomous concept of statehood that is central to both of the twin imperatives. Each of the imperatives—secession and deep territoriality—insists, in effect, on a strict binary choice. Either/or is their default position. Pretenders to sovereignty tend to act as if the only serious alternative to perpetual sub-nationalism is full-fledged independence. The choice is limited to secession or assimilation. Conversely, defenders of deep territoriality generally act as if the only alternative to exclusive territorial control is no control at all. State authority over a contested piece of land must be either absolute or erased. In each case, the starting point is the Westphalian principle of sovereign equality among territorially defined states. The two imperatives agree that the independent territorial state is the world's basic unit of governance. If there is tension between the two, ironically it is because in their underlying assumptions they are actually convergent. Together, they share a common understanding of sovereignty as a fundamentally binary choice.

But what if the choice is not necessarily binary? What if the central notion of sovereignty can be disaggregated to allow for various hybrid forms of state authority? Back in Chapter 2, I suggested that a dichotomous conceptualization of statehood may well be too rigid. Now, with the benefit of a fuller appreciation of the many types and risks of dream states that must be faced, we are in a position, finally, to return to that potentially powerful idea. Reconsideration of both of the twin imperatives is called for.

Dream States. Benjamin J. Cohen, Oxford University Press. © Oxford University Press (2025).
DOI: 10.1093/9780197811672.003.0015

182 DREAM STATES

Secession reconsidered

First, think again about the goal of secession (a.k.a. self-determination). Obviously, it is a quantum leap to go all the way from the first faint stirrings of separatist feelings to something like full-scale secession. The range of possible types of dream states in between—from daydreams to drexits to rebels and clients—is broad. There is absolutely no reason why full independence needs to be considered the only legitimate alternative to continued sub-nationalism. Between the poles of secession or assimilation, we may conceive of many plausible hybrid solutions that successfully *redistribute* sovereign powers in one way or another. The lesson is clear: To best address the tensions involved, we need to formally conceptualize sovereignty as a continuous attribute, plastic in nature rather than strictly dichotomous—a spectrum of compromise choices among intermediate trade-offs rather than one stark either/or.

Recall that sovereignty is inherently multidimensional. Since the Montevideo Convention of 1933, international law has come to recognize at least four basic criteria for statehood: (1) a defined territory; (2) a permanent population; (3) a government; and (4) a capacity to enter into relations with other states. (Stephen Krasner rephrased the four dimensions under the labels of domestic sovereignty, interdependence sovereignty, international legal sovereignty, and Westphalian sovereignty.[1]) The choice between the twin imperatives is binary only for communities at the extremes— groups that either fully satisfy all four criteria or else manifest none at all. In the real world, it is more likely that candidates for club membership will fit somewhere in between, satisfying some criteria but not necessarily every one and fulfilling some dimensions rather more strongly than others. For these groups, hybrid trade-offs are the name of the game. Magic is not needed to negotiate a mutually agreed redistribution of formal authority.

Undoubtedly, the conceptualization of sovereignty as a continuous variable has disadvantages. The main problem is that in most cases the notion calls for potentially controversial judgments. How firm is a candidate's authority over the territory it claims as its homeland (Krasner's Westphalian sovereignty)? How strong a degree of command does it exercise over political and economic activities within or across its frontiers (Krasner's domestic sovereignty and interdependence sovereignty)? How influential are the states that have offered the candidate formal recognition

(Krasner's international legal sovereignty)? Judgments on such matters are inherently subjective—questions on which sincere parties may sincerely disagree.

But there are advantages as well—most importantly, a significant gain of flexibility in the identification of policy options. Once the strait jacket of a binary approach is relaxed, we can see clearly that in practice there is really a much more extensive menu of potential hybrid solutions available—intermediate distributions of authority short of full statehood that might be offered to appease a minority's aspirations without threatening an incumbent government's overall sovereign status. A number of these options have already bubbled up at times in preceding chapters.

Chapter 5, for instance, while speaking of the four R's (reconciliation, repression, reform, and rebellion), identified in passing a number of practical reform possibilities, including in particular support for expressions of distinctive sub-national cultures. Inter alia, protection might be promised for instruction in minority languages or for the practice of ancient faiths. Likewise, while outlining the logic of federalism, Chapter 11 drew attention to the opportunities for local autonomy created by the notion of subsidiarity. Self-rule at lower levels of a federal hierarchy can take any number of forms depending on how political and economic powers are shared or divided. Britain calls it devolution—administrative decentralization (Chapter 5). Canada calls it sovereignty association (Chapter 6). Both Britain and Canada have offered formal recognition to restless sub-national groups—Scotland and Wales in the case of Britain, Quebec in Canada—as "nations" within a larger sovereign state. Large multiethnic federations like India, Russia, or Ethiopia have all aimed for much the same by defining constituent entities mostly along ethnic or linguistic lines (Chapter 11).

And yet other hybrid arrangements have tried to placate a militant minority by authorizing separate participation in various regional or global settings. Canada has demonstrated one possibility by allowing francophone Quebec to operate its own Ministry of International Relations in some eighteen foreign countries. The United States (US) has highlighted another by condoning Puerto Rico's independent participation in international sporting events. Back at the end of World War II, as we saw in Chapter 2, Joseph Stalin underscored how the approach might be abused by demanding full membership in the newborn United Nations (UN) for his so-called "republics" of Belarus and Ukraine.

184   DREAM STATES

In most cases, however, compromise solutions like these tend, at best, to be tolerated rather than welcomed. Negotiated redistributions of power are treated as regrettable exceptions rather than an integral feature of the Westphalian model. The bias is understandable. Incumbent states are understandably reluctant to surrender any significant element of their sovereign authority unless compelled to do so. Moreover, there is no guarantee that any such options may be enough to fully sate the ambitions of separatists. But as the saying goes, it's a start.

Territoriality reconsidered

Much the same may be said about the goal of deep territoriality. Here too the typical assumption is binary. Who will exercise legal authority over a contested parcel of land—the incumbent government or an emergent dream state? Once again, the default position is generally thought to be strictly either/or. Control is expected to be exclusively in the hands of one side or the other. And here too we may argue that as a practical matter, the range of possible options between the polar alternatives is in fact broader than conventionally thought. Once again, we may conceive of many plausible hybrid solutions. The key is to think in terms of some form of *shared* authority—in effect, joint sovereignty—rather than monopoly control by a single entity. A popular synonym for joint sovereignty is *condominium*, derived from the Latin words *cum* (with) and *dominium* (rule).

The idea of joint sovereignty has a long history, preceding by centuries the signing of the Peace of Westphalia in 1648. Indeed, before the emergence of the Westphalian principle of sovereign equality, the practice of shared authority was not at all uncommon. In Chapter 1, I emphasized the complexity of pre-Westphalian political geography. Governing authority was diffuse, and there were as yet no fixed or exclusive sovereignties. In that mixed setting, established authorities often agreed to exercise their powers jointly in some designated or disputed territory. One of the world's earliest examples is provided by Andorra, a microstate located in the Pyrenees Mountains between France and Spain (and a member of the United Nations since 1993). Ever since gaining independence in 1278, Andorra's rights and liberties have been jointly guaranteed by the President of France and the Bishop of Urgell in Spain, who share the position of Andorran head of state *ex officio*—an arrangement that has persisted all the way down to the present day. Similarly, many other past examples were offered by the medieval Holy Roman Empire, which in its time hosted numerous condominiums within its boundaries. Perhaps best known was the city of Maastricht, which existed as a condominium for some five centuries under the shared rule of the Bishopric of Liège and the Duchy of Brabant until absorption by the Dutch Republic in 1794. (It was no accident that more recently, in 1992, Maastricht was chosen for the signing of the treaty formally creating today's European Union. The symbolism was unmistakable.)

Once Westphalian norms began to spread, the idea of shared authority might have been expected in time to fade from the scene. Joint sovereignty, after all, seemed the antithesis of the territorial state model. Yet contrary to expectations, the practice has continued in a number of signal instances, demonstrating that in reality some forms of condominium are not at all incompatible with the rules of today's sovereignty club. Recall Antarctica, for instance, where competing land claims by the United States and a number of other governments have been frozen for years. Instead, we have a de facto condominium governed by the twenty-nine Consultative Parties to the long-standing Antarctic Treaty. In Central America, the governments of El Salvador, Honduras, and Nicaragua exercise joint sovereignty over portions of the Gulf of Fonseca and nearby territorial waters. In the United States and Canada, versions of shared authority have been formalized in treaties with Native American tribes and Canada's First Nations. And in Northern Ireland under the terms of the Good Friday Agreement, Britain and the Republic of Ireland combine responsibility for keeping the peace between the still feuding Catholic and Protestant communities of Northern Ireland.

In fact, here too, as in disputes over the distribution of sovereign powers, an extensive menu of potential hybrid solutions can be imagined. Most are variations on one or the other of two basic models—what may be called either *combined* sovereignty or *divided* sovereignty.[2] In a regime of combined sovereignty, governance in a contested territory is exercised in *tandem* along the lines of the consociational arrangement laid down in the Good Friday Agreement. Two or more condominium powers agree on a fixed set of rules to exercise authority over a territory together. In a regime of divided sovereignty, by contrast, control is exercised in *parallel fashion* by means of a non-territorial separation of distinct ethnic or religious groups. Each minority community within a designated territory is authorized to govern itself

186   DREAM STATES

under its own customs and traditions. Self-rule may be strictly limited to "personal" matters such as marriage and divorce or may be more extensive, up to and including even the power to levy taxes.

An apt historical example of legally combined sovereignty was the Anglo-Egyptian Sudan, a British-Egyptian condominium that lasted from 1899 until 1956 when Sudan was granted independence. An apt example of divided sovereignty was the so-called *millet* system that long existed throughout the Ottoman Empire, authorizing independent courts of law ("millets") for each major religion under its rule. Each court enforced its own separate legal code—Muslim sharia, Christian canon law, Jewish halakha—for its own people wherever they were located within the frontiers of the empire.

Here too, of course, we find that most such solutions are treated as regrettable exceptions to prevailing norms—tolerated at best, rather than welcomed. And of course here too there is little assurance that separatist passions can be fully quenched by either model. Whether we are talking of combined sovereignty or divided sovereignty, the condominium approach cannot be expected to work well without some spirit of compromise and a minimum of good will. But again, it's a start.

A path forward

So magic is not needed after all. Once each of the twin imperatives is properly reconsidered, a workable path forward begins to emerge.

There is no foolproof solution, of course. But as an old adage suggests, we should not let the perfect be the enemy of the good. There is plenty of room to negotiate a constructive compromise if we keep our ambitions reasonably modest. Our goal is dual: to minimize, to the extent possible, the risk of disruptive conflict while at the same time not ignoring the interests of separatist minorities. Dream states need not provoke nightmarish combat. Disruptions can be contained, perhaps in many cases even deterred, if we satisfactorily address two central questions. First, what are (or should be) the rules of the game? And second, how can we assure that the rules will be properly implemented? The clearer we are in answering these two questions, the more likely it is that we can prevent smoldering hot spots from erupting into all-consuming infernos.

Rules of the game

The answer to the first question, by now, ought to be evident. The rules of the game need to be redefined to relax the strait jacket of binary choice. The aim should be to bring intermediate options in from the cold: to include power redistribution or sovereignty sharing as legitimate choices, not distasteful exceptions, in today's international system. Full-scale secession need not be treated as the only credible alternative to permanent sub-national status; nor should the idea of joint authority be considered acceptable only in the rarest of political circumstances. Statehood should be seen as a matter of degree, a continuous variable, rather than either/or.

The reason is plain to see. To insist on a strictly binary approach under all circumstances is to make the choice between imperatives far more challenging than it needs to be. Exclusion of intermediate options simply adds unnecessarily to the difficulty of averting stalemate or violent separatist conflict. Why risk triggering an armed rebellion so long as some calibrated measures of reform might hold out hope for a less disruptive outcome? Previously, I emphasized the fragility of daydreams, which could be likened to an "unstable equilibrium"—a delicate soap bubble that at any moment might pop, triggering the birth of a drexit or militant rebellion. Legitimization of a broader range of potential hybrid solutions reduces the risk that separatists will conclude that armed resistance is their only alternative. Intermediate options act like a solvent to reduce frictions.

And how can that legitimization be accomplished? Earlier chapters described how since the birth of the United Nations, our understanding of national sovereignty has been gradually refined by two kinds of action from the UN General Assembly. On the one hand, the Assembly plays a quasi-executive role in determining who gets to join the organization—thus functioning, in effect, as a de facto admissions committee for the global sovereignty club. At the same time, it also plays a quasi-legislative role through the sponsorship of a series of declarations and resolutions seeking to clarify finer points of conventional international law. Particularly influential was the Friendly Relations Declaration of 1970. As noted in the preceding chapter, that resolution was ostensibly intended to offer support for the waves of decolonization then in full swing in the Global South. With its notorious "saving clause," however, the statement also managed to reinforce a strictly dichotomous concept of statehood. Between the twin imperatives of

188   DREAM STATES

secession and deep territoriality, no intermediate option was contemplated by the declaration or even mentioned in passing.

A workable path to legitimization, therefore, could focus on effectively repealing the saving clause. Recall that the Friendly Relations Declaration reads as follows:

> Nothing in the foregoing paragraphs shall be construed as authorizing or encouraging any action which would dismember or impair, totally or in part, the territorial integrity or political unity of sovereign and independent states.

In plain English, this translates as: *No redistribution of sovereign powers and no joint sovereignty*. The choices are strictly binary. My proposal is that the saving clause should be revised to *authorize*, not prohibit, intermediate hybrid solutions, subject only to one important qualification: There must be no overt coercion. Any action shall be mutually agreed upon by the parties directly involved. Hence, a new declaration might read as follows (with emphasis supplied for the key revisions):

> Nothing in the foregoing paragraphs shall be construed as *preventing* any action which would, *by mutual agreement*, dismember or impair, totally or in part, the territorial integrity or political unity of sovereign and independent states.

With these seemingly small changes of wording, a major revolution could be wrought in the practice of state sovereignty. With luck, it might even significantly dim the lurking nightmare of separatist violence.

Implementation

Rules alone, however, will not suffice. In a Westphalian world, where each state is presumed to be entirely in control within its own borders, respect for international law is at best provisory—accepted when it happens to be convenient, defied when it does not. It would be naive to suggest otherwise. Hence the second question: What can be done to make effective implementation of the rules more likely? One hundred percent adherence is improbable, given the realities of world politics. But even a marginal shift toward less contested outcomes would surely make the game worth the candle.

Ideally, we need a global institution with specific responsibility for facing up to the disruptive challenge of secession. A title like "United Nations Agency for Dream States" (UNADS) might be a bit too fanciful but captures the spirit of the idea. At present, quite remarkably, the international system has no unit specifically designated to address separatism as a practical problem. In place of a watchful eye, there is a vacuum. That lack of institutional attention is evidence of just how underappreciated the lurking nightmare truly is. The vacuum is also potentially tragic given the ubiquity of secession movements: the multitude of brush fires that smolder around the world, primed to ignite into yet more armed combat. The sovereignty club's posture, typically, tends to be reactive rather than pro-active—intervening slowly, timidly, and only as a last resort. As one source laments, the UN "usually waits for a conflict to break out and then considers sending a peace-keeping mission to restore law and order."[3] We ought to be able to do better.

In practical terms, a UN Agency for Dream States would combine three functions: (1) certification; (2) mediation; and (3) surveillance. Successful execution of this trio of responsibilities would go a long way toward moderating the risk of prolonged and ever more costly conflicts.

(1) *Certification*. First, we need to know who merits attention. Which secession movements must be taken seriously? Many dream states are little more than fantasies or daydreams. The agency's first responsibility would be to certify who may be considered a genuinely legitimate applicant for membership in the sovereignty club.

One way to do this, some might think, would be simply to look to the roster of entities supported by the Unrepresented Nations and Peoples Organization (UNPO; which I first mentioned back in Chapter 1). UNPO was established in 1991 to help undergird the aspirations of marginalized peoples everywhere. Its formal goal is to promote self-determination for communities that are generally not represented diplomatically at the UN or in other major international institutions. Currently, its membership runs to some forty-four separatist movements claiming to represent more than 300 million people.

190 DREAM STATES

UNPO's roster, however, is an imperfect guide at best. Reliance on the organization's membership list would be *too* simple. On the one hand, the UNPO list includes entities whose credentials are, at a minimum, questionable. Is Brittany really anything more than a sentimental daydream? Does the District of Columbia, America's federal district, truly seek some form of separation from the United States? On the other hand, some key players are excluded, exposing critical gaps in coverage. Where, for example, is Quebec, one of the world's best known drexits? Or what about the Kurds, spread as they are across much of the Middle East? Perhaps most puzzling of all, why are there so many separatist movements that once belonged to UNPO but now are listed as "former members"? If any degree of accuracy is to be attained, a more systematic approach is needed.

A more reasonable approach, I submit, would be to build directly on the same four criteria that are typically used to define "statehood." We have seen how some variation of this quartet of standards is conventionally applied to produce what amounts to a census of the Westphalian world (Chapter 2). So why not make use of these same standards to produce a census of plausible applicants as well? As already noted, the four criteria are: (1) a defined territory; (2) a permanent population; (3) a government; and (4) a capacity to enter into relations with other states. The first responsibility of UNADS would be to certify which of the world's many separatist movements would seem to meet—or show realistic promise of being able to meet—at least some if not all of the four criteria. Certification would be reviewed regularly. New candidates would be added to the list once they appear to have crossed the threshold of acceptability. Older names might be dropped if their credentials seem to be waning.

Incumbent governments might object, of course. Certification of plausible applicants would seem to create a new class of international actors—entities that are less than wholly sovereign but more than mere assimilated subnationalisms. In fact, however, there is nothing new about this kind of hybrid, however anomalous it may seem. What might be called "demi-states" or "semi-sovereign states" have long been reluctantly tolerated in the Westphalian system as a convenient fudge to handle exceptionally awkward cases. At the United Nations, for example, we have the category of "permanent non-member observer," a designation currently applied to Palestine and the Vatican City. Though neither of these two entities is a full member of the global club, each enjoys at least some of the privileges of formal national sovereignty. And in East Asia we have Taiwan, long coveted by mainland

A MODEST PROPOSAL 191

China. Despite every effort by the People's Republic to limit Taiwanese autonomy, the island is welcomed in many international venues under the unique identity of "Chinese Taipei."

Analogously, in Europe, we see a special label for prospective new members of the European Union (EU) that has long been used as part of the bloc's procedure for expansion. The EU admission process begins when a government in the European neighborhood expresses an interest in joining. Once the applicant meets certain initial conditions, it becomes an "official candidate," permitting it to move on to formal membership negotiations. In effect, the applicant is certified as part of a special class of nations with one foot outside and one foot inside the EU—legitimate prospects but not yet full members. We might call them "demi-members." The negotiations themselves may take years, even decades, depending on how quickly candidates are able to satisfy the requirements of EU law (known as the *acquis communautaire*). And of course politics may also intervene. Some applicants, such as Poland or Hungary, had little difficulty getting through the process once the Cold War ended. Turkey, on the other hand, formally applied in 1987 and still is nowhere near acceptance as a full member.

Another analogy can also be seen in the North Atlantic Treaty Organization, where for many years any country applying for membership has been obliged first to fulfill an elaborate Membership Action Plan. These states too might be called "demi-members," half in the alliance and half not yet.

In short, with their taste for obfuscation, diplomats have little difficulty in coming up with new class titles when needed. So why not one more category for credible dream states?

(2) *Mediation*. Once credible dream states have been certified, the next step is—or should be—negotiation. Can an incumbent government and representatives of a certified secession movement be persuaded to sit down together to talk peaceably about their mutual future? That would be the second responsibility of UNADS. The agency would act as a mediator: a neutral intermediary doing all it can to promote and facilitate productive bargaining by the two sides. UNADS would provide an appropriate venue for talks and handle all related logistics. It should also be prepared to chair discussions and offer useful compromise proposals when needed. And at all times, it should endeavor to remind the parties involved how much the rules of the game have evolved to relax the strait jacket of binary choice.

192 DREAM STATES

Most importantly, UNADS should seek to make the negotiation agenda clear. At stake, ultimately, are the four R's that were first highlighted back in Chapter 5: reconciliation, repression, reform, and rebellion. If separatists cannot be convinced to reconcile themselves to a permanent sub-national status, every effort must be made to avoid provoking either repression by the incumbent national government or armed rebellion by secessionists. Coercion of any sort must be discouraged. The role of UNADS would be to keep everyone's eye on the ball: to keep the focus on reforms that might help to stabilize the unstable equilibrium. Can reconciliation be promoted by promises of greater political or economic autonomy? Can repression be deterred by assurances of a genuine openness to compromise? Can rebellion be forestalled before all patience is lost?

Even with the best of intentions, of course, mediation ultimately might fail to prevent an eruption of destructive violence. But as I have said before, it's surely worth a try.

(3) *Surveillance.* Finally, UNADS would be responsible for keeping an eye on the involved parties over time. Once an agreement of some kind emerges from the negotiation process, systematic surveillance may be needed for years to come to ensure that there is no back-sliding or betrayal by one side or the other. UNADS might be authorized to monitor ongoing developments or engage in periodic inspections in order to ensure a suitable degree of compliance all round. The agency might even be charged to produce an annual report evaluating the performance of both incumbent governments and their separatist counterparts. On such delicate matters as sovereignty and territory, accords—however well-intentioned—cannot be expected to fly on autopilot alone. As Ronald Reagan was wont to say back in the 1980s when negotiating with the Soviet Union (which he called the Evil Empire): Trust but verify!

No miracle cure

Needless to say, my modest proposal is just that: modest. New rules together with a new agency do not add up to a miracle cure. In place of mutual trust, both sides might just dig in their heels. Incumbent governments may stubbornly resist any redistribution or sharing of powers; separatists may be unwilling to settle for anything less than full sovereignty and territorial control. But at what price? The lurking nightmare is real. The number of dream states is large and growing, and separatist violence is on the rise with no end in sight. Are we doomed to endure a future of ever more—and more costly—wars of secession? Many lives hang in the balance.

Notes

Chapter 1

1. The term "dream state" is my invention. There is no standardized terminology in the formal academic literature, which refers variously to "contested states," "de facto states," "para-states," "proto-states," "pseudo-states," "quasi-states," or "unrecognized states." For useful overviews, see e.g., Pegg 2019; Florea 2020; Kursani 2021; Blakkisrud 2023. One journalist has popularized the term "shadowlands" (Winn 2018).
2. Fazal and Griffiths 2014: 82.
3. Radan 2023.
4. Griffiths 2016.
5. Griffiths 2021: 14.
6. Beary 2008.
7. Griffiths 2021: 2.
8. See e.g., Gurr 2000; Walter 2006; Coggins 2011; Fazal and Griffiths 2014; Griffiths 2016; Muro 2023.
9. Fazal 2007: 3.
10. Clark et al. 2019: 587.
11. Horowitz 2003: 73.
12. Altman 2020.
13. Zacher 2001.
14. Carter and Goemans 2011, 2014.
15. Fearon and Laitin 2003; Sorens 2012.
16. Walter 2009: 3.
17. Buchanan 1997: 301.
18. Sauerbrey 2022.
19. Griffiths 2016: 4.
20. *The Economist* 2023e.
21. Griffiths 2021.
22. Agnew 1994b: 89.
23. Washington 2023: 197.
24. Anderson 1983.
25. Harmelink 1972.
26. Anderson 1983: 6.
27. Rosenberg 1994: 99, 103.
28. Agnew 1994a.
29. Krasner 1993: 260.
30. Anderson 1983: 3.
31. Griffiths 2021.
32. Jackson and Rosberg 1982.
33. Weber 1972: 1.
34. Krasner 1999: 9.
35. Walter 2006; Griffiths 2021.
36. Giffiths 2010.

Chapter 2

1. Russett, Singer, and Small 1968.
2. The COW project's latest estimates date to 2016. See www.correlatesofwar.org/data-sets.
3. See e.g., Gleditsch and Ward 1999; Bremer and Ghosn 2003; Coggins 2011; Griffiths and Butcher 2013; Schvitz et al. 2021.
4. Griffiths 2016: 1.

NOTES 195

5. Weber 1972: 1.
6. Jackson and Rosberg 1982.
7. Jackson and Rosberg 1982.
8. Carley 1996; Bremer and Ghosn 2003.
9. Schvitz et al. 2021: 154.
10. Lake and O'Mahony 2004.
11. See e.g., Bolton and Roland 1997; Alesina and Spolaore 1997, 2003; Hiscox 2003; Lake and O'Mahony 2004.
12. Eisenberg and Spinner-Halev 2005.
13. Boutros-Ghali 1992: 9.
14. Schaeffer 2008: 1891.
15. Gellner 1983/2006: 43.
16. Griffiths 2021: 16.

Chapter 3

1. Anderson 2004a: 101–102.
2. Sunstein 1991; Anderson 2004b; Brandon 2014; Read 2014.
3. Pogue 2022.
4. Abramsky 2023: 17.
5. Sotille 2018.
6. Corbin 2023; Baker and Swift 2023.
7. Southern Poverty Law Center 2022.
8. Naylor 2008.
9. For a comprehensive listing, see Erwin 2007.
10. Kreitner 2020.
11. Pew Research Center 2010.
12. CBS News 2013.
13. Zogby 2017.
14. Pelaez 2020.
15. Barnes 2021.
16. Hall 2022.
17. Dicamillo 2017.
18. Chan et al. 2022.
19. Sharlet 2023: *ix, xi.*
20. Sharlet 2023.
21. Lepore 2023.
22. Chemerinsky 2024: *xiii.*
23. Lepore 2023.
24. Baker 2017.
25. Priscilla Southwell, a professor emerita of political science at the University of Oregon, as quoted by Miles Baker 2023.
26. See e.g., Marche 2022; Simon and Stevenson 2022; Walter 2022.
27. As quoted by Wallace-Wells 2024.
28. Darrell West, as quoted in Hall 2022.
29. Blight 2022; Chemerinsky 2024.
30. Buckley 2020: 17–18.
31. Buckley 2020: 18.
32. Naylor and Willimon 1997: 25–26.
33. Kreitner 2020: 374.
34. Ricks 2017.
35. Wright 2017.
36. Baker 2017.
37. As quoted in Bouie 2023.
38. Gordon 1998.

Chapter 4

1. See e.g., Ryan et al. 2006.
2. Ceceri and Thompson 2014; Baek 2020.

196   NOTES

3. https://www.imdb.com/title/tt0475195/
4. *The Economist* 2021a.
5. Rosa 2020.
6. *The Economist* 2021b.
7. https://www.imdb.com/title/tt10287954/
8. www.nme.com/reviews/film-reviews/rose-island-review-netflix-sydney-sibilia-2835832
9. Wibberley 1955.
10. https://www.imdb.com/title/tt0053084
11. http://www.quatloos.com/groups/melchiz.htm
12. *The Washington Post* 1995.
13. Sinclair 2004.
14. Sinclair 2004: 26.

Chapter 5

1. Baldwin 1956.
2. Cohen 2021.
3. Sambanis and Siroky 2023.
4. Kidd 2003.
5. What Scotland Thinks (https://whatscotlandthinks.org/opinion-polls). Last retrieved: August 13, 2022. The precise shares were 58 percent in December 2014 and 62 percent in March 2015.
6. YouGov (https://yougov.co.uk/topics/politics/explore/issue/Welshpolitics). Last retrieved: August 13, 2022.
7. BBC (http://news.bbc.co.uk/1/hi/wales/3527673.stm). Last retrieved: August 13, 2022.
8. The Local (http://www.thelocal.fr/20130192/brittany). Last retrieved August 13, 2022.
9. "Falls Around Her" (2018), Samuel Goldwyn Films, Darlene Naponse Director.
10. Futterman 2023.
11. Boutros-Ghali 1992: 9. Previously cited in Chapter 2.

Chapter 6

1. *The Economist* 2022b.
2. *The Economist* 2023d.
3. Massie 2023.
4. Castle 2023.
5. *The Economist* 2023b.
6. As quoted in Frost 2024.

Chapter 7

1. https://www.imdb.com/title/tt0048545.
2. Beary 2008: 87.
3. Griffiths 2021: 14.
4. "List of Wars of Independence," Wikipedia. Last retrieved: October 2, 2022.
5. Florea 2020: 1016.
6. As quoted in *The Economist* 2024.
7. Ong 2023.

Chapter 8

1. Beary 2008: 97.
2. Toal 2017: 58.
3. Rich 2024.
4. As quoted in Nechepurenko 2023.
5. Schmidt 2014.

Chapter 9

1. *The Economist* 2022c.
2. Dworkin 2022.
3. Lijphart 2004.
4. Hogg 2023.

NOTES   197

5. Winn 2024.
6. *The Economist* 2023a.
7. Mergo and Kejela 2021.

Chapter 10

1. Netanyahu 2022.
2. *The Economist* 2022a.
3. *The Economist* 2023c.
4. Election Study Centre, National Chengchi University.
5. Cohen 1998.
6. Srinivasan 2022.

Chapter 11

1. The full list of formal federal states is as follows: Argentina, Australia, Austria, Belgium, Bosnia, Brazil, Canada, Comoros, Cyprus, Ethiopia, Germany, India, Malaysia, Mexico, Micronesia, Nepal, Nigeria, Pakistan, Russia, Saint Kitts and Nevis, South Africa, Spain, Switzerland, United Arab Emirates, and United States of America.

Chapter 12

1. Gudkov 2021.
2. Coffey 2022; Kuzio 2022; Sussex 2022; Fix and Kimmage 2023.
3. Friedman 2023a.
4. Gall 2023.
5. MacFarquhar 2023.
6. Baker and Swift 2023.
7. See *Wikipedia*, "Dissolution of Russia."
8. Putin 2011.
9. Abbas Gallyamov, as quoted by Kurmanaev 2024.
10. Fix and Kimmage 2023.
11. Fandom.com 2022.
12. Leon Aron, as quoted by Friedman 2023b.
13. Ostrovsky 2022.
14. Coffey 2022: 3.
15. Fix and Kimmage 2023: 11–12.

Chapter 13

1. Griffiths 2016: 162.
2. As quoted in Bartkus 1999: 58.
3. Griffiths 2016: 170.
4. Kohli 1997; Griffiths 2016.
5. Yasir and Raj 2023.
6. Austen and Isai 2023.
7. Mashal 2023.
8. As quoted by Raj et al. 2023.
9. *The Hindu* 2010.
10. Chowdhury 2023.
11. Nanda 2023.
12. Cohen 2000.
13. Raj 2023.
14. As quoted in The *New York Times* 2023.
15. Mashal et al. 2023.
16. Chowdhury 2023.

Chapter 14

1. Waters 2023: 123.
2. Zacher 2001.
3. Horowitz 2003; Radan 2023.

198 NOTES

4. Carley 1996; Beary 2008.
5. Anderson 2023.
6. Radan 2023: 31.
7. Kartsonaki 2023: 192–193; Waters 2023: 123–124.
8. The full title was "Declaration on Principles of International Law Concerning Friendly Relations and Co-Operation Among States in Accordance with the Charter of the United Nations."
9. United Nations General Assembly 1970: Principle 5, paragraph 1.
10. United Nations General Assembly 1970: Principle 5, paragraph 7.
11. Gellner 1983/2006: 43.
12. Nicholson 2023.
13. Carley 1996: 8.
14. Abulof 2023: 26.
15. Anderson 2023.
16. The observer was Graham Fuller of the RAND Corporation, as quoted by Carley 1996: 9.

Chapter 15

1. Krasner 1999.
2. Wolff 2002.
3. Beary 2008: 92.

References

Abulhof, Uriel (2023), "The Emergence and Evolution of Self-Determination," in Ryan D. Griffiths, Aleksandar Pavković, and Peter Radan, eds., *The Routledge Handbook of Self-Determination and Secession* (London and New York: Routledge), 16–29.

Abramsky, Sasha (2023), "The Takeover," *The Nation*, June 12/19, 16–23.

Agnew, John A. (1994a), "The Territorial Trap: The Geographical Assumptions of International Relations Theory," *Review of International Political Economy* 1:1, 53–80.

Agnew, John A. (1994b), "Timeless Space and State-Centrism: The Geographical Assumptions of International Relations Theory," in Stephen J. Rosow, Naeem Inayatullah, and Mark Rupert, eds., *The Global Economy as Political Space* (Boulder, CO: Lynne Reinner), ch. 4.

Alesina, Alberto and Enrico Spolaore (1997), "On the Number and Size of Nations," *Quarterly Journal of Economics* 112:4, 1027–1056.

Alesina, Alberto and Enrico Spolaore (2003), *The Size of Nations* (Cambridge, MA: MIT Press).

Altman, Dan (2020), "The Evolution of Territorial Conquest After 1945 and the Limits of the Territorial Integrity Norm," *International Organization* 74:3, 490–522.

Anderson, Benedict (1983), *Imagined Communities: Reflections on the Origin and Spread of Nationalism* (London: Verso).

Anderson, Glen (2023), "Who Are the 'Peoples' Entitled to the Right of Self-Determination?," in Ryan D. Griffiths, Aleksandar Pavković, and Peter Radan, eds., *The Routledge Handbook of Self-Determination and Secession* (London and New York: Routledge), 41–59.

Anderson, Lawrence M. (2004a), "Exploring the Paradox of Autonomy: Federalism and Secession in North America," *Regional and Federal Studies* 14:1, 89–112.

Anderson, Lawrence M. (2004b), "The Institutional Basis of Secessionist Politics: Federalism and Secession in the United States," *Publius: The Journal of Federalism* 34:2, 1–18.

Austen, Ian and Vjosa Isai (2023), "Justin Trudeau Accuses India of a Killing on Canadian Soil," *The New York Times*, September 18.

Baek, Wyatt S. (2020), *Create Your Own Micronation: Grow Your Nation Fast, Get Noticed, and Build Active Citizens* (Las Vegas, NV: self-published).

Baker, Kevin (2017), "It's Time for a Bluexit: A Declaration of Independence from Trump's America," *The New Republic*, March 9.

Baker, Mike (2023), "A Small Boat, a Vast Sea and a Desperate Escape from Russia," *The New York Times*, January 29.

Baker, Miles (2023), "In a Year of Capitol Feuds, Oregon Has a Political Breakdown," *The New York Times*, June 4.

REFERENCES

Baker, Miles and Hilary Swift (2023), "Oregon's Rural-Urban Divide Sparks Talk of Secession," *The New York Times*, March 18.

Baldwin, James (1956), *Giovanni's Room* (New York: Vintage Books).

Barnes, Adam (2021), "Shocking Poll Finds Many Americans Now Want to Secede from the United States," *The Hill*, July 15, https://thehill.com/changing-america/enrichment/arts-culture/563221-shocking-poll-finds-many-americans-now-want-to/. Last retrieved May 18, 2023.

Bartkus, V.O. (1999), *The Dynamics of Secession* (New York: Cambridge University Press).

Beary, Brian (2008), "Separatist Movements: Should Nations Have a Right to Self-Determination?," *CQ Global Researcher* 2:4, 85–114.

Blakkisrud, Helge (2023), "Surviving Without Recognition: De Facto States," in Ryan D. Griffiths, Aleksandar Pavković, and Peter Radan, eds., *The Routledge Handbook of Self-Determination and Secession* (New York: Routledge), 343–358.

Blight, David W. (2022), "The Irrepressible Conflict," *The New York Times Magazine*, December 25.

Bolton, Patrick and Gerard Roland (1997), "The Breakup of Nations: A Political Economy Analysis," *Quarterly Journal of Economics* 112:4, 1057–1090.

Bouie, Jamelle (2023), "Marjorie Taylor Greene Has a Dream," *The New York Times*, February 24.

Brandon, Mark E. (2014), "Secession and Nullification in the Twenty-first Century," *Arkansas Law Review* 67, 91–102.

Boutros-Ghali, Boutros (1992), *An Agenda for Peace: Preventive Diplomacy, Peacemaking, and Peacekeeping* (New York: United Nations).

Bremer, Stuart A. and Faten Ghosn (2003), "Defining States: Reconsiderations and Recommendations," *Conflict Management and Peace Science* 20:1, 21–41.

Buchanan, Allan (1997), "Self-Determination, Secession, and the Rule of Law," in Robert McKim and Jeff McMahan, eds., *The Morality of Nationalism* (Oxford: Oxford University Press).

Buckley, F.H. (2020), *American Secession: The Looming Threat of a National Breakup* (New York: Encounter Books).

Carley, Patricia (1996), *Self-Determination: Sovereignty, Territorial Integrity, and the Right of Secession* (Washington, DC: United States Institute of Peace).

Carter, David B. and H.E. Goemans (2011), "The Making of the Territorial Order: New Borders and the Emergence of Interstate Conflict," *International Organization* 65:2, 275–309.

Carter, David B. and H.E. Goemans (2014), "The Temporal Dynamics of New International Borders," *Conflict Management and Peace Science* 31:3, 285–302.

Castle, Stephen (2023), "Will U.K. Rejection of Scottish Gender Bill Bolster Independence Movement?," *The New York Times*, January 26.

CBS News (2013), CBS News Poll, Question 5, October.

Ceceri, Kathy and Chad Thompson (2014), *Micronatons: Invent Your Own Country and Culture* (White River Junction, VT: Nomad Press).

Chan, Sewell, Aneri Pattani, and Matthew Watkins (2022), "No, Texas Can't Legally Secede from the U.S., Despite Popular Myths," *Texas Tribune*, June 20, https://www. texastribune.org/2021/01//29/texas-secession/. Last retrieved June 6, 2023.

Chemerinsky, Erwin (2024), *No Democracy Lasts Forever: How the Constitution Threatens the United States* (New York: Liveright).

Chowdhury, Debasish R. (2023), "India Is on the Brink," *The New York Times*, August 9.

Clark, Cory J., Brittany S. Liu, Bo M. Winegard, and Peter H. Ditto (2019), "Tribalism is Human Nature," *Current Directions in Psychological Science* 28:6, 587–592.

Coffey, Luke (2022), "*Preparing for the Final Collapse of the Soviet Union and the Dissolution of the Russian Federation,*" Policy Memo (Washington, DC: Hudson Institute).

Coggins, Bridget (2011), "Friends in High Places: International Politics and the Emergence of States from Secessionism," *International Organization* 65:4, 433–467.

Cohen, Benjamin J. (1998), *The Geography of Money* (Ithaca, NY: Cornell University Press).

Cohen, Benjamin J. (2021), *Lucky Jerry: The Life of a Political Economist* (Bloomington, IN: Archway Publishing).

Cohen, Stephen P. (2000), "India Rising." brookings.edu/articles/india-rising. Last retrieved February 14, 2023.

Corbin, Clark (2023), "Idaho House Passes Nonbinding Measure Calling for Formal 'Greater Idaho' talks," *Idaho Capital Sun*, February 15.

DiCamillo, Mark (2017), "Berkeley IGS Poll," Release No. 2017-01, March 28, https:// www.mercurynews.com/wp-content/uploads/2017/03/2017_01-trump-1-11.pdf. Last retrieved May 18, 2023.

Dworkin, Anthony (2022), "*North Africa Standoff: How the Western Sahara Conflict is Fueling New Tensions Between Morocco and Algeria,*" Policy Brief (Berlin: European Council on Foreign Relations).

The Economist (2021a), "No Me Pises: Argentina's Libertarians," October 9.

The Economist (2021b), "A Stop in the Ocean," December 4.

The Economist (2022a), "Balkan Barricades," December 24.

The Economist (2022b), "Isolated But Not Independent," October 8.

The Economist (2022c), "The Sands They Are A-Swirling," March 26.

The Economist (2023a), "Asia's Multi-Headed Conflict," February 4.

The Economist (2023b), "Briefing: Europe's Hard Right," September 16.

The Economist (2023c), "Frontline Formosa," Special Report, March 11.

The Economist (2023d), "A Straw in the Wind," September 2.

The Economist (2023e), "Why Are Civil Wars Lasting Longer?," April 22.

The Economist (2024), "Nagorno-Karabakh, the Republic that Disappeared Overnight," January 1.

Eisenberg, Avigail and Jeff Spinner-Halev, eds. (2005), *Minorities Within Minorities: Equality, Rights and Diversity* (New York: Cambridge University Press).

Erwin, James L. (2007), *Declarations of Independence: Encyclopedia of American Autonomous and Secessionist Movements* (Westport, CN: Greenwood Press).

202 REFERENCES

Fandom.com (2022), "Dissolution of the Russian Federation." second-renaissance.fandom.com/wiki/dissolution_of_the_Russian_federation. Last retrieved January 17, 2023.

Fazal, Tanisha M. (2007), *State Death: The Politics and Geography of Conquest, Occupation, and Annexation* (Princeton, NJ: Princeton University Press).

Fazal, Tanisha M. and Ryan D. Griffiths (2014), "Membership Has Its Privileges: The Changing Benefits of Statehood," *International Studies Review* 16:1, 79–106.

Fearon, James and David Laitin (2003), "Ethnicity, Insurgency, and Civil War," *American Political Science Review* 97:1, 75–90.

Fix, Liana and Michael Kimmage (2023), "Putin's Last Stand: The Promise and Peril of Russian Defeat," *Foreign Affairs* 102:1, 8–21.

Florea, Adrian (2020), "Rebel Governance in De Facto States," *European Journal of International Relations* 26:4, 1004–1031.

Friedman, Thomas L. (2023a), "Putin, Prigozhin and the Danger of Disorder," *The New York Times*, June 27.

Friedman, Thomas L. (2023b), "Vladimir Putin is the World's Most Dangerous Fool," *The New York Times*, May 9.

Frost, Natasha (2024), "Dozens Killed after Gunfight in Papua New Guinea," *The New York Times*, February 18.

Futterman, Matthew (2023), "An Indigenous Olympic Lacrosse Team Push Gets a Boost from Biden," *The New York Times*, December 6.

Gall, Carlotta (2023), "Now Fighting for Ukraine: Volunteers Seeking Revenge Against Russia," *The New York Times*, January 8.

Gellner, Ernst (1983/2006), *Nations and Nationalism*, second edition (Ithaca, NY: Cornell University Press).

Gleditsch, Kristian S. and Michael D. Ward (1999), "A Revised List of Independent States Since the Congress of Vienna," *International Interactions* 25:4, 393–413.

Gordon, David, ed. (1998), *Secession, State, and Liberty* (New Brunswick, NJ: Transaction Publishers).

Griffiths, Ryan D. (2010), "Security Threats, Linguistic Homogeneity, and the Necessary Conditions for Political Unification," *Nations and Nationalism* 16:1, 169–188.

Griffiths, Ryan D. (2016), *Age of Secession: The International and Domestic Determinants of State Birth* (Cambridge: Cambridge University Press).

Griffiths, Ryan D. (2021), *Secession and the Sovereignty Game: Strategy and Tactics for Aspiring Nations* (Ithaca, NY: Cornell University Press).

Griffiths, Ryan D. and Charles R. Butcher (2013), "Introducing the International System(s) Dataset (ISD), 1816-2011," *International Interactions* 39:5, 748–768.

Gudkov, Lev (2021), "The Unity of the Empire in Russia is Maintained by Three Institutions: The School, the Army, and the Police," interview, December 26, https://www.levada.ru/en/2021/05/12/lev-gudkov-the-unity-of-the-empire-in-russia-is-maintained-by-three-institutions-the-school-the-army-and-the-police/. Last retrieved February 23, 2023.

Gurr, Ted Robert (2000), *People Versus States: Minorities at Risk in the New Century* (Washington, DC: US Institute of Peace).

Hall, Richard (2022), "Texas Republicans Want to Secede from the United States. Could They Do It?," *The Independent*, June 20, https://www.independent.co.uk/news/world/americas/us-politics/texas-secession-republicans-donald-trump-b2105461.html. Last retrieved May 19, 2023.

Harmelink, Herman (1972), letter to *The New York Times*, January 12.

The Hindu (2010), "Naxalism Biggest Threat to Internal Security: Manmohan," May 24, https://www.thehindu.com/news/national/Naxalism-biggest-threat-to-internal-security-Manmohan/article16302952.ece. Last retrieved February 5, 2023.

Hiscox, Michael J. (2003), "Political Integration and Disintegration in the Global Economy," in Miles Kahler and David A. Lake, eds., *Governance in a Global Economy: Political Authority in Transition* (Princeton, NJ: Princeton University Press), 60–86.

Hogg, Clare Dwyer (2023), "Northern Ireland is Far Too Quiet," *The New York Times*, April 9. Ms. Hogg is a playwright and poet.

Horowitz, Donald L. (2003), "A Right to Secede?," in Stephen Macedo and Allen Buchanan, eds., *Secession and Self-Determination: Nomos XLV* (New York: New York University Press), 50–76.

Jackson, Robert H. and Carl G. Rosberg (1982), "Why Africa's Weak States Persist: The Empirical and the Juridical in Statehood," *World Politics* 82:1, 1–24.

Kartsonaki, Argyro (2023), "Debating the Right to Secede: Normative Theories of Secession," in Ryan D. Griffiths, Aleksandar Pavković, and Peter Radan, eds., *The Routledge Handbook of Self-Determination and Secession* (London and New York: Routledge), 191–204.

Kidd, Colin (2003), *Subverting Scotland's Past: Scottish Whig Historians and the Creation of an Anglo-British Identity, 1689-1830* (Cambridge: Cambridge University Press).

Kohli, A. (1997), "Can Democracies Accommodate Ethnic Nationalism? Rise and Decline of Self-Determination Movements in India," *Journal of Asian Studies* 56:2, 325–344.

Krasner, Stephen D. (1993), "Westphalia and All That," in Judith D. Goldstein and Robert O. Keohane, eds., *Ideas and Foreign Policy: Beliefs, Institutions, and Political Change* (Ithaca, NY: Cornell University Press), 235–264.

Krasner, Stephen D. (1999), *Sovereignty: Organized Hypocrisy* (Princeton: Princeton University Press).

Kreitner, Richard (2020), *Break It Up: Secession, Division, and the Secret History of America's Imperfect Union* (New York: Little, Brown).

Kurmanaev, Anatoly (2024), "Protests in Russia Put Spotlight on Wartime Ethnic Grievances," *The New York Times*, January 18.

Kursani, Shpend (2021), "Reconsidering the Contested State in Post-1945 International Relations: An Ontological Approach," *International Studies Review* 23:3, 752–777.

Kuzio, Taras (2022), "Putin's Russian Empire Is Collapsing Like Its Soviet Predecessor, *Ukraine Alert*, September 17, atlanticcouncil.org/blogs/ukrainealert/putins-russian-empire-is-collapsing-like-its-soviet-predecessor. Last retrieved January 17, 2023.

Lake, David A. and Angela O'Mahony (2014), "The Incredible Shrinking State: Explaining Change in the Territorial Size of Countries," *Journal of Conflict Resolution* 48:5, 699–722.

204 REFERENCES

Lepore, Jill (2023), "How to Stave Off Constitutional Extinction," *The New York Times*, July 1.

Lijphart, Arend (2004), "Constitutional Design for Divided Societies," *Journal of Democracy* 15:2, 96–109.

MacFarquhar, Neil (2023), "They Refused to Fight for Russia. The Law Did Not Treat Them Kindly," *The New York Times*, April 30.

Marche, Stephen (2022), *The Next Civil War: Dispatches from the American Future* (New York: Avid Reader Press).

Mashal, Mujib (2023), "India Faces Questions about Another Reported Foreign Assassination Plot," *The New York Times*, November 23.

Mashal, Mujib, Hari Kumar, and Sameer Yasir (2023), "Killing on Live TV Renews Alarm about India's Slide Toward Extrajudicial Violence," *The New York Times*, April 17.

Massie, Alex (2023), "For Scotland, Leaving Will Always Be an Option," *The New York Times*, August 7.

Mergo, Teferi and Kebene Kejela (2021), "Ethiopia's Breakup Doesn't Have to Be Violent." www.foreignpolicy.com/2021/11/27. Last retrieved November 24, 2021.

Muro, Diego (2023), "The Causes of Secession," in Ryan D. Griffiths, Aleksandar Pavković, and Peter Radan, eds., *The Routledge Handbook of Self-Determination and Secession* (New York: Routledge), 133–145.

Nanda, Showkat (2023), "India is Arming Villagers in one of Earth's Most Militarized Places," *The New York Times*, March 8.

Naylor, Thomas H. (2008), *Secession: How Vermont and All the Other States Can Save Themselves from the Empire* (Port Townsend, WA: Feral House).

Naylor, Thomas H. and William H. Willimon (1997), *Downsizing the U.S.A.* (Grand Rapids, MI: William B. Eerdmans Publishing).

Nechepurenko, Ivan (2023), "Refugees Flee to Armenia as Breakaway Enclave Comes Under Azerbaijan's Control," *The New York Times*, September 24.

Netanyahu, Benjamin (2022), *Bibi: My Story* (New York: Simon and Schuster).

The New York Times (2023), "India's Proud Tradition of a Free Press Is at Risk," editorial, February 12.

Nicholson, Rowan (2023), "The Meaning of Self-Determination," in Ryan D. Griffiths, Aleksandar Pavković and Peter Radan, eds., *The Routledge Handbook of Self-Determination and Secession* (London and New York: Routledge), 3–15.

Ong, Andrew (2023), *Stalemate: Autonomy and Insurgency on the China-Myanmar Border* (Ithaca, NY: Cornell University Press).

Ostrovsky, Arkady (2022), "What Next for Russia?," in "The World Ahead 2023," *The Economist*, supplement, December.

Pegg, Scott (2019), *International Society and the De Facto State* (London: Routledge). First published in 1998 (Ashgate).

Pelaez, Robert (2020), "Hofstra Poll Shows 40 Percent of Likely Voters Would Favor State Secession Depending on Election Results," *The Island Now*, September 30.

Pew Research Center (2010), "Poll: Trust in Government," Question 90.

Pogue, James (2022), "Notes on the State of Jefferson," *Harper's*, April.

REFERENCES 205

Putin, Vladimir (2011), "Separation of the Caucasus from Russia Will Lead to the Collapse of the Country" (in Russian). Archived from the original. https://rg.ru/2011/12/20/reg-skfo/gudermes-anons.html. Last retrieved January 14, 2023.

Radan, Peter (2023), "The Meaning of Secession," in Ryan D. Griffiths, Aleksandar Pavković and Peter Radan, eds., *The Routledge Handbook of Self-Determination and Secession* (London and New York: Routledge), 30–38.

Raj, Suhasini (2023), "New Indian Textbooks Purged of Muslim History and Hindu Extremism," *The New York Times*, April 6.

Raj, Suhasini, Mujib Mashal, and Hari Kumar (2023), "Sikh Separatism is a Nonissue in India, Except as a Political Boogeyman," *The New York Times*, September 28.

Read, James H. (2014), "Changing the Rules, Leaving the Game: Nullification, Secession, and the American Future," *Arkansas Law Review* 67, 103–112.

Rich, Motoko (2024), "A Russian Bank Account May Offer Clues to a North Korean Arms Deal," *The New York Times*, February 6.

Ricks, Thomas E. (2017), "Will We Have a 2nd Civil War?," *Foreign Policy*, March 7, https://foreignpolicy.com/2017/03/07/will-we-have-a-2ndcivil-war-youtell-me. Last retrieved May 22, 2023.

Rosa, Giorgio (2020), *Rose Island: The Real Story of a Utopian Micronation* (Bologna: Casa Editrice Persiani).

Rosenberg, Justin (1994), "The International Imagination: IR Theory and 'Classic Social Analysis,'" *Millennium: Journal of International Studies* 23:1, 85–108.

Russett, Bruce M., J. David Singer, and Melvin Small (1968), "National Political Units in the Twentieth Century: A Standardized List," *American Political Science Review* 62:3, 932–951.

Ryan, John, George Dunford, and Simon Sellars (2006), *Micronations: The Lonely Planet Guide to Home-Made Nations* (Oakland, CA: Lonely Planet Publications).

Sambanis, Nicholas and David S. Siroky (2023), "The Lifecycle of Secession: Interactions, Processes, and Predictions," in Ryan D. Griffiths, Aleksandar Pavković, and Peter Radan, eds., *The Routledge Handbook of Self-Determination and Secession* (London and New York: Routledge), 146–163.

Sauerbrey, Anna (2022), "This was the Year that Everything Changed in Germany," *The New York Times*, December 25.

Schaeffer, Robert K. (2008), "Secession and Separatism," in Lester Kurtz, ed., *Encyclopedia of Violence, Peace, and Conflict*, second edition (Cambridge, MA: Academic Press), 1887–1892.

Schmidt, Helmut (2014), "Wir Schlafwandler" (We Sleepwalkers), Die Zeit, October 9.

Schvitz, Guy, Luc Girardin, Seraina Rüegger, Nils B. Weidmann, Lars-Erik Cederman, and Kristian S. Gleditsch (2021), "Mapping the International System, 1886-2019: The CShapes 2.0 Dataset," *Journal of Conflict Resolution* 66:1, 144–161.

Sharlet, Jeff (2023), *The Undertow: Scenes from a Slow Civil War* (New York: Norton).

Simon, Steven and Jonathan Stevenson (2022), "These Disunited States," *New York Review of Books*, September 22, 51–54.

Sinclair, David (2004), *The Land That Never Was: Sir Gregor MacGregor and the Most Audacious Fraud in History* (Boston: Da Capo Press).

206 REFERENCES

Sorens, Jason (2012), *Secessionism: Identity, Interest, and Strategy* (Montreal: McGill-Queen's University Press).

Sotille, Leah (2018), "Something's Brewing in the Deep Red West," *Rolling Stone*, October 23.

Southern Poverty Law Center (2022), "Neo-Confederate." https://www.splcenter.org/fighting-hate/extremist-files/ideology/neo-confederate. Last retrieved May 16, 2023.

Srinivasan, Balaji (2022), *The Network State*. thenetworkstate.com/kindle.gif. Last retrieved November 5, 2024.

Sunstein, Cass R. (1991), "Constitutionalism and Secession," *University of Chicago Law Review* 58, 633–670.

Sussex, Matthew (2022), "Could Russia Collapse?," *The Conversation*. theconversation.com/could-russia-collapse193013. Last retrieved January 17, 2023.

Radan, Peter (2023), "The Meaning of Secession," in Ryan D. Griffiths, Aleksandar Pavković, and Peter Radan, eds., *The Routledge Handbook of Self-Determination and Secession* (New York: Routledge), 30–38.

Toal, Gerard (2017), *Near Abroad: Putin, the West and the Contest over Ukraine and the Caucasus* (New York: Oxford University Press).

United Nations General Assembly (1970), *Declaration on Principles of International Law Concerning Friendly Relations and Co-Operation Among States in Accordance with the Charter of the United Nations*, Resolution 2625, October 24.

Wallace-Wells (2024), "How Trump Captured Iowa's Religious Right," *The New Yorker*, January 7.

Walter, Barbara F. (2006), "Information, Uncertainty, and the Decision to Secede," *International Organization* 60:1, 105–135.

Walter, Barbara F. (2009), *Reputation and Civil War* (Cambridge: Cambridge University Press).

Walter, Barbara F. (2022), *How Civil Wars Start: And How to Stop Them* (New York: Crown).

Washington, John (2023), *The Case for Open Borders* (Chicago: Haymarket Books).

The Washington Post (1995), "The Ruse That Roared," November 5.

Waters, Timothy W. (2023), "The Map Makes the People: The Territorial Nature of Self-Determination," in Ryan D. Griffiths, Aleksandar Pavković, and Peter Radan, eds., *The Routledge Handbook of Self-Determination and Secession* (London and New York: Routledge), 117–130.

Wibberley, Leonard (1955), *The Mouse That Roared* (Boston: Little, Brown).

Winn, Patrick (2018), *Hello, Shadowlands: Inside the Meth Fiefdoms, Rebel Hideouts and Bomb-Scarred Party Towns of Southeast Asia* (London: Icon Books).

Winn, Patrick (2024), *Narcotopia: In Search of the Asian Drug Cartel that Survived the CIA* (New York: Public Affairs).

Wolff, Stefan (2002), *Disputed Territories: The Transnational Dynamics of Ethnic Conflict Settlement* (New York and Oxford: Berghahn).

Wright, Robin (2017), "Is America Headed for a New Kind of Civil War?, *The New Yorker*, August 14.

Yasir, Sameer and Suhasini Raj (2023), "Internet Blocked in Indian State as Security Forces Pursue Separatist," *The New York Times*, March 21.

Zacher, Mark W. (2001), "The Territorial Integrity Norm: International Boundaries and the Use of Force," *International Organization* 55:2, 215–250.

Zogby, John (2017), "New Poll on Americans' Support for Secession," John Zogby Strategies, September 18, http://johnzogbystrategies.com/new-poll-on-americans-support-for-secession. Last retrieved May 22, 2023.

Weber, Max (1972), *Politics as a Vocation* (Philadelphia: Fortress Press).

Index

For the benefit of digital users, indexed terms that span two pages (e.g., 52–53) may, on occasion, appear on only one of those pages.

A

Abkhazia
  as Client of Russia, 97–98, 112–113
  declaration of sovereignty by, 4
  as international pariah, 98
  international recognition lacking for, 14–15, 98
  origins of, 4
  Russia's recognition of, 4, 97–98, 112–113
  sovereignty conditions for, 14–15
Abraham, 122
Abraham Accords (2020), 125–126
Abu Sayyaf, 108–109
Adams, John Quincy, 41
Adivasi people, 160–161
Aerican Empire (fantasy dream state) (Canada), 45
African examples of Drexits, 72–74
Akhzivland (Israel), 47
al-Baghdadi, Abu Bakr, 130
Alexander the Great, 154–155
Algeria
  Berbers in, 72–73, 110
  Clients used by, 101–103, 109–110
  hydrocarbon resources in, 110
  Kabylia self-determination and, 72–73, 110
  Morocco's strained relations with, 110
  Movement for the Self-Determination of Kabylie in, 72–73
  Polisario supported by, 101–102, 109–110
  Sahrawi supported by, 101–102, 109–110
  secession movements in, 72–73, 110
America. *See* United States (US)
American Samoa, 30
Anderson, Benedict, 11–13, 55, 58–59, 61, 129–130, 178
Andorra
  joint sovereignty of, 184–185
  location of, 184–185
  as microstate, 22
  UN membership of, 22

Anglo-Egyptian Sudan, 82–83, 186
Angolan secession movements, 73–74
Anjouan (Comoros Islands)
  colonial history of, 86
  independence of, 86
  location of, 86
  war of secession in, 86, 93–94
Antarctic Treaty (1959), 179–180, 185
Aquinas, Thomas, 133
Arab League, 101–102, 109–110
Argentina
  federation in, 132–133
  Mendoza district in, 69, 137
  Patagonia secession movement in, 69, 137
  secession movements in, 69, 137
Armenia
  Azerbaijan's conflicts with, 7, 87, 98
  displaced inhabitants of Nagorno-Karabakh fleeing to, 87, 98
  homeland of, 63–64
  Nagorno-Karabakh Wars and, 86–87
  Russia as sacrificing Armenians of Nagorno-Karabakh in, 107
Around the World in Eighty Days (Verne), 68
Articles of Confederation (US), 32
Artsakh war of secession, 86–87
Asian examples of Drexits, 74–76
August War (2008), 97–98
Australia
  federation in, 132–133, 136
  First Peoples in, 64–65
  Quad membership of, 169
  Sikh émigrés to, 159–160
  Voice to Parliament movement loss in, 65
Austria
  federation in, 136
  Kugelmugel independence declared in Vienna in, 47
Azawad
  external intervention in war of secession in, 95

INDEX 209

MNLA declaration of sovereignty for, 87–88
secession movement in, 87–88, 95
Tuareg Berbers in, 87–88
war of secession in, 87–88
Azerbaijan
Armenia's conflicts with, 7, 87, 98
Artsakh war of secession in, 86–87
as Client of Russia, 98
displaced inhabitants of Nagorno-Karabakh
fleeing from, 87, 98
homeland of, 63–64
Lachin corridor military action in, 87
Nagorno-Karabakh Wars in, 86–87, 98
refugees fleeing from, 87
Russian approval of military strike against
Nagorno-Karabakh of, 98

B
Baker, Kevin, 38–39, 42
Baldwin, James, 54–55
Balkan wars, 7–8, 85, 99–100, 116, 138
Bangladesh
atrocities committed against, 81
brief nature of war of secession in, 93
Concert for, 81
Indian intervention in war of secession of,
81–82, 94
international recognition of, 80–81
origins of, 80–81
Rohingyas driven from ancestral homes
into, 57
success conditions of war of secession in,
81–82
surrender of Pakistan following war against,
80–81
war of secession in, 80–82, 94, 174–175
Western support for, 81
Basque Country
cessation of violence in, 88
distinctive language and culture of, 88
ETA in, 88
"Europe's longest war" in, 93
homeland in, 63–64
secession movement in, 71–72, 86, 88, 93
war of secession in, 86, 88, 93
Belarus
Kyivan Rus as cultural ancestor of, 140–141
pogroms in, 55–56
UN membership as exceptional for, 20, 183
Belgium
federation in, 132–133, 137
as forced marriage, 71–72

secession movements in, 71–72, 137
Vlaams Belang party in, 71–72
Berbers
Algerian Berbers, 72–73, 110
dispersed nature of, 24, 72–73, 178
distinctness of, 72–73
secession movements including, 24, 72–73,
87–88
Tuareg Berbers in Azawad, 87–88
Berlin Wall falls (1989), 84–85, 146, 149–150
Bhutan's UN membership, 156
Biafra
independence declaration of, 89
oil resources in, 89, 93–94
surrender of Igbo militants fighting for, 89
war of secession in, 86, 89, 93
Biden, Joe, 64–65
Bluexit (US), 42
Bolivian secession movements, 69
Bosnia
Dayton Agreement ending war in, 85
independence declaration in, 84–85
origins of, 6
secession movement in, 6, 70, 80
Serbia's desire to consolidate, 6
US diplomatic efforts in, 94
war of secession in, 80, 85
Boutros-Ghali, Boutros, 25, 65–66
Brazil
federation in, 132–133
secession movements in, 69
Britain. See also England; Scotland; United
Kingdom (UK); Wales
African colonialism by, 72
Anglo-Egyptian Sudan jointly ruled by,
82–83, 186
devolution of authority strategy of, 70, 183
economy of, 154
federation in, 136
Indian colonialism by, 80–81, 154–159, 162,
165
Lagoan Isles independence declaration in, 45
regional assemblies recognized by, 136
Republic of Ireland's shared authority with,
185
Roman Britain, 60
secession movements in, 24, 91, 136
British East India Company, 155
Brittany
administrative autonomy of, 60, 63
Celtic identity of, 56–58, 60–62
French ownership of, 58–60, 63

210 INDEX

Brittany (*Continued*)
    name of, 60
    public opinion of Breton identity in, 62
    reform outcome in, 63
    symbols of Celtic identity in, 61
Buckley, F.H., 40
Burns, Robert, 158

C
Canada. *See also* Québec
    Aerican Empire in, 45
    federation in, 132–134
    First Nations in, 64–65, 185
    formal recognition of Québec as distinct
      nation in, 68–69, 136, 183
    India's diplomatic war with, 159–160
    secession movements in, 64, 68–69, 136
    shared authority with First Nations in, 185
    Sikh activist assassinated in, 159–160
    sovereignty association in, 183
Carter, Jimmy, 29
Catalonia
    administrative autonomy of, 70
    arrests of regional leaders and activists in,
      70–71
    history of, 70
    homeland in, 63–64
    independence referendums in, 70–71
    industrial and tourist importance of, 70
    location of, 70
    Madrid's relations with, 70–71
    political fractures widening in, 71
    secession movement in, 24, 63–64, 70–71,
      137
Catherine the Great, 141
Celtic Congress, 60–61
Celtic Connections (Scotland), 61
Celtic Fringe. *See also* Brittany; Cornwall;
      Ireland; Isle of Man; Scotland; Wales
    alternative names for, 59
    Celtic identity promotion in, 60–62
    Declaration of Arbroath and, 59
    definition of, 58
    festivals promoting Celtic identity in, 61
    history of, 59–60
    imagined communities and, 61
    incorporation of, 59–60
    institutions promoting Celtic identity in,
      60–61
    location of, 58
    member nations of, 58
    outcomes of daydreams in, 62–63

    public opinion on Celtic identity in, 62
    sovereignty of, 58–59
    sports as contributing to Celtic identity in,
      61
    as sub-nationalisms, 58–59
    symbols of Celtic identity in, 61
Celtic League, 60–61
Chad's aid to Mali, 87–88
challenge of dream states
    binding constraint and, 180
    daunting nature of, 173
    decolonization and, 178
    federations and, 179
    formal right to secession absent and,
      174–177
    identity politics and, 173
    imagined communities and, 178
    incompatible imperatives as, 173–174
    legitimacy of secession movements and,
      174–176
    Montevideo Convention and, 174
    overview of, 4, 25, 173–174
    remedial secession and, 175
    self-determination as ambiguous term and,
      176–178
    territoriality and, 173, 178–180
    Texas v. White and, 174–175
    UN and, 174–175
    Westphalian model and, 173–174, 178–180
Chase, Salmon P., 31
Chechnya
    constitutional reintegration into Russia of,
      89–90, 147
    de facto independence gained in, 89–90
    location of, 89–90
    Republic of Ichkeria declared in, 89–90
    Russia's wars against, 7, 80, 86, 89–90, 92–93,
      147, 152
    Soviet Union's dissolution and, 89–90, 147
    United Mountain Dwellers of the North
      Caucasus in, 145
Chemerinsky, Erwin, 38
Cherokee Nation movement (US), 36, 42
China
    centralization of, 132–133
    civil war in, 75
    Han majority of, 75
    Inner and Outer division in, 75
    Kashmir area disputed by, 163
    population of, 139, 154
    secession movements in, 75–76, 178
    South China Sea confrontations of, 109

INDEX 211

Taiwan claimed by, 20–21, 128–129, 190–191
Tibet secession movement in, 75, 178
Uyghurs repressed in, 57
Xinjiang secession movement in, 75
Churchill, Winston, 165–166
Civil War (film), 39
Civil War (US), 31–32, 34–35, 38–39, 43
Clients
  Algeria as example of using, 101–102
  Armenia as example of, 98
  Azerbaijan as example of, 98
  breaking stalemates and, 103
  definition of, 9, 95
  degree of conflict risk of, 95
  Georgia as example of, 97–98
  lessons learned from, 102–103
  Moldova as example of, 97
  overview of, 95–96
  risks involved in, 102–103
  Russia as example of using, 95–100
  Turkey as example of using, 100–101
  Ukraine as example of, 99–100
  US interests and, 96
  Yemen as example of using, 102
Cold War
  anti-communist revolutions at end of, 84–85, 146
  Berlin Wall falls at end of, 84–85, 146, 149–150
  German reunification at the end of, 15–16, 178–179
  new nations following end of, 6, 15–16, 64, 80, 84–85, 138
  nuclear arms race during, 49
Concert for Bangladesh (1971), 81
Conch Republic (fantasy dream state) (US)
  as fantasy, 45
  origins of, 4, 45
  scope of, 45
  tongue-in-cheek nature of, 4, 15
  as tourism booster, 45
  unserious nature of, 15, 45
conflict risk. *See* degree of conflict risk
constitutional order of the US
  amendment provisions in, 38
  Articles of Confederation as predecessor to, 32
  centrifugal forces as reason for secession and, 32
  Civil War as challenge to, 31–32
  commonwealths recognized by, 30

compact theory of, 31–32
complexity of, 29–30
cultural integrity as reason for secession and, 32
dependencies recognized by, 30–31
District of Columbia in, 30
dysfunction as reason for secession and, 32
economic self-interest as reason for secession and, 32
federalism in, 134
as frozen in time, 38
House of Representatives in, 30
mutual suspicion as reason for secession and, 32
origins as reason for secession and, 32
partisan divide's impact on, 38–39
political morality as reason for secession and, 32
principle of perpetuity established in, 31–32
reasons for secession as possibility in, 32–34, 40
secession as possibility in, 31–34
Senate in, 30
sovereignty and, 31–32
states as core constituents of, 29–30
Union of, 31–32
Westphalian model and, 31–32
Cornwall
  Celtic identity of, 58, 61–62
  Kingdom of England's incorporation of, 59–60
  public opinion on Celtic identity in, 62
  symbols of Celtic identity in, 61
Covid-19 pandemic, 24
Crick, Francis, 122
Crimea
  Karaims from, 24–25
  Russia's annexation of, 7, 99–100, 118–119, 141–142, 178–179
  Tatar deportations in, 148–149
Croatia
  international recognition of, 85
  origin of, 6, 84–85
  War of Independence (Homeland War) in, 85
  war of secession in, 80
Cyprus
  coup by Greek nationalists in, 100–101
  enosis and *taksim* movements in, 100–101
  ethnic division of, 100–101
  independence of, 100–101, 178–179
  Ottoman rule of, 100–101

212 INDEX

Cyprus (*Continued*)
secession movements in, 100–101
Turkish invasion of and military presence in, 100–101, 119
Czech Republic's separation with Slovakia, 178–179

D

David Copperfield (Dickens), 103
Daydreams
aims and causes of, 54–56
author experiences with, 55–56
Celtic Fringe example of, 58–63
commonplace nature of, 65–66
crowd sourced nature of, 54–55
definition of, 9, 54
degree of conflict risk of, 54
disruptive potential of, 66
Drexits as easy evolution of, 76–77
examples of, 58–65
four R's possibilities for, 56–58, 66
fragility of, 55–56, 65–66
identity politics as basis of, 54–56
Indigenous Peoples and, 64–65
as intermediate category, 54, 56
lessons learned from, 65–66
limited ambition as distinguishing feature of, 55
nationalism at odds with some, 56
overview of, 54–55
rebellion outcomes of, 58
reconciliation outcomes of, 56–57
reform outcomes of, 57–58
repression outcomes of, 57
sentimental attachments involved in, 54–56
statehood and, 55
supplemental nature of, 55
symbolic level of operation of, 55–56
transitional nature of, 66
ubiquity of, 63–65
variation in outcomes of, 56–58
Declaration of Arbroath (1320), 59
decolonization
challenge posed by secession movements and, 178
Friendly Relations Declaration created to support, 175, 187–188
new nations resulting from, 19, 22–23, 79, 178
Rebels with a Cause influenced by, 79, 86
UN membership increased through, 19, 175, 187–188

de Gaulle, Charles, 68
deglobalization, 24
degree of conflict risk. *See also* special cases
classification of, 9
Clients and, 95
combustion risks, 107–108
Daydreams and, 54
definition of, 9
dream states and, 9, 15–16
Drexits and, 67, 137
Ethiopia and, 8, 108, 115–116, 137–138
familiar faces in, 107–108
Fantasies and, 44, 52–53
federations and, 135, 137–138
fragility and, 119–120
Georgia and, 112–113, 119–120
India and, 160, 164, 168–169
Katanga and, 112
Kurdistan and, 116–118
Myanmar and, 114–115, 119–120
Northern Ireland and, 111
overview of, 107–108
Philippines and, 108–109
quantification of, 119
Rebels with a Cause and, 78–79
Russia and, 147–152
Sahrawi and, 109–110
stalemates and frozen conflicts and, 107
time as factor in, 107
Top Ten Combustibles in, 108–119
Ukraine and, 118–119
Yemen and, 113–114
Democratic Party (US), 37–40, 42
Democratic Republic of the Congo (DRC). *See also* Katanga (DRC)
colonial history of, 73–74
independence of, 112
secession movements in, 73–74, 112
Denmark
Faroe Islands and Greenland secession movements in, 71–72
Freetown Christiania in, 47
secession movements in, 47, 71–72
Dominica and St. Kitts UN membership, 22
Dominion of Melchizedek, 50–51
Don Cossacks, 145, 148–149
Don Republic, 145
dream states. *See also* challenge of dream states; Clients; Daydreams; Drexits; Fantasies; modest proposal on dream states; Rebels with a Cause
age of secession and, 5–7

aims of current volume on, 15–16
armed conflicts traced to, 7–8
as chief source of violence in the world, 7
dangers posed by, 15–16
definition of, 3–4
degree of conflict risk classification of, 9
demand-side dimensions of, 23–25
domestic heterogeneity as factor in
motivation for, 23–25
as dominant source of friction on global
stage, 7
emergence of, 4–5
formal right of secession absent for, 174–177
fragmentation of national identity as leading
to, 6, 24–25
globalization and, 24
identity politics as root of, 3, 5–6, 24–25
importance of, 5–8
intensity of feeling underlying, 6
interstate disputes as giving way to, 7
key questions surrounding, 4
labels for categories of, 9
lack of standardized taxonomy of, 8–9
legitimacy of, 174–176
less attention paid to, 16
level of trade barriers as factor in motivation
for, 23–24
local politics constituting, 6
loyalty's relation to, 6
minorities-within-minorities issue and,
24–25
motivations for, 23–25
number of, 5–8
optimal size of nations research and, 23–24
overview of, 4–5
reasons for emergence of, 4–5
rise of movements based on, 7–8
secession as aim of, 3–5
self-determination as synonym of, 4
separatism as synonym of, 4
sovereignty's relation to, 3, 8, 13–15
supply-side dimensions of, 17–23
tribalism underlying, 5–6
types of, 8–9
validation as goal of, 3
wars of, 7–8
Westphalian model and, 10–13
Drexits
African examples of, 72–74
aims and causes of, 67
Asian examples of, 74–76
Canada as example of, 68–69

commonplace nature of, 67
Daydream's easy evolution into, 76–77
definition of, 9, 67
degree of conflict risk of, 67, 137
disruptive potential of, 77
European examples of, 70–72
examples of, 67–76
Latin American examples of, 69
lessons of, 76–77
no lower limit on size of, 77
Oceanian examples of, 76
overview of, 67
Westphalian model and, 67
Duchy of Grand Fenwick, 49–50
Duck Soup (film), 47
Dylan, Bob, 81

E
Egypt
Anglo-Egyptian Sudan jointly ruled by,
82–83, 186
Gaza controlled by, 125
ISIS province declared in, 130–131
Israel invaded by, 125
Jewish exodus from, 122–123
peace treaty with Israel of, 125–126
Syria's merger attempt with, 15–16
Elizabeth I, 59
England. *See also* Britain; Cornwall; United
Kingdom (UK)
Cornwall incorporated into, 59–60
Isle of Man incorporated into, 59–60
Kingdom of, 59–60
Scotland annexation attempts by, 59
Wales incorporated into, 59–60
Eritrea
colonial borders of, 81–82
international cognition of, 81–82
Italian colonial claims to, 81–82
lack of external intervention in war of
secession in, 94
national identity of, 82
reasons for length of war of secession in, 82,
93
sovereignty of, 81–82
success conditions of war of secession in, 82
Tigrayan People's Liberation Front allied
with, 115–116
UN resolution combining Ethiopia with,
81–82
war of secession in, 79–80, 81–82, 93,
115–116, 174–175

214   INDEX

Estonia
  independence of, 64, 144–145, 152
  international recognition of, 64
Ethiopia
  brush fires in, 116
  cease-fire in, 115–116
  constitutional reform in, 115–116
  degree of conflict risk in, 8, 108, 115–116,
    137–138
  Derg government overthrown in, 82
  disintegration potential of, 116
  Eritrea's war of secession against, 79–80,
    81–82, 93, 115–116, 174–175
  ethnic conflict in, 11, 115–116
  federation in, 132–133, 138, 179, 183
  fragility of, 119–120
  Gulf of Aden port offered by Somaliland to,
    73
  Italian colonial claim in, 81–82
  secession movements in, 11, 73
  Somalia dispute with Somaliland of, 73
  Somaliland proposed recognition by, 73
  Tigrayan People's Liberation Front in,
    115–116
European examples of Drexits, 70–72
European Union (EU)
  Kosovo-Serbia conflict and, 127
  official candidate status in, 191
  prospective new members of, 191
  subsidiary principle adopted by, 133
  Turkey's application to, 191
  Ukraine's relation to, 99–100
Euskadi Ta Askatasuna (ETA) (Basque
    Country), 88

F
Falls Around Her (film), 64
Fantasies
  aims and causes of, 44–45, 46–48, 50–51
  definition of, 9
  degree of conflict risk of, 44, 52–53
  examples of, 45–51
  fraud forms of, 50–52
  joke forms of, 45–46
  Kingdom of Lovely example of, 46
  libertarian forms of, 46–47, 49
  as mostly benign, 44, 52–53
  overview of, 9, 44
  Poyais example of, 51–52
  regulatory forms of, 46–50
  Rose Island example of, 48–49
  seasteading as form of, 49

statehood and, 45, 50
  varieties of, 44
federations
  big three of, 138–139
  business class of, 136–137
  challenge posed by secession movements
    and, 179
  classes of federations and, 135
  coach class of, 137–138
  compromise solutions in, 134–135
  definition of federalism, 133–135
  degree of conflict risk in, 135, 137–138
  EU's adoption of subsidiary principle and,
    133
  fragile forms of, 132–133, 138–139
  large multiethnic unions as, 132–133
  natural law basis of, 133
  overview of, 132–133
  premier class of, 135–136
  scarcity of, 132–133
  sovereignty in, 133
  subsidiarity principle in, 133
financial crisis of 2008, 24
First Nations (Canada), 64–65, 185
First Peoples (Australia), 64–65
Founding Fathers, 30
"Fourteen Points" (Wilson), 177–178
fragmentation of national identity, 6, 24–25
France. See also Brittany
  Andorra's sovereignty guaranteed by,
    184–185
  colonial history of, 68, 72, 86
  ETA's use of, 88
  formation of, 56–57
  French Guiana, 69
  Le Saugeais in, 45
  Mali aided by, 87–88, 93–94
  reconciliation outcome in, 56–57
  secession movements in, 71–72
  territories gained by, 178–179
Franco, Francisco, 70
Free Territory of Trieste (1954), 178–179
Freetown Christiania (Denmark), 47
French and Indian Wars (1754-1763), 68
French Guianese secession movement, 69
Friendly Relations Declaration (1970) (UN),
  175, 177–178, 187–188

G
Gagauz secession movement, 146
Gellner, Ernst, 25, 63, 176
Georgia. See also Abkhazia

INDEX   215

August War against Russia in, 97–98
degree of conflict risk in, 112–113, 119–120
frozen conflict with Russia in, 97–98, 112–113
homeland in, 63–64, 112–113
independence of, 97–98
location of, 97–98
Russian support for secession movements in, 97–98, 119
South Ossetia breakaway region in, 97–98, 112–113
Soviet Union's disintegration and, 97–98, 112–113
Germany
Berlin Wall falls in, 84–85, 146, 149–150
federation in, 136
Länder communities in, 64
Nazi Germany, 178–179
reunification of, 15–16, 178–179
Giovanni's Room (Baldwin), 54–55
Glacier Republic (Chile), 47–48
global financial crisis of 2008, 24
globalization, 24
God Made Trump (video), 39–40
Grand Duchy of the Lagoan Isles, 45
Great Britain. *See* Britain
Great Recession (2008), 24
Greene, Marjorie Taylor, 42
Griffiths, Ryan, 8–9
Gudkov, Lev, 144
Gulf of Fonseca, 185

H

Haudenosaunee Confederacy, 64–65
Hebridean Celtic Festival (HebCelt) (Isle of Lewis), 61
Henry V (Shakespeare), 10
Henry VIII, 59–60
Hezbollah, 126
Holy Roman Empire, 10–11, 184–185
How to Start Your Own Country (documentary), 46
Hussein, Saddam, 7, 117

I

identity politics
challenge of dream states and, 173
Daydreams based in, 54–56
definition of, 5, 24
dream states rooted in, 3, 5–6, 24–25
fluidity of identity and, 25

fragmentation of national identity resulting from, 6, 25
tribalism as fundamental to human nature and, 6
imagined communities
Celtic Fringe and, 61
challenge of dream states and, 178
definition of, 11–12
India as a, 168
ISIS as a, 129–130
"naturalness" perceptions and, 11–12, 17, 178
religion as factor in, 168
Spain as a, 71
statehood as form of, 11–12
territoriality and, 178
US as a, 29
Westphalian model and, 11–12, 71, 129–130
Incredible Story of Rose Island, The (film), 49
India. *See also* Kashmir
accommodating nature of, 166
anti-Muslim actions and sentiment in, 167–168
Assam secession movements in, 162
Ayodhya historic Ram temple site in, 167–168, 178
Bangladesh war of secession intervention of, 81–82, 94
Bharatiya Janata Party (BJP) in, 157, 167–169
Bhutan's separation from, 156
Bodoland autonomous region in, 162
British colonial rule of, 80–81, 154–159, 162, 165
British East India Company rule in, 155
Canada's diplomatic war with, 159–160
challenges of self-rule in, 155, 157–158
concentration potential in, 167–169
Congress Party in, 157
constitutional order of, 155–157, 163, 166
degree of conflict risk in, 160, 164, 168–169
disintegration potential of, 165–167
ethnic and linguistic diversity of, 75–76, 155, 157–158, 165–166
federation in, 132–133, 154–157
fragility of, 154, 164–165
future of, 164–170
Golden Temple occupation in, 159
Hindutva principle in, 157, 167–168
historical development of, 154–155
as imagined community, 168
independence of, 154–155

216 INDEX

India (*Continued*)
    as indestructible union of destructible states, 156–157
    Indian Rebellion of 1857 in, 155
    Islam and Muslims in, 11, 154–155, 157, 164–165, 167–169
    Khalistan secession movement in, 158–160
    languages recognized in, 75–76
    Manipur secession movements in, 162
    Meiteis secession movement in, 162
    minorities-within-minorities issue in, 162
    Myanmar secession movements and, 115
    Naxalite-Maoist insurgency movement in, 160–161
    northeast secession movements in, 161–163
    overview of, 154, 169–170
    Pakistan's conflicts with, 7, 164–166
    partitioning of, 155
    population of, 75, 139, 154
    Punjab Reorganization Act and, 159
    secession movements in, 75–76, 157–164
    secession ruled out constitutionally in, 156
    Seven Sister states in, 161–162, 165
    Sikhism in, 158–159
    size of, 75
    sovereignty of, 154, 156–158
    Sri Lankan peacekeeping force of, 90
    states and union territories in, 156
    States Reorganization Act in, 156–157
    subsidiarity principle in, 155–156
    Union, State, and Concurrent Lists in, 157
    US interests and, 169
Indigenous Peoples, 64–65, 89, 185
Indonesia
    Free Papua Movement in, 74–75, 92
    location of, 83
    Muslim population in, 168–169
    secession movements in, 74–75
    Timor-Leste war of secession with, 14, 79–80, 83
International Monetary Fund (IMF), 176–177
Iran
    Baloch Liberation Army in, 75
    Gaza war of 2023 funded by, 24
    Hamas supported by, 24
    Kurds in, 65, 117–118
    Revolutionary Guards Corps of, 74–75
    secession movements in, 74–75
    Yemen supported by, 102
Iraq
    ISIS control of territory in, 13, 130
    Kurds in, 65, 117–118

    secession movements in, 74
Ireland. *See also* Northern Ireland
    Acts of Union and, 60
    creation of, 60
    Easter Rising of 1916 in, 60, 62–63
    famine in, 60
    Good Friday Agreement in, 62–63
    partition of, 62–63
    Provisional IRA in, 62–63
    rebellions in, 60
    repression in, 62–63
    Republic of Ireland, 58–59, 185
    symbols of Celtic identity in, 61
    United Kingdom's relation to, 60, 91
Irish Free State, 60, 62–63
Irish Republican Army (Provisional IRA), 62–63, 91, 111
Irish Republican Army (Real or New IRA), 111
Islamic State (ISIS)
    caliphate revival as goal of, 129–130
    continued threat of, 130–131
    founding of, 130
    as harbinger of future movements, 131
    as imagined community, 129–130
    international recognition lacking for, 13
    leader of, 130
    losses of, 130
    MNLA backed by, 87–88
    religious claims to sovereignty of, 129–131
    rise to prominence of, 130
    as special case, 129–131
    territorial control gained by, 13, 130–131
    Westphalian model rejected by, 129–131
Isle of Man
    Celtic identity of, 58
    Kingdom of England incorporation of, 59–60
    Manx cat of, 61
    as offshore financial center, 62
    reconciliation outcome in, 62
    symbols of Celtic identity of, 61
    three legs of man flag design of, 61
Israel
    Abraham Accords and, 125–126
    Akhzivland in, 47
    Arab alliance of 1948 against, 125
    Arab uprisings preceding, 124
    biblical origins and claims to, 50, 122–124
    double secession struggle of the I-P conflict, 121–124
    Egypt's peace treaty with, 125–126
    founding of, 121–122

INDEX 217

Gaza war of 2023 with, 24, 92, 114, 126
international recognition of, 110, 125–126
Israeli-Palestinian conflict, 121–126
Jewish diaspora as desiring founding of,
122–123
Jewish immigration to, 124
Jordan's peace treaty with, 125–126
Morocco's recognition of, 110, 125–126
occupied territories by, 125
Palestine's UN membership blocked by,
20–21
population of, 123–124
Six-Day War of, 125
Temple Mount in Jerusalem and, 178
UN membership of, 125
UN partition plan preceding, 123–125
violence following partition plan in, 125
war of independence of, 125
Zionist movement for, 123–124
Italy. *See also* Rose Island (Italy)
colonial history of, 81–82
Eritrea claimed by, 81–82
Ethiopia claimed by, 81–82
Fascist period of, 81–82
Free Territory of Trieste and, 178–179
secession movements in, 71–72
sovereignty of, 48–49

J
Jedlička, Vít, 46–47
Jefferson state movement (US), 42

K
Kadyrov, Ramzan, 89–90, 92, 147
Kanu, Nnamdi, 89
Kashmir
degree of conflict risk in, 164
division of, 163
as double secession conflict, 164
India's dream state as including, 163–164
intractability of, 163
juridical status disputed of, 163
limited autonomy of, 163
location of, 163
name of, 163
ongoing violence in, 164
origins of conflict in, 164
partition of, 164
secession movement in, 163–166, 169
significance of, 163–164
UN-backed cease-fire in, 164
wars fought over, 164

Katanga (DRC)
degree of conflict risk in, 112
independence of, 112
Mai-Mai Kata Katanga offensive in, 112
secession movements in, 73–74, 112
Union Minière du Haut Katanga support for
rebellion in, 112
UN peacekeeping forces in, 112
Kennedy, Ted, 81
Khalistan movement
Golden Temple occupation by, 159
historical development of, 158–159
India-Canada diplomatic war and, 159–160
militaristic dimensions of, 159
name of, 158–159
origins of, 159
Punjab Reorganization Act and, 159
suppression of, 159–160
Kingdom of Lovely, 46
Kosovo
EU negotiations with Serbia and, 127
independence declaration of, 84–85,
126–127
Kosovo Liberation Army in, 85
Matryoshka doll metaphor for
understanding, 129
minorities-within-minorities issue in, 71–72,
126–127
NATO intervention in, 85, 94, 126–127
renewed conflict potential in, 92, 127–128
secession of, 6, 85, 92, 126–127
Serbian secession movement in, 71–72,
126–127
Serbia's refusal to recognize independence
of, 84–85, 92, 126–127
as special case, 126–128
UN membership blocked by Serbia for,
20–21
war of 1998-1999 in, 80
Yugoslavia experiences of, 126–127
Krasner, Stephen, 12, 14, 17, 19, 32, 182–183
Kugelmugel (Austria), 47
Kurdistan
autonomous status of, 117
degree of conflict risk in, 116–118
Desert Storm and, 117
dispersed nature of Kurds and, 65, 116–117,
178
fragility of, 117
Iranian Kurds, 117–118
Iraqi Kurdistan, 117–118

218 INDEX

Kurdistan (*Continued*)
  Kurds as largest minority without a
    jurisdiction to call their own, 65
  leading families in, 117
  no-fly zones declared over, 117
  PKK and, 117
  population of, 65
  statehood ambitions of, 24
  Syrian Kurds, 65, 116–118
  Turkish Kurds, 65, 70, 116–118
  US interests and, 118
Kuwait invaded by Iraq, 7

L

Latin American examples of Drexits, 69
Latvia
  independence of, 144–145
  international recognition of, 64
Law in Wales Act (1535 and 1542), 59–60
League of Nations, 124
Lepore, Jill, 38
Le Saugeais (France), 45
Levada Center, 144
Liberation of Azawad (MNLA), 87–88, 93–94
Liberation Tigers of Tamil Eelam (Tamil
  Tigers), 90
Liberland, 46–47
libertarian dream states, 43, 46–47, 49
Liberty state movement (US), 42
Libya
  Berbers in, 72–73
  ISIS province in, 130–131
  secession movements in, 72–73
  UN membership as exceptional for, 20
Liechtenstein
  inspiration for other ministates of, 46–47
  UN membership of, 22
Lincoln, Abraham, 43, 119
Lithuania
  independence of, 24–25, 144–145
  international recognition of, 64
  Karaims in, 24–25
  minorities-within-minorities issue in, 24–25
  Republic of Užupis in, 47
  secession movement in, 24–25
  Soviet Union's absorption of, 64

M

MacGregor, Gregor, 51–52
Malaysia
  federation in, 137–138
  renewed conflict potential in, 137–138

  secession movements in, 74–75, 108–109,
    137–138
Mali
  French intervention in, 93–94
  ISIS support for MNLA in, 87–88
  MNLA in, 87–88, 93–94
  secession movements in, 86–88, 94
  Tuareg Berbers in, 72–73, 94
Malraux, André, 81
Mao Zedong, 160
Massie, Alex, 70
Mauritanian Western Sahara, 4
Mexican secession movements, 137
minorities-within-minorities issue
  definition of, 24–25
  dream states and, 24–25
  India as example of, 162
  Kosovo as example of, 71–72, 126–127
  Lithuania as example of, 24–25
  Oceanian examples of, 76
  recursive nature of, 25, 43
  secession movements in the US and, 43
  statehood and, 25
MNLA (Liberation of Azawad), 87–88, 93–94
modest proposal on dream states
  certification function of UNADS in, 189–191
  dichotomous statehood and, 181, 187–188,
    190
  federations in, 183
  Friendly Relations Declaration and, 187–188
  global institution proposed in, 189–192
  hybrid forms of state authority in, 181–187
  implementation of, 188–192
  joint sovereignty in, 184–185, 187–188
  lack of miracle cure in, 192–193
  legitimization of secession in, 186–192
  mediation function of UNADS in, 191–192
  Montevideo Convention and, 182
  overview of, 181
  reconsidering the twin imperatives in,
    181–184
  redistribution of sovereign powers and, 182,
    184, 187–188, 192–193
  reform possibilities in, 183, 192
  rules of the game and, 187–188
  secession reconsidered in, 182–184
  self-determination reconsidered in, 182
  sovereignty reconsidered in, 181–186
  statehood reconsidered in, 181–183,
    187–188, 190
  surveillance function of UNADS in, 192

territoriality reconsidered in, 181, 184–186, 187–188
UN Agency for Dream States proposed in, 189–192
UNPO and, 189–190
Westphalian model and, 181–182
Modi, Narendra, 157, 167
Moldova
  as Client of Russia, 97, 119
  cultural divide in, 97
  frozen conflict with Russia in, 97
  Gagauzia region in, 146
  independence of, 97
  location of, 97
  Russian support of secession movement in, 95–97
  Soviet Union's disintegration and, 97
  Transnistria in, 97
Montenegro
  independence of, 84–85
  Kosovo repression by, 85
Montevideo Convention (1933)
  challenge posed by secession movements and, 174
  modest proposal on dream states and, 182
  statehood criteria in, 19–20, 79, 97, 182
  UN informed by, 19, 174
Montreal World's Fair (1967), 68
Morocco
  Algeria's strained relations with, 110
  Arab League's backing of, 101–102, 109–110
  Berbers in, 72–73
  Border Wall built along border of Sahrawi by, 101
  Israel recognized by, 101–102, 125–126
  Polisario's threats against, 110
  Rif Independence Movement in, 72–73
  Sahrawi claim of, 4, 101, 109–110
  Sahrawi's conflict with, 4, 92, 101–102, 109–110
  secession movements in, 4, 72–73, 92, 109–110
  UN membership of Sahrawi blocked by, 20–21
  US recognition of claim to sovereignty over Sahrawi by, 101–102, 109–110
Movimiento Independentista Patagónico (Argentina), 69
Muhammad, 123, 129–130
Myanmar
  colonial history of, 114
  coup d'état in, 114–115

degree of conflict risk in, 114–115, 119–120
ethnic conflict in, 74–75, 92, 114–115
India's construction of fence along length of, 115
intervention risk in, 115
Kachin Independence Army in, 114–115
population of, 114
relational autonomy of United Wa State Army in, 92
Rohingya repressed and exiled in, 57
secession movements in, 74–75, 92, 114–115
UN membership as exceptional for, 20
Wa people in, 92, 114

N

Nagorno-Karabakh
  Armenian population forced to flee of, 87, 98
  Azerbaijan's lightning military strike on, 98
  Russia as sacrificing Armenians of, 107
  wars in, 86–87, 98
national identity. See identity politics; imagined communities
national identity fragmentation, 6, 24–25
nationhood. See statehood
NATO. See North Atlantic Treaty Organization (NATO)
Nauru, 22, 76
Navassa Island, 30–31
Naxalite-Maoist insurgency
  Adivasi support for, 160–161
  India's inability to fully suppress, 160–161
  Maoist roots of, 160
  Operation Green Hunt against, 161
  Operation Steeplechase against, 161
  origins of, 160–161
  reinvigoration of, 168–169
Nazi Germany, 178–179
Nehru, Jawaharl, 156
Netanyahu, Benjamin, 123–124
New Zealand
  co-governance rejected in, 65
  joint sovereignty in, 70
  Maori in, 64–65
  Whangamōmona in, 45
Nigeria. See also Biafra
  colonial history of, 89
  ethnic diversity of, 89
  federation in, 138, 179
  independence of, 89
  lack of external intervention in war of secession in, 94
  oil reserves in, 89

220 INDEX

Nigeria (*Continued*)
  population of, 89
  religious and ethnic conflict in, 89
  renewed conflict risk in, 138
  Republic of Biafra declared in, 89
  secession movements in, 73–74, 89, 112, 119
Nijjar, Hardeep Singh, 159–160
North Atlantic Treaty Organization (NATO)
  Britain's ability to contribute to, 111
  Kosovo intervention of, 85, 94, 126–127
  Membership Action plan of, 191
North Dumpling (US), 47
Northern Ireland
  border counties eased in, 111
  consociational model of democracy and,
    111, 185–186
  creation of, 60
  degree of conflict risk in, 111
  devolution of authority strategy in, 63
  disarmament of Provisional IRA in, 111
  Good Friday Agreement and, 91, 111, 136,
    185–186
  MI5 threat assessment for, 111
  Provisional IRA in, 91, 111
  Real (or New) IRA threat to, 111
  regional assembly in, 136
  secession movements in, 62–63, 91, 111, 127
  Sinn Féin elected in, 111
  Troubles conflict in, 62–63, 91, 111
  United Kingdom membership of, 62–63
Northern Mariana Islands, 30

O
Oceanian examples of Drexits, 76
Operation Blue Star (India), 159
optimal size of nations research, 23–24, 77, 132
Oregonian secession movements, 39

P
Pakistan. *See also* Kashmir
  Baluchi separatists in, 75
  Bangladesh war of secession from, 79–81
  federation in, 132–133, 138, 154–155, 179
  India's conflicts with, 7, 164–166
  ISIS province in, 130–131
  renewed conflict risk in, 138
  secession movements in, 75
Palau, 22, 76
Palestine
  Arab uprisings in, 124
  double secession struggle of the I-P conflict,
    121–124

Gaza war of October 2023 in, 24, 92, 126
Hamas in, 24, 126
international recognition of, 13, 20–21
Israeli-Palestinian conflict, 121–126
limited possibilities for rebellion in, 92
Nakba suffered by, 125–126
observer status in UN of, 20–21
occupied territories in, 125–126
origins of conflict with Israel of, 123
PLO's declaration of independent state in
  Jerusalem in, 126
settler colonialism view in, 124
Six-Day War and, 125–126
stalemate of war of secession in, 92
Temple Mount in Jerusalem and, 178
territorial control as not required for
  recognition in, 13
UN membership blocked for, 20–21
UN partition plan of, 123–125
Pannun, Gurpatwant Singh, 159–160
Papua New Guinea
  Bougainville island in, 76
  secession movements in, 74, 76
Peace of Westphalia (1648), 10–11, 174,
  179–180, 184–185
Pedley, Mark, 50
Peter the Great, 141, 150–151
Philippines
  armed conflicts in, 108–109
  Bangsamoro Autonomous Region in,
    108–109
  casualties of secession movements in,
    108–109
  degree of conflict risk in, 108–109, 119–120
  fragile peace in, 92
  ISIS province in, 130–131
  Jabidah massacre in, 108–109
  Mindanao secession movement in, 108–109
  Moro conflict in, 108–110
  population of, 108–109
  religious division in, 108–109
  secession movements in, 74–75, 92, 108–109
  US interests in, 109
Pledge of Allegiance (US), 37
Poland
  EU membership of, 191
  secession movement in, 71–72
  territories lost and gained by, 178–179
Poyais (fictional kingdom)
  bursting of bubble of, 52
  creation of, 51
  fraud committed through, 52

INDEX 221

institutions and culture of, 52
location of, 51
name of, 51
overview of, 51–52
Principality of Freedonia (US), 47
Puerto Rico
  commonwealth relationship with US of, 21,
    30
  House of Representative shooting involving
    Nationalist Party of, 91
  independence votes in, 36
  international sports participation of, 21, 183
  Nationalist Party in, 91
Punjab Reorganization Act (1966), 159
Puntland
  aim of, 4
  autonomous functioning of, 73
  emergence of, 4
  Somalia's disintegration as leading to, 4
  sovereignty conditions for, 14
Putin, Vladimir
  Chechen wars under, 7, 89–90, 93–94
  failure in Ukraine as raising possibility of
    leadership change from, 151
  invasion of Ukraine as "last stand" of, 150
  New Russia return desired by, 99
  separatism risk acknowledged by, 150–151
  Soviet Union's disintegration as catastrophe
    for, 96, 150
  Ukrainian invasion under, 7, 24, 100,
    118–119, 148–151

Q

Québec
  Coalition Avenir Québec in, 68–69
  economic status resented in, 68
  formal recognition as distinct nation by
    Canada of, 68–69, 136, 183
  home rule of, 21
  loss to British of, 68
  Ministry of International Relations of, 21
  national identity in, 68–69
  origins of, 68
  Parti Québécois in, 68–69, 136
  Quiet Revolution in, 68
  reconciliation option in, 68–69
  referenda on exit in, 68
  secession movement's birth in, 68
  sovereignty association model in, 68
  "*Vive le Québec libre*" slogan in, 68

R

Ramayana (Hindu epic), 167–168
Rashtriya Swayamsevak Sangh (RSS), 167
Rebels with a Cause
  Anjouan as example of, 86
  Artsakh as example of, 86–87
  Azawad as example of, 87–88
  Bangladesh as example of, 80–81
  Basque Country as example of, 88
  Biafra as example of, 89
  Chechnya as example of, 89–90
  classic vs fatal wars of secession in, 79–80
  decolonization as factor in, 79, 86
  definition of, 9, 78–79
  degree of conflict risk of, 78–79
  ease of starting compared to finishing, 93
  Eritrea as example of, 81–82
  international recognition as condition for
    winning form of, 79
  interventions in support of, 81, 83–84, 93–94
  lessons learned from, 93–94
  longevity of, 93
  losing movements based on, 86–90
  number of, 78, 91
  overview of, 78–79
  reintegration as failure condition of, 86
  relational autonomy leading to stability
    following, 92
  South Sudan as example of, 82–83
  stalemates based on, 91–92
  success conditions of, 79–81, 82–84
  Tamil Eelam as example of, 90
  Timor-Leste as example of, 83–84
  UN membership as condition for winning
    form of, 79
  US interests and, 79
  winning movements based on, 79–85
  Yugoslavia as example of, 84–85
Rebel Without a Cause (film), 78
Republican Party (US), 37–40, 42
Republic of Artsakh war of secession, 86–87
Republic of Ireland, 58–59, 185
Republic of Lakota movement (US), 36
Republic of Užupis (Lithuania), 47
Republika Srpska (Serbia dream state), 6
risk of conflict. *See* degree of conflict risk
Romanian secession movement, 71–72
Roosevelt, Franklin, 20
Rosa, Giorgio, 48
Rose Island (Italy)
  aim of, 48
  demolition of, 48–49
  emergence of, 48

222 INDEX

Rose Island (Italy) (*Continued*)
   Esperanto as official language of, 48
   as example of seasteading, 49
   film based on, 49
   funding for, 48
   independence declaration of, 48
   inspiration for other projects of, 49
   location in international waters of, 48–49
   overview of, 48–49
   tourism to, 48–49
Russia
   Abkhazia as Client of, 97–98, 112–113
   Armenians of Nagorno-Karabakh sacrificed
     by, 107
   autocracy in, 72, 143
   Azerbaijan as Client of, 98
   Bolshevik Revolution in, 144–146
   borders of, 141
   breakdown potential of, 140, 149–152
   Chechen wars of, 7, 80, 89–90, 147, 152
   Clients used by, 95–100
   constituent entities of, 141–142
   constitution of, 141–142
   Cossacks in, 148–149
   Crimea annexed by, 7, 99–100, 118–119,
     141–142, 178–179
   degree of conflict risk in, 147–152
   desire to recapture traditional sphere of
     influence by, 96
   discontent in, 147–149
   ethnic diversity of, 72, 141, 148–149
   Eurasian national identity in, 150
   expansion of, 141
   federation of, 132–133, 140–143
   future of, 147–152
   Georgian secession movement supported
     by, 97–98, 119
   historical development of, 140–141, 144–147
   imperial history of, 96, 141
   Kyivan Rus as origins of, 140–141
   Moldova as Client of, 97, 119
   North Korean military hardware obtained
     by, 98
   origins of, 140–141
   overview of, 152–153
   public opinion on secession sentiments
     lacking in, 144
   Romanov dynasty in, 141
   Sámi people in, 63–64
   secession movements sponsored by, 96–100,
     119
   size of, 72, 140–141

   South Ossetia as Client of, 97–98, 113
   sovereignty of, 141, 147, 157–158
   Soviet Union's dissolution and, 146–147
   Tatars in, 146, 148–149
   Transnistria as Client of, 98
   Turkey trade reliance of, 98
   Ukrainian invasion of, 7, 24, 100, 118–119,
     148–151
   Ukrainian secession movement supported
     by, 99–100
   use of minorities in Ukrainian special
     military operation by, 149
   US interests and, 140

S
Sahrawi (Western Sahara)
   Algeria as supporter of, 101–102, 109–110
   Arab Democratic Republic of, 4, 92, 101
   cease-fire in, 109–110
   colonial history of, 4
   degree of conflict risk in, 109–110
   emergence of, 4
   frozen state of conflict in, 110
   Morocco and Mauritania given initial
     ownership of, 4
   Morocco's conflict with, 4, 92, 101–102,
     109–110
   Polisario Front's desire for, 101, 109–110
   sovereignty conditions for, 14
   stalemated nature of conflict involving,
     101–102
   UN membership blocked by Morocco of,
     20–21
   US interests and, 110
Sangh Parivar (Sangh Family), 167
San Marino UN membership, 22
Schmidt, Helmut, 99
Scotland
   British relations with, 70
   Celtic identity of, 58, 61–62
   devolution of authority strategy in, 63, 111,
     136
   emotional resonance of independence idea
     in, 70
   independence referendum in, 70
   Isle of Man ownership of, 59–60
   Kingdom of, 59
   national identity development in, 59
   public opinion on Celtic identity in, 62
   regional assembly in, 136
   Scottish National Party (SNP) in, 70
   Scottish Parliament established in, 63

INDEX 223

secession movement in, 24, 70
symbols of Celtic identity in, 61
United Kingdom membership of, 59, 68–69
Seasteading Institute, 49
Seborga, 46–47
secession movements. *See* Clients; Daydreams;
    dream states; Drexits; Fantasies; Rebels
    with a Cause; US secession movements
self-determination
    ambiguity of, 176–178
    appeal of, 6
    dream state as synonym of, 4, 6
    external form of, 177–178
    Fourteen Points and, 177–178
    fragmentation of national identity and, 25
    historical development of, 177–178
    modest proposal on dream states and, 182
    number of plausible claims to, 25
    reconsideration of, 182
    UNPO and, 189
    UN recognition of, 25, 177–178
Sellers, Peter, 49
Serbia
    Bosnia desired by, 6
    EU negotiations with, 127
    Kosovo independence not recognized by,
        84–85, 92, 126–127
    Matryoshka doll metaphor for
        understanding, 129
    NATO intervention in, 85
    Republika Srpska dream state of, 6
    secession movements in Kosovo and, 71–72,
        126–127
    UN membership of Kosovo blocked by,
        20–21
Shakespeare, William, 6, 10
Shankar, Ravi, 81
Singh, Amritpal, 159–160
Slovakia's separation with Czech Republic,
    178–179
Slovenia
    independence of, 6, 84–85
    international recognition of, 85
    War of Independence (Ten-Day War) in, 85
Somalia. *See also* Puntland; Somaliland
    anarchy in, 4
    Ethiopia and Somaliland dispute with, 73
    fragility of, 119
    secession movements in, 73, 92
    Somaliland breakaway area in, 73
    UN membership as exceptional for, 20
Somaliland

autonomous functioning of, 73
colonial history of, 73, 81–82
Ethiopia's proposed recognition of, 73
Somalia's dispute with Ethiopia and, 73
South Ossetia as client of Russia, 97–98
South Sudan
    colonial rule of, 82–83
    independence referendum in, 82–83
    location of, 82–83
    name of, 82–83
    origins of, 15–16, 82–83
    petroleum resources as success condition in,
        83
    reasons for length of war of secession in, 83,
        93
    success conditions of war of secession in, 83
    UN membership of, 19
    war of secession against Sudan in, 15–16,
        82–83, 174–175
sovereignty. *See also* statehood
    absolute sovereignty, 10–12
    belonging as component of, 13
    challenge of, 13–15
    club of, 13–14, 17–19, 22–23
    combined sovereignty, 185–186
    complex and controversial nature of, 14–15
    as continuous attribute, 21–22
    core dimensions of, 14, 17
    development of, 10–13
    divided sovereignty, 185–186
    domestic sovereignty, 14, 19, 32, 182–183
    dream states' relation to, 3, 8, 13–15
    federations and, 133
    hybrid forms of, 181–184
    interdependence sovereignty, 14, 19, 32,
        182–183
    international legal sovereignty, 14, 19, 50,
        182–183
    joint sovereignty, 184–185, 187–188
    modest proposal on dream states and,
        181–186, 187–188
    multidimensional nature of, 182
    practical sovereignty, 12
    recognition as basis for qualifying for, 13
    reconsideration of, 181–186
    redistribution of, 182, 184, 187–188,
        192–193
    territoriality as insufficient for, 13–14
    Westphalian model of, 10–12, 14, 182,
        184–185

224   INDEX

Soviet Union
  anti-communist revolutions following,
    84–85, 146
  Bolshevik Revolution establishing, 141,
    144–146
  Decossackization repression in, 145
  Don Republic declared against, 145
  ethnic minorities in, 145
  Idel-Ural State declared against, 145
  imperial borders replicated by, 141
  new states resulting from disintegration of, 4,
    15–16, 19, 22–23, 64, 80, 97–98, 138,
    141–142, 146–147, 178–179
  Putin's belief that disintegration was greatest
    geopolitical catastrophe, 96, 150
  rebellions against, 145–146
  Red-White Civil War preceding, 148–149
  United Mountain Dwellers of the North
    Caucasus declared against, 145
  UN membership increases following, 19
Spain. *See also* Basque Country; Catalonia
  Andorra's sovereignty guaranteed by,
    184–185
  colonial history of, 4, 72
  federation in, 132–133, 137
  heterogeneity of, 71
  as imagined community, 71
  Mexico's independence from, 137
  secession movements in, 70–71, 89, 137
special cases
  ISIS as a, 129–131
  Israeli-Palestinian conflict as a, 121–126
  Kosovo as a, 126–128
  overview of, 121
  Taiwan as a, 128–129
  themes and variations of, 131
  unusual hot spots, 121
Sri Lanka
  Indian peacekeeping force in, 90
  Tamil Eelam secession movement in, 74–75,
    90
Stalin, Joseph, 20, 183
statehood. *See also* sovereignty
  Correlates of War project and, 18
  Daydreams and, 55
  definition of, 11–13, 18–20, 79, 97, 182
  dichotomous conception of, 21, 181,
    187–188
  effective control as basis for, 19
  elasticity of, 21–22
  emergence of, 11–12
  empirical and juridical dimensions of, 13

exceptions to qualifications for, 20–22
  extralegal dimensions of, 174–175
  Fantasies and, 45, 50
  fragmentation potential of, 25
  as imagined communities, 11–12
  international recognition as basis for, 19
  minorities-within-minorities issue and, 25
  modest proposal on dream states and,
    181–183, 187–188, 190
  Montevideo Convention criteria for, 19–20,
    79, 97, 182
  national identity and, 11–12
  nation-state system in, 10–13
  natural basis assumed for, 11–12
  number of plausible claims to, 25
  population as condition for, 19, 22–23
  post-1945 increase in, 18–19
  reconsideration of, 181–183, 187–188, 190
  size as condition for, 22–23
  territoriality as condition for, 13, 19
  UN membership and, 18–20
  Westphalian model of, 10–13
Sudan
  Anglo-Egyptian Sudan preceding, 82–83,
    186
  civil wars in, 82–83
  colonial history of, 82–83, 186
  independence of, 82–83
  Israel recognized by, 125–126
  South Sudan's war of secession against,
    15–16, 79–80, 83
Switzerland
  canton communities in, 64, 135
  constitutions of, 135
  federation in, 132–133, 135
  Old Swiss Confederacy in, 135
  secession movements absent from, 135
Syria
  Egypt's merger attempt with, 15–16
  Golan Heights of, 125
  ISIS territorial gains in, 13, 130–131
  Israel invaded by, 125
  Kurds in, 65, 116–118
  secession movements in, 74

T
Tanganyika's absorption of Zanzibar, 15–16
Taiwan
  China's claim to, 20–21, 128–129, 190–191
  Chinese Taipei identity of, 190–191
  history of, 128
  population of, 128

INDEX 225

public opinion on independence of, 128–129
risk of conflict in, 129
self-determination claims in, 128–129
as special case, 128–129
successor state not named for, 128–129
Treaty of San Francisco and, 128–129
UN membership blocked by China of, 20–21
US interests in, 128
Tamil Eelam
Liberation Tigers of, 90
name of, 90
secession movement of, 74–75, 86, 93
war of secession in, 90
territoriality
binding nature of, 180
challenge posed by dream states and, 173, 178–180
deep territoriality, 173–174, 178–181, 184, 187–188
definition of, 7
hybrid forms of, 184–186
imagined communities and, 178
modest proposal on dream states and, 181, 184–186, 187–188
reconsideration of, 181, 184–186, 187–188
sovereignty as requiring more than, 13–14
statehood conditioned by, 13, 19
territorial integrity norm based on, 7, 173, 179–180
Westphalian model establishing as basis for authority of, 10–13, 179–180
Texas v. White (1869), 31–32, 38, 43, 174–175
Thiel, Peter, 49
Thomas Aquinas, 133
Timor-Leste
colonial history of, 83
independence of, 14–16, 83
Indonesian occupation of, 83
location of, 83
national identity as success condition in, 84
oil and gas deposits in, 93–94
reasons for length of war of secession in, 93
Revolutionary Front for an Independent East Timor in, 83
sovereignty of, 14
success conditions of war of secession in, 84
UN membership of, 19, 83
war of secession in, 15–16, 79–80, 83–84
Tito, Josip Broz, 84–85
Transnistria
name of, 97

Russian use as model of secession of, 97–98, 99–100
secession of, 7, 97
Treaty of San Francisco (1951), 128–129
Trudeau, Justin, 159–160
Trump, Donald
America First slogan of, 167
armed conflict as possibility under, 39
Espionage Act indictment of, 39
fragmentation of US under, 38
Morocco's sovereignty over Western Sahara recognized by, 101–102
new civil war potential under, 39–40
religious beliefs surrounding chosenness of, 39–40
rumors of creating red-state army in second term of, 39
Tuareg Berbers, 87–88
Turkey
caliphate abolished in, 129–130
Clients used by, 100–101
Cyprus as client of, 100–101, 119
EU application of, 191
Kurds in, 65, 70, 116–118
Russia's trade with, 98
secession movements sponsored by, 70, 95–96, 100–103

U

UK. *See* United Kingdom (UK)
Ukraine
Crimea annexed by Russia from, 7, 99–100, 118–119, 141–142, 178–179
degree of conflict risk in, 118–119
Donbas region in, 7, 99–100
EU economic relations plan of, 99–100
Euromaidan protests in, 99–100
frozen period in Russian conflict against, 99–100
historical ties to Russia of, 99
Kyivan Rus in, 99, 140–141
population of, 99
Putin's views on Russian ownership of, 99
Russian empire role of, 99
Russian invasion of, 7, 24, 100, 118–119, 148–151
Russian minorities joining fight alongside, 149
Russian support for secession movements in, 99–100
sovereignty of, 99
Soviet Union cornerstone of, 99

226 INDEX

Ukraine (*Continued*)
    UN membership as exceptional for, 20, 183
    Yanukovych overthrown in, 99–100
UN. *See* United Nations (UN)
Union of the Comoros, 86
United Kingdom (UK). *See also* Britain;
    England; Northern Ireland; Scotland;
    Wales
    Acts of Union forming, 60
    creation of, 60
    devolution of authority strategy of, 63
    Ireland's relation to, 60, 91
    model of, 68–69
    Northern Ireland's membership in, 62–63
    Scotland's membership in, 59, 68–69
    sovereignty of, 58–59
United Mountain Dwellers of the North
    Caucasus, 145
United Nations (UN)
    Agency for Dream States proposal for,
      189–192
    blocked membership to, 20–21
    challenge posed by dream states and,
      174–175
    decolonization as increasing membership of,
      19, 175, 187–188
    exceptions and omissions to, 20–21
    Friendly Relations Declaration of, 175,
      177–178, 187–188
    General Assembly of, 18–19
    international law's development influenced
      by, 19
    international recognition through, 18–19
    languages recognized by, 25
    lonesome foursome nations to, 20–21
    membership process for, 18–19
    microstates permitted by, 22
    modest proposal on dream states and,
      189–192
    Montevideo Convention informing, 19, 174
    permanent non-member observer status of,
      190–191
    post-1945 increase in membership of, 18–19
    safeguard clause of, 175
    self-determination recognized by, 25,
      177–178
    size as condition for membership in, 22–23
    Soviet Union's disintegration as prompting
      membership to, 19
    statehood and, 18–20
    Yugoslavia's disintegration as prompting
      membership to, 19

United States (US). *See also* constitutional
    order of the US; US secession movements
    Alaska Purchase in, 179
    American Samoa as overseas territory of, 30
    blue states in, 42–43, 179
    Civil War in, 31–32, 34–35, 38–39, 43
    constitutional order of, 29–31
    Democratic Party in, 37–40, 42
    dependencies of, 30–31
    District of Columbia of, 30
    disuniting of, 40
    e pluribus unim slogan of, 11
    federation in, 132–133
    Guam as overseas territory of, 30
    as imagined community, 29
    Indigenous People in, 64–65
    interest in global secession movements of,
      44, 79, 96, 109, 110, 140, 169
    internal challenge of, 29, 43
    Louisiana Purchase of, 179
    Mexican-American War of, 179
    national identity of, 29
    overview of, 29, 43
    partisan divide in, 38–40, 43
    population and size of, 29
    red states in, 39, 42–43
    Republicans in, 37–40, 42
    secession as possibility in, 31–34
    second Civil War potential in, 38–41
    Spanish-American War of, 179
    states as core constituents of, 29–30
    Tenth Amendment of, 123
    territoriality and, 179
    Texas v. White in, 31–32, 38, 43, 174–175
    Union of, 31–32
Unrepresented Nations and Peoples
    Organization (UNPO), 5, 189–190
Ural Republic, 146
US secession movements
    aims of, 34–35
    Alaska Independence Party movement, 36
    American history as precedent in, 36–37
    armed conflict as possibility in, 39–40
    bold forms of, 34–35
    centrifugal forces argument for, 40
    Cherokee Nation movement, 36
    Civil War as precedent to, 38, 43
    common ground missing in, 38–39, 41
    complications for peaceful dissolution
      through, 41–43
    dissolution potential of, 38–41
    dysfunction argument for, 41

future of, 38
Greater Idaho movement, 35
grouping of state secession in, 42
Hawaiian Sovereignty Movement, 36
increasing risk of, 40
Jefferson state proposal, 35
Kentucky as precedent for, 34–35
Liberty Star movement, 35
as logical culmination of political
   polarization, 40
Maine as precedent for, 34–35
mild forms of, 34–35
minorities-within-minorities issue in, 43
mutual suspicion argument for, 40
Neo-Confederate Movements, 35
open questions on feasibility of, 41–43
order of state secession in, 42
overview of, 6, 34–36
partisan division informing, 38–40
post-presidential election polls on, 37
public opinion on, 36–37, 38–40
Puerto Rico independence movement, 36
reasons for secession as possibility in, 40
redrawing of state lines in, 42–43
regional variation in, 35, 37
Republic of Lakota movement, 36
responses to polls on, 37
second civil war potential and, 38–41
Second Vermont Republic, 36
shifting nature of, 38
slow civil war in, 38–40
sovereignty and, 35
state secession polls on, 37
Texas Nationalist Movement, 36
Trump's impact on, 38–40
West Virginia as precedent for, 34–35
Yes California movement, 36

V

Vaitcan City (Holy See), 20–21, 190–191
Verne, Jules, 68

W

Wales
   Celtic identity of, 58, 61
   devolution of authority strategy in, 63, 183
   Kingdom of England incorporation of,
      59–60
   Law in Wales Act and, 59–60
   public opinion on Celtic identity in, 62
   regional assembly in, 136
   secession movement in, 62, 70, 136

   symbols of Celtic identity in, 61
   Welsh Assembly established in, 63
Wallace, Danny, 46
Waris Punjab De (Heirs of Punjab), 159–160
Watson, James, 122
Weber, Max, 13, 19, 180
Western Sahara. *See* Sahrawi (Western Sahara)
Westphalian model
   absolute sovereignty established by, 10–12
   belonging challenge to, 13
   challenge posed by dream states and,
      173–174, 178–180
   constitutional order of the US and, 31–32
   definition of, 10–11
   dream states and, 10–13
   Drexits and, 67
   imagined communities and, 11–12, 71,
      129–130
   importance of, 10–11
   international law and, 12
   limitations of, 11–12
   minority populations as conflicting with, 11
   modest proposal on dream states and,
      181–182
   naturalness of states assumed in, 11–12, 71
   negotiated redistributions of power as
      exception to, 184
   overview of, 10–13
   prevalence of, 179–180
   recognition as basis for qualifying for, 13
   secession as illegal violation of, 31–32
   sovereignty according to, 10–12, 14, 182,
      184–185
   statehood in, 10–13
   territoriality as legitimate basis of authority
      established by, 10–13, 179–180
Whangamōmona, 45
White, Texas v. (1869), 31–32, 38, 43, 174–175
Wibberley, Leonard, 49
Wilson, Woodrow, 177–178
Wy (Australia), 47

Y

Yanukovych, Viktor, 99–100
Yemen
   Clients in, 102
   degree of conflict risk in, 113–114
   Gaza war of 2023 and, 114
   Houthis in, 102, 113–114
   Iran's support for, 102

228 INDEX

Yemen (*Continued*)
    merger attempt between North and South Yemen, 15–16
    People's Democratic Republic of Yemen in, 113–114
    Presidential Leadership Council in, 113–114
    Saudi Arabia and UAE bombing of, 102, 113–114
    secession movements in, 74, 95–96, 102
    Sunni-Shiite proxy war in, 102
    UN-backed cease-fire failures in, 114
    UN membership as exceptional for, 20
Yugoslavia. *See also* Bosnia; Croatia; Montenegro; Serbia; Slovenia
    author experiences in, 84
    casualties of wars of secession in, 85
    centrifugal forces in, 84
    as example of national identity leading to fragmentation, 6
    Free Territory of Trieste and, 178–179
    inter-ethnic tensions in, 84
    new states resulting from disintegration of, 6, 15–16, 19, 22–23, 79–80, 84–85, 138
    origin of, 6, 84
    as primed for failure, 85
    Tito's rule in, 84
    UN membership increases following, 19
    wars of secession following disintegration of, 8, 84–85

Z

Zanzibar absorbed by Tanganyika, 15–16